A *Forever Story:*
The People and Community
of the Fond du Lac Reservation

Thomas D. Peacock, Editor

Fond du Lac Band
of Lake Superior Chippewa

Library of Congress Catalog Number: 99.90215
Peacock, Thomas.
    A forever story: The people and community of the Fond du
Reservation/Thomas Peacock
        p. 320.
            1. Indians of North America, Fond du Lac Reservation

Printed in the United States of America

"This material is based upon work assisted by a grant from the
Department of the Interior, National Park Service. Any opinions,
findings, and conclusions or recommendations expressed in this
material are those of the author(s) and do not necessarily reflect
the views of the the Department of the Interior."

ISBN 0-9670645-0-3

Cover photo:
Ojibwe Family
Photo by Olaf Olson
Collection of Carlton County Historical Society

The life cycle of the Creation is endless.
We watch the seasons come and go,
life into life forever.
The child becomes parent who then
becomes our respected elder.
Life is so sacred,
it is good to be a part of all this.

A Forever Story:
The People and Community of the Fond du Lac Reservation

Page

Preface

Contributors

This collection was done by a group of volunteers unofficially calling themselves the Fond du Lac history group. Over a period of several years, members of the Fond du Lac history group solicited articles, pictures and documents for this collection. We received much more than could be printed in this volume. Other stories need to be told and someone in the future will take it upon themselves to do just that. Many pictures and documents of the reservation's collections are included in the book.

Writers:

Elizabeth Albert
Dan Anderson
Betty Dahl
Michael LeGarde
Bonita Sutliff
Jerrold Ojibway
Robert "Sonny" Peacock
Thomas Peacock
Brenda Pollak
Bonnie Wallace
Isabelle Whelan

Photographs or Documents:

Elizabeth Albert
Harvey Danielson
Carol Jaakola
Dorothy Olson
Michael Peacock
Sandy Shabiash
Charles Walt
Isabelle Whelan
Lawrence Murray
Joyce Troseth
Mary Northrup

Document/Photo Reproduction/Layout:
Rocky Wilkinson
Dan Anderson
Hand tinting of book cover by Marlene Wisuri

Photo credits:
MHS – Minnesota Historical Society
NEMHC – Northeastern Minnesota Historical Center
CCHS – Carlton County Historical Society

Preface

Across the earth everywhere
making my voice heard

Many years ago, ethnologist Frances Densmore traveled throughout Ojibwe country recording the traditional songs of the Ojibwe people. Later, the songs were published by the Smithsonian Institution, Bureau of American Ethnology. According to Densmore, the above song describes a singer's interpretation of the approach of a summer thunderstorm.

The song could be analogous to the voices of the Ojibwe heard in this book. Unlike other histories and descriptions of our culture (which were often written by others), this book was written, edited or overseen primarily by Ojibwe people. Where non-Indians did contribute, their works were included because of their special expertise and knowledge. The contributors avoided concentrating solely on the history of Indian and white contact that has sometimes erroneously been passed off as American Indian history. Moreover, this is not a history taken from the notes of the missionaries who first arrived to live amongst our ancestors, or a compilation of the descriptive notes of ethnologists or anthropologists. This collection of writings reflects a holistic picture of the people and community of the Fond du Lac Reservation, melding historical fact, cultural and spiritual beliefs, personal stories, occasional fiction based on fact, and reflection. Several non-Fond du Lac band members contributed articles, photographs, editing, and technical expertise, but Fond du Lac band members were the editorial board for every word, photograph and illustration in this book. This is *our* story.

Why did we feel it important to tell our own story? Because it had not been done and needs to be done. Because what had been published in the past as the truth may have been only one fraction of the truth. Because we want to tell the story of people and communities over that of institutions.

Readers will notice the book doesn't contain *everything* that could ever be written about Fond du Lac history. Other individual interviews could have been included. Histories of institutions, including tribal governments, economic development, human service systems, or schools could have been included. Other pictures could have been included. The articles, reprints, pictures and format were the work of a group of volunteers, and works and pictures were solicited through local newspapers and word of mouth. Consider the book a sampling, a volume one of what we hope will lead to other collections.

Readers will notice we chose to use 'Ojibwe' in describing ourselves as a people; however, we kept 'Ojibway', 'Chippewa', or 'Anishinabe' in previously published materials and documents. All of these terms are often used to describe us as a distinct tribal entity.

More than anything else, we felt is was critical to have a written and pictorial record of the *people* of the Fond du Lac Reservation for our children, grandchildren and for their children. We want them to fully understand their place in the history of the Ojibwe people of the Fond du Lac Reservation. We want them to understand that we are all part of a story that has gone on for thousands of years: Since the days of our migrations, to settling in this area, to the comings and goings of recent times. We are all part of a story that goes on forever. Our children continue our story, and their children continue theirs.

This is a forever story.

Thomas D. Peacock, Editor

Acknowledgements

We thank the tribal council for authorizing and providing the funds and equipment for use by the Fond du Lac History Group to gather the history of the band. For a generous publication grant, we thank the National Park Service. For the time and resources to work on this project these last two years, we thank the University of Minnesota-Duluth. For their assistance in word processing and editorial assistance, we thank Elizabeth "Betsy" Albert, Linda Witzke, Amy Ziegenhaugen, and Bonita Sutliff. For their contributions of both primary and secondary reference materials, we thank Dan Anderson, Betty Dahl, Marlene Wisuri (Carlton County Historical Society) and the College of St. Scholastica. For getting the book press-ready (layout, photo and document scanning and technical expertise) we thank Rocky Wilkinson. And for the editing and proofreading we thank Andrea Junker. For allowing the Band to reprint a significant amount of previously published interview material, we thank the Duluth Indian Education Committee and the Minnesota Historical Society. For readers who gave generously of their time, expertise, counsel and humor, we thank Dan Anderson, Elizabeth Albert, Sonny Peacock.

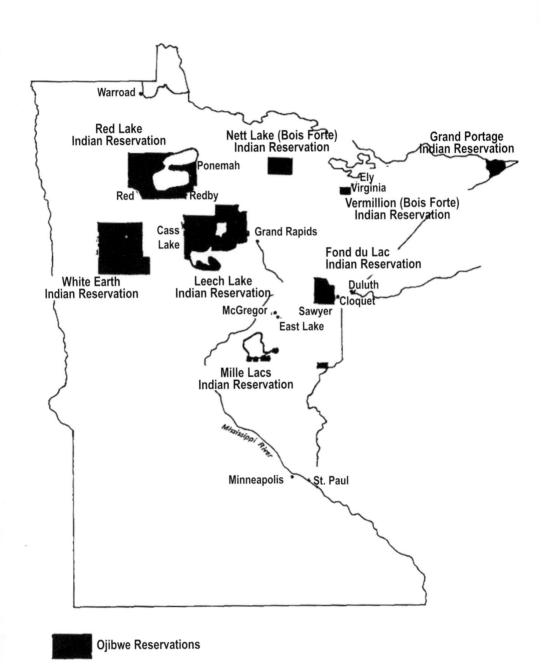

Warroad

Red Lake
Indian Reservation

Nett Lake (Bois Forte)
Indian Reservation

Grand Portage
Indian Reservation

Ponemah

Red   Redby

Ely
Virginia
Vermillion (Bois Forte)
Indian Reservation

Cass
Lake

Grand Rapids

Fond du Lac
Indian Reservation

White Earth
Indian Reservation

Leech Lake
Indian Reservation

Duluth
Cloquet

McGregor

Sawyer

East Lake

Mille Lacs
Indian Reservation

Mississippi River

Minneapolis   St. Paul

Ojibwe Reservations

Map by Dianne Schaefer. Based in part on Brown, Tideman and Calkins, 1969.

Fond du Lac Indian Reservation

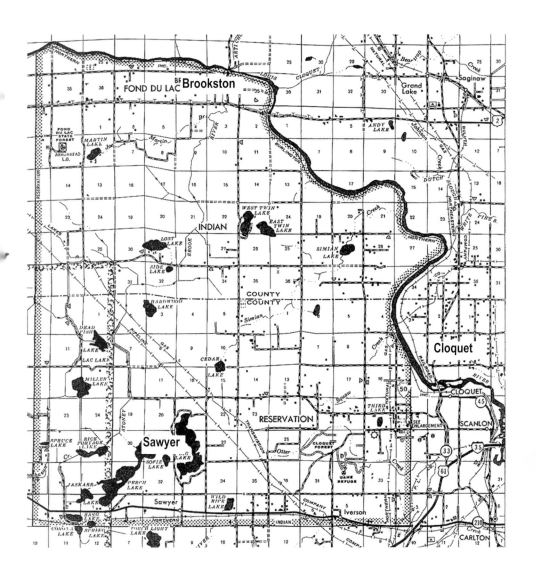

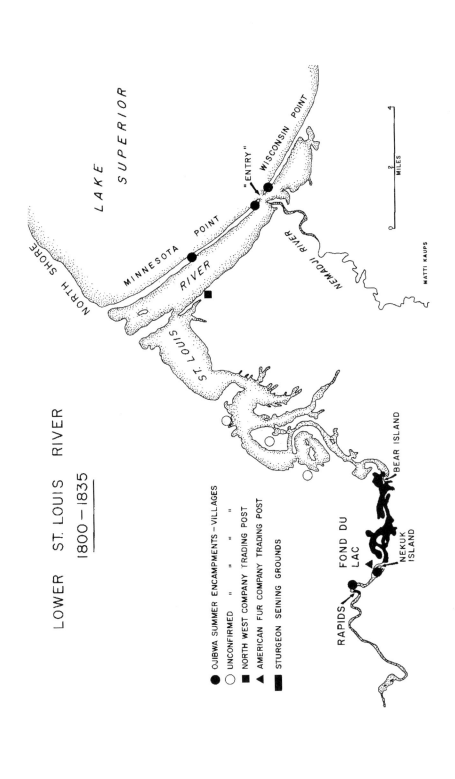

LOWER ST. LOUIS RIVER
1800 – 1835

● OJIBWA SUMMER ENCAMPMENTS – VILLAGES
○ "   "   "   "   UNCONFIRMED
■ NORTH WEST COMPANY TRADING POST
▲ AMERICAN FUR COMPANY TRADING POST
■ STURGEON SEINING GROUNDS

LAKE SUPERIOR

NORTH SHORE

MINNESOTA POINT

"ENTRY"

WISCONSIN POINT

ST. LOUIS RIVER

NEMADJI RIVER

BEAR ISLAND

NEKUK ISLAND

FOND DU LAC

RAPIDS

MATTI KAUPS

0   2   4
MILES

Chapter One: Coming to This Place

There is a clearing in the woods just north of Cloquet, Minnesota, on a hill overlooking the river that flows through Nahgahchiwanong (Fond du Lac Reservation). As a young boy, I walked the old trails that intersect it with my brothers and cousins. And each spring and fall the meadow would show part of its story to me: Old stone foundations of homes of the old village that had stood there before the great fire of 1918, rusted kettles and old pottery, a cluster of trees that once served as shade and for the children of that time to climb. Even as a child, it seemed each time I stood in that place it would sing to me. And I would wonder about all of the stories of that place, of the people who spent their lives there and who also reflected on its powerful presence.

Now as a grandfather, I often return and walk the old road that follows the hills that overlook the river up to that small parcel of earth. In some places, the horse drawn wagons which passed through there many years ago still show some effects, the road being worn deep into the hill. Often I sit in the tall grass and listen to the sounds of wind, the creak of trees and all the voices of life that celebrate this sacred place.

I know I belong here. My great-grandparents and grandparents and parents and cousins and brothers and sister all walked these same hills. Their bones lay buried just several hundred yards further up the river road, in the old reservation cemetery. It is the very existence of their memory that separates us from all other people on this place we call Turtle Island. We have been here for many thousands of years. Our ancestors are a part of this place, their physical beings long ago recycled into the very trees and grasses and flowers and animals that now celebrate the dance of life. That is why this place is sacred (Momaday, p. 114):

> To encounter the sacred is to be alive at the deepest center of human existence. Sacred places are the truest definitions of the earth; they stand for the earth immediately and forever; they are its flags and shields. If you know the earth for what it really is, learn it through its sacred places.
>
> Sacred ground is in some way earned. It is consecrated, made holy with offerings, song and ceremony, joy and sorrow, the dedication of the mind and heart, offerings of life and death.

All of us have our own sacred places. Places seen through our child-

1

hood eyes. Places associated with grandmas and grandpas. When we become adults we return to them because their powerful and healing ways cause us to reflect. They offer solace and respite in difficult times. They offer us a direct pathway to the Creator, because when we are in these places we can feel His presence in every blade of grass, every flower and leaf, every wisp of cloud and wind and smell. And if we are gone for many years and we return to these places, it is as though we are greeted by our Ojibwe grandmother after a long journey. It is as though we climb into her lap and she holds us in her arms and we become buried deep in her bosom.

We are honored to live in such a place.

– T. Peacock

Part One:
The Origin of the Anishinabe

—- Jerrold Ojibway

I have been asked to tell a story to explain our existence. I have been asked to be a man, and I have been asked to share with you the creation of the Anishinabeg. People nowadays are very inquisitive as to where they came from. *They came from their mothers.*

Over the years I have been wondering myself where I came from. I too came from my *mother.* But before me, where did she come from – and her mother, and her mother. Where did she come from...yes, from her *mother* too;

But where did we come from?

I remember a trip our family took to Chippewa Falls, Wisconsin to visit our relatives. On this trip I was somehow more aware of my surroundings. We traveled for a time...we needed a rest...so we stopped at a store along the way (Highway 53 in Wisconsin at this time was very bare and did not have the many stops it has now). It was in this store that I began to ask where I came from.

In this store, I found an interesting object. It was a postcard of a big Indian man, and strewn around him were all different kinds of people; yellow people, black people, red people, people dressed in different clothing. He appeared to be talking to them. This interested me. *I called my mother over and asked her what and who this man was on the postcard.* I was kindly told that when we got back into the car she would tell me about the postcard and with the quickness of her hand snatched up the postcard, which was to be used as a reference later on.

"My son, this man that you are asking about does exist and the postcard is from the people who think they know who this man is.

"But what you need to understand is that there is a story that tells of this man and how he came to be the way he is shown in the postcard.

"The man is called Waynahbooszhoo. He is a man who can and has done a lot for the Anishinabeg."

(This man that I came to know that day has become a very important part of my life and some of his doings, I have done myself).

"The story goes like this, I hope I can remember, but if I do not remember we can always ask Gramma...

"Before Man came to be on this world, a spirit woman lived in the sky, who was married to a spirit man. They had been together for a long time.

3

"After a while the woman began to become uneasy and every day she would look down at the earth world and say to herself, 'I wonder how it would be to live there?' She did not understand this urge to go to the earth world, but it became more and more a part of her thoughts. *She was able to look at the earth through a hole in the sky.*

"One day, while she was looking and wishing and wondering about the earth, she fell. Her fall was not of haste, but of floating like a feather toward the earth. Once on earth, she could hear, smell, taste, and feel how beautiful the earth was. Plants and animals were all over the place, they were not hurting each other, and all the earth could speak to each other. The woman walked for miles and miles. She laid down to sleep, and she dreamt of her husband and felt bad for leaving him. She cried.

"She cried for someone to help her and her mother came to her, the same way she had come to be on the earth. They were both happy. Soon after this, the woman gave birth to two boys, twins. She died giving birth to the babies.

"The Gramma took care of the babies for a long time. She watched them grow into two very big, healthy boys. One day, one of the boys asked where he came from, and the Gramma told him the story of how they came to be on the earth. This boy wanted to return where he came from. So Gramma called for and prayed for the Father to hear what his son had to say. The boy left for his father.

"The remaining boy did not want to go. His name was Waynahboo–szhoo."

I was curious, so I asked, "Mother, so what does this have to do with the man ON THE POSTCARD?"

She replied, "Son, this is the man that the white man thinks is our Waynahbooszhoo." My mother began to explain to me how he came to help us as a people. "There are many oral translations about this man. Before you can understand who this man in the postcard is, you need to understand that Waynahbooszhoo does not look like this man at all. He looks just like me and you."

I tried to understand what she meant, but for the love of me how could this man be like me and her? I was a man and she was a woman! How could he be both of us?

Then she told me the story of when Waynahbooszhoo went looking for

4

his father after the Gramma told him that his father lived in the West. Then she told me the story of how he gave the Kingfisher his red eyes, beak, and no tail. She told me of when he had fought with his father, because he blamed his father for leaving him. She told me the story of how he gave earth back to the people when the earth was flooded. He found himself with the animals on the turtles back. The animals tried to dive for a piece of earth in the water of the flood and the muskrat, the smallest of them all, saved the earth because he could dive farther than the other animals.

After hearing these tales of the man, I began to understand how he gave the human beings life and how he did these things for human beings. He also showed them how to learn from his teachings and doings! One important lesson he taught was that humans should not to be so hard on themselves for being human means everyone makes mistakes and you are to learn from these mistakes. *But most of all, he said not to use being a human being as a means to get what you want.*

Then I asked the question about the picture on the postcard.

"Ohhh," she said. "The picture does tell of what Waynahbooszhoo had done."

Long time ago, when Waynahbooszhoo was younger, he became very lonely. And he called for the help from the Spirits and he asked of his Spirit helpers what should he do, saying, 'how can I not be lonely anymore?' Then he lay down to sleep. During his sleep he had a dream. In this dream he was told by his spirit helpers what he needed to do so he would not be lonely anymore.

A description of the postcard: The man is pictured kneeling by a fire. He is breathing on a person made from clay. The fire is used for the coloring of the people: brown/red for the original people of Turtle Island. Black for the people across the sea. Yellow for the people from the east. White for the people who were yet to come to Turtle Island. Also on the postcard are other clay figures at different stages of coloration, some from being close to the fire and others from not being close to the fire. The people are all joined in merriment and are expressing themselves as friends to each other.

What the picture is saying is that the dream had told Waynahbooszhoo he had the power of life and that with this power he could do or be anything he wanted to be. But with this power came the responsibility of guiding the people to become a people that were of his being and stature.

My mother stated the picture is not accurate about how we as people came to be. The picture is accurate with respect to the person who was breathed upon first, the people of Turtle Island. The others did come along, but not of his doing.

I will never forget this trip, as this was the trip where I began to be acknowledged as a person, who was to become a man.

The mother that was spoken about in the beginning of this story is the Mother Earth...

Part Two:
The People's Journey: Migrations of the Ojibwe
– *Thomas D. Peacock*

The Anishinabe (now sometimes referred to as the Ojibwe) people are not originally from this area, but at this point in history this place is what we call home. We didn't always live on Northrup or Lockling Road or Scotty Drive. Historically, these are new and within the recent memories of many people, these places were once woods and fields occasionally connected by trails or wagon roads. This area was a vast forest for thousands of years, interrupted occasionally by glacial periods. Our contemporary home was, until just a few hundred years ago, the home of the Dakota. Before them, it was the home of the people before the Dakota. This chapter tells one version of the journey our ancestors made to the place where many of us live today. Surely, there are other versions or stories of how we got to be where we are today, but this version is the one we have chosen to tell.

Our journey to Fond du Lac began many thousands of years ago. First was the migration of the Lenni Lenape (known today as the Delaware), the Grandfathers, across this great continent from the west to the east. The Lenni Lenape are the original people from which many tribal nations, including the Anishinabe, can linguistically and culturally trace their ancestry. The story of this period of our migration is what connects us as cousins to western and Midwestern tribes – Blackfeet, Cheyenne, Cree, Shawnee, and Miami to name a few. Next was the journey to northern New England and southeastern Canada, a part of the migration that connects us as relatives to the eastern nations – the Passamaquaddy, Penobscot, Wampanoag to name a few. More recently, our ancestors began a westward migration as one people with the Ottawa and Potawatomi, only to separate along the way and become the three distinct tribal nations we know today. This journey eventually led us to Madeline Island (just offshore Red Cliff, Wisconsin), then to Wisconsin and Minnesota Points at the tip of Lake Superior, Fond du Lac village in far west Duluth, the old village in Fond du Lac (just north of Cloquet on a bluff overlooking the St. Louis River) then to the other villages and settlements of present-day Fond du Lac Reservation.

Our journey doesn't end here. There have been more recent migrations as some families were forced west to the White Earth Reservation during the period of the Chippewa Commission of the late 19th century. During that time, the federal government attempted to move all the Ojibwe people west of the Mississippi River to the White Earth Reservation. There was the policy of relocation by the Bureau of Indian Affairs during the 1940's through the 1960's, which sent many families to Oakland, San Francisco, Cleveland, Chicago, Seattle and other large urban areas. There was the movement of families to the Minneapolis/St. Paul and Duluth areas. Toward the end of the millennium, we have seen a migration back to the reservation.

There are some people who assume we have always been here and will always be. But the story of humankind is filled with the movement, displacement and the migrations of people. Will we as a tribal people be in this place we call Fond du Lac one hundred years from now? Probably. A thousand years? We don't know. Tens of thousands of years? Most probably not. Our presence in this time on the earth is part of a larger story that began with our ancestors and will continue with the ongoing story of our children, grandchildren and their children. This story goes on forever, and it is a story of journeys and migrations, breaking off and melding with other tribal nations, absorbing other peoples and being absorbed at the same time. The story of our migrations is partially based on fate, timing and happenstance. Ultimately, it is based upon divine plan.

Journey of the Grandfathers

The migration of the ancient ancestors, the Lenni Lenape (the Grandfathers), was told in the Wallum Olum, an epic song which was recorded on bark tablets and song sticks (McCutchen, 1993). This historical record is the oldest recorded account of people in North America, possibly dating back to 1600 B.C. (McCutchen, 1993):

> Among Native Americans – whose elders are given respect and for whom a title of age is proof of honor and influence – the Lenni Lenape were known as the "Grandfathers"; they were acknowledged as the progenitor tribe of what the French called the "grand old Algonquan Family".

The Wallum Olum describes a journey from the west to the Atlantic Ocean; of the eventual dispersion of the people as they branched out and became their own nations, took on new names and evolved into the tribes we know today. The journey has our ancestors as far west as California, the home of our Lenape relatives, the Yuroks and Wiyots. Amelia LeGarde, a highly respected Ojibwe storyteller, noted that at one time our people were in the west, 'as far as California.' The Wallum Olum tells of the encounters as the people journeyed east and came upon the indigenous people of the Rocky Mountains and the Great Plains, the great mound builders of the Mississippi, and eventually with our traditional enemies, the people of the Iroquois Federation. Other tribes with Lenape roots, including the Cheyenne, Arapaho, Cree, Blackfoot, Shawnee, and Miami, may have settled as others made their eastward journey, or like the Ojibwe, moved east only to move westward in another migration. Eventually, the Lenni Lenape reached the Atlantic Ocean and settled along the Delaware River. From there, some of them branched out to the north to New England, to become our relatives, the Montauk, Wampanoag, Pequot, Narraganset, Nipmuc, Penobscot, Passamaquaddy, and others. Others, including the Ojibwe, moved north to the St. Lawrence River area in what is now Newfoundland, and then west. The last entry of the Wallum Olum was written in 1638 to announce the arrival of a boatload of European settlers. The entry is both chilling and prophetic, saying simply, "Who are they?"

The migration from the East Coast

The Anishinabe (Ojibwe) lived on the shores of the Atlantic Ocean over 600 years ago near the mouth of the St. Lawrence River (Warren, 1974) for so long that most forgot their true origins lay in the west (Johnston, 1976). We began the westward journey as one people with the Ottawa (Odawa, or traders) and Pottawatomi (keepers of the perpetual fire), but separated at the Straits of Michilimacinac (where Lake Michigan converges with Lake Huron). Some Ojibwe went north (known as the northern Ojibwe) and are the ancestors of the Canadian Ojibwe and some of the people of Grand Portage Reservation in Minnesota. A larger group went south and west. Most of the original Ojibwe inhabitants of the Fond du Lac Reservation are descendants of these southern Ojibwe. The Ottawa remained near Sault St. Marie and the Pottawatomi moved into northern Michigan. Warren describes how he learned of the westward migration while listening in on a Midewiwin ceremony. The speaker took a Me-da-me-gis (a small sea shell), saying (p. 78-79):

> "While our forefathers were living on the great salt water toward the rising sun, the great Megis (sea-shell) showed itself above the surface of the great water, and the rays of the sun for a long period were reflected from its glossy back. It gave warmth and light to the Anishinabeg. All at once it sank into the deep, and for a long time our

ancestors were not blessed by its light. It rose to the surface and appeared again on the great river which drains the waters of the Great Lakes, and again for a long time it gave life to our forefathers, and reflected back the rays of the sun. Again it disappeared from sight and it rose not, till it appeared to the eyes of the Anishinabeg on the shores of the first great lake. Again it sank from sight, and death daily visited the wigwams of our forefathers, till it showed its back, and reflected the rays of the sun once more at Boweting (Sault. St. Marie). Here it remained for a long time, but once more, and for the last time, it disappeared, and the Anishinabeg was left in darkness and misery, till it floated and once more showed its bright back at Moningwunakauning [Madeline Island in Lake Superior], where it has ever since reflected back the rays of the sun, and blessed our ancestors with life, light and wisdom. Its rays reach the remotest village of the widespread Ojibways."

The speaker then offered an interpretation to his listeners (p. 79-80):

"My grandson," said he, "the megis I spoke of, means the Me-da-we [midewiwin] religion. Our forefathers, many string of lives ago, lived on the shores of the Great Salt Water in the east. Here it was, that while congregated in a great town, and while they were suffering the ravages of sickness and death, the Great Spirit, at the intercession of Manabosho, the great common uncle of the Anishinabeg, granted them this rite wherewith life is restored and prolonged. Our forefathers moved from the shores of the great water, and proceeded westward. The Me-da-we lodge was pulled down and it was not again erected, till our forefathers again took a stand on the shores of the great river where Mon-ne-aung (Montreal) now stands.

In the course of time this town was again deserted, and our forefathers still proceeding westward, lit not their fires till they reached the shores of Lake Huron, where again the rites of the Me-da-we were practiced.

Again these rites were forgotten, and the Me-da-we lodge was not built till the Ojibways found themselves congregated at Boweting (outlet of Lake Superior) where it remained for many winters. Still the Ojibways moved westward, and for the last time, the Ma-da-we lodge was erected on the Island of LaPointe [Madeline Island], and here, long before the pale face appeared among them, it was practiced in its purest and most original form."

Madeline Island, which lies several miles offshore Red Cliff, Wisconsin, was once the home of the Ojibwe. All the bands of the southern Ojibwe, including the people of the Fond du Lac Reservation, originally came from Madeline Island. Living on the island protected them from their enemies, the Fox and Dakota nations. Our ancestors lived congregated together in a town estimated to contain over 10,000 people (Warren, 1974, p. 96-97):

> ...for greater security they were obliged to move their camp [the Ojibwe had first settled Long Island] to the adjacent island of Moningwunakauning (place of the golden-breasted woodpecker, but known as LaPointe). Here, they chose the site of their ancient town, and it covered a space about three miles long and two broad, comprising the western end of the island.

> While hemmed in on this island by their enemies, the Ojibways lived mainly by fishing. They also practiced the arts of agriculture to an extent not since known amongst them. Their gardens are said to have been extensive, and they raised large quantities of Mundamin (Indian corn), and pumpkins.

> The more hardy and adventurous hunted on the lake shore opposite their village, which was overrun with moose, bear, elk and deer. The buffalo, also, are said in those days to have ranged within a day's march from the lake shore, on the barrens stretching towards the headwaters of the St. Croix River.

The Ojibwe lived in their island community for 120 years. The sudden departure of the people from the island has several explanations. Some of Warren's informants indicated the coming of the white race (and introduction of the firearm) led to a rapid expansion of the Ojibwe into Wisconsin and Minnesota, where they overwhelmed the Fox and woodland Dakota with their superior weaponry. With guns, there was no need to rely on the relative safety of the island to protect then from their enemies. Other informants told of a time of evil on the island, of cannibalism and starvation, and disease. Needless to say, the island was evacuated by the Ojibwe, some of whom moved back east toward Sault St. Marie, while others pressed on west to Fond du Lac and beyond.

Regardless of how or why the island was nearly abandoned by our ancestors, it remains a special and sacred place to the Anishinabe. To many contemporary Anishinabe, it is disconcerting to hear some historians dismiss the significance of our presence on Madeline Island. If a colonial settlement of 10,000 souls dispersed mysteriously in the span of a few years, it would be deemed of great historical significance in any historical accounting; however, I remember some years ago sitting in a Bayfield County Historical Society (Wisconsin) presentation on the Apostle Islands (of which Madeline Island is the largest), and hearing only scant mention made of the great nation of the Anishinabe. Nothing was said of the Indian village of LaPointe. Nothing was said of their migration from the eastern shores. Moreover, it was also disconcerting to hear that several years ago tourists attempted to build a croquet playing area on the Indian graves of Madeline Island. Ojibwe residents from the nearby village of Red Cliff had to stand guard over the area to ensure that was not done. These struggles to have an equal voice in the great American story exemplify the need to tell the stories of all people of this country.

What makes the story of our migration to Madeline Island, even more intriguing was something I heard while listening to Iris Heavy Runner, a Blackfeet. We were talking about how our two tribes were related, and she said something which almost took my breath away.

"The creation story for my people," she said, "begins on Madeline Island."

The first settlement at Fond du Lac

The Ojibwe takeover of former Fox and Dakota homelands happened very quickly. The Fox people were forced to abandon this area and moved to southern Wisconsin by the early part of the 17th century. Soon, the Ojibwe moved west to Fond du Lac (Warren, p. 129-130):

> Soon after the above occurrence [removal of the Fox at St. Croix], the Ojibways pressed up the lakeshore, and Wa-me-gis-ug-o, a daring and fearless hunter, obtained a firm footing and pitched his wigwam permanently at Fond du Lac [far west Duluth], or Wi-a-quah-ke-che-gume-eng. He belonged to the Marten Totem family, and the present respected chiefs of that now important village, Shin-goop and Nug-aun-ub, are his direct descendants. [Editors note: Esther Nahgahnub

maintains her family is actually from the Bear Dodaim, and that Warren was in error to make the above statement.] Many families of his people followed the example of this pioneer, erecting their wigwams on the islands of the St. Louis River, near its outlet into the lake for greater security.

The Ojibwe lived at the present day village of Fond du Lac in far west Duluth and on Wisconsin Point, Minnesota Point, and in and around the hills of what is now the city of Duluth, for many years. Following the signing of the Treaty of 1854, which established the Fond du Lac Reservation, efforts were made to have people move onto reservation land. Some families were already well settled onto reservation land near the ricing lakes (Perch, Dead Fish and Rice Portage). In the 1870's, an Indian village was established just north of the present city of Cloquet (between what is now Jarvi Road and Holy Family Mission Church on the east side of Reservation Road) on a bluff overlooking the St. Louis River. Fifty or more homes, a school and blacksmith shop were built and the people lived there until the early part of the 20th century, when a dispute over land ownership, a governmental effort to have people move to their land allotments, and a great forest fire all combined to its near abandonment. But the fields and old foundations, rusted kettles and pottery of our ancestors still haunt that place.

Forced and coerced dispersals

Two attempts were made to get reservation Indians to move off the reservation. The first was the Chippewa Commission, during the latter part of the 19th century. The idea was to move all Ojibwe to the White Earth Reservation, and some families did move; however, most refused to leave the area.

The second attempt was the period of relocation from the 1940's to the 1960's, during which the Bureau of Indian Affairs paid Indians to relocate to large urban areas. Many Fond du Lac band members moved to Chicago, Cleveland, Oakland, Minneapolis, and other areas during this period. The interview of Les Northrup contained in this book tells one story of relocation.

A returning full circle

There are many individual stories of migration and journeys. This is mine.

As a graduate student, I had a dear friend who was a member of the

Penobscot people from Indian Island, Maine. Indian Island is a large island on the Penobscot River just outside Old Town, where the canoes bearing the name are made. Often we would sit in Conroy Commons [the campus student center] on the Harvard University campus and tell our stories to each other.

"We know you people are from out here," she would say. "We had stories about you back then." Then she would laugh.

Sometimes we take a journey without knowing the reasons, only to find upon reaching the destination the answers were provided in the journey itself. Several years ago, while interviewing teachers of American Indian students, I became intrigued while listening to a taped interview a friend had done with Wayne Newell, a Passamaquoddy language and culture teacher from Maine. I had a sense I needed to talk to him in person, so I booked a flight to Boston, then rented a car and drove the six hour trip to northern Maine. It was a long drive and all the way I wondered why I was doing it. But once I got off the freeway onto a two lane, and finally to an old dirt road that led to the reserve, I began to realize there was purpose in this journey. There, on a picnic bench outside a small reserve school I listened as a gentle, knowledgeable and profoundly wise person told the story of his people.

Have you ever met someone for the first time and felt you have known him forever? This was one of those people and one of those times. We told hauling-moose-out-of-the-woods stories, and rabbit-snaring stories, drinking and fighting stories, and stories of our activist days. We both acknowledged how difficult it has been as teachers and educators to force schools to tell the story of our people, to include it as part of the American story that is taught in most schools. He showed me the brown ash basketry woven by his students and gave me a large bunch of freshly harvested sweet grass to take home.

"We know of your people," he said. "We remember when you were from here. We have stories from then."

I thought of Warren's description of the long ago Anishinabe conquest over a people known as the Mundua, who lived in a East Coast town described as being (p. 92), "so large that a person standing on a hill which stood in its center, could not see the limits of it." The Mundua who were not killed or driven off were incorporated into the Anishinabe.

Newell told of a time he came west as far as Iowa to a conference, and while sitting in a room where only Mesquakie (the tribal people who live near Tama, Iowa) and Ojibwe were being spoken, he was able to converse in his language and be understood. He told me his people's story of our westward migration.

"We sent you west. Some of us stayed. We knew the only way to retain who we were would be to send some people west."

When he said that, I was thinking that would be the likely story of those left behind.

What remained of their traditional culture was clearly like that of our tribe. The brown ash basketry was nearly the same as our black ash basketry. Their birchbark and sweet grass crafts was nearly the same. The land they lived on looked the same as ours – lakes and pine forests filled with deer, moose and other animals which they harvested as part of their treaty rights. Clearly, these people were our relatives.

"What do your people call themselves in your language?" I asked.

"Waubun anung (morning star)," he said. "People of the dawn."

When he said that, I knew why I had traveled so far to meet him.

A forever journey

When I lived in Massachusetts I would drive back and forth to Minnesota during the summers to visit relatives. One time I drove back to the Boston area along the Trans-Canadian Highway. In many respects, my eastward journey retraced the path our ancestors had made on their westward journey. On our way we stopped in Red Cliff, Wisconsin and visited relatives. We passed Chequamegon Bay in Lake Superior, and off in the distance I could see Madeline Island, the great homeland of the Anishinabe. That evening we stayed in an inexpensive roadside motel just outside Sault St. Marie, Michigan, another place our ancestors stopped during their journey. The next day we drove across Canada through Sudbury, North Bay and the Canadian capitol of Ottawa. Our ancestors traveled a similar path many years ago. The third day we drove along the St. Lawrence River through Montreal and then down to Boston. The story of our people takes us down the St. Lawrence River and through what is now present day Montreal.

I vividly remember the last time I drove back home from the East Coast to the reservation. For the most part the trip was uneventful. But for one moment. There is a hill along Highway 53 in northern Wisconsin about twenty miles out of the city of Superior where Lake Superior first comes into view. The view affords a great expanse of forest melding into the blue of the lake. I remember being overcome by the sight of the lake because I knew I was returning home after a journey to many different places that had taken me many, many years.

"Home," I was thinking. "I am home."

Now I live and walk the paths along the hills and pastures that overlook the river that flows through Nahgahchiwanong (Fond du Lac). And my children and grandchildren walk the same paths.

References

Johnston, B. (1976). Ojibway heritage. Lincoln, Nebraska: University of Nebraska Press.

McCutchen, D. (1993). The red record: The Wallum Olum. Garden City, New York: Avery.

Momaday, N. (1997). Man made of words. New York: St. Martin's Press.

Warren, W. (1974). History of the Ojibway nation. Minneapolis: Ross and Haines.

Chapter Two: Perspectives of the Ojibwe at Fond du Lac

Much of what has been referred to as American Indian history is actually a history of Indian-white contact. Non-Indian people kept written records of their early encounters with Indian people in personal and trader journals, missionary chronicles, government and church documents, newspaper accounts, and the written documents of early European explorers. The collective consciousness of American Indian people has paid dearly for this omission because some of what has been recorded as history is a reflection of only one perspective of the forest of reality, one fraction of the truth. Throughout much of Indian country, the story of the indigenous people, told from the perspective of the indigenous, remains untold. So the history which explains our place in the great story of this land becomes a mystery for more and more American Indian people with the passing of time. In some tribes it becomes forever lost to time with the passing of the few remaining elders who know the old stories. And to a great extent, the same has been true for colonized people all over the world, who also suffer from the loss of languages, cultures, and historical knowledge (Memmi, 1965, p. 102):

> We should ask that he draws less and less from his past. The colonizer never even recognized that he had one; everyone knows that the commoner whose origins are unknown has no history. Let us ask the colonized himself: who are his folk heroes? His great popular leaders? His sages? At most, he may be able to give us a few names, in complete disorder, and fewer and fewer as one goes down the generations. The colonizer seems condemned to lose his memory.

Many Indian people have gone through their formalized education with a special dislike for history. Perhaps it was because we realized the American history we were taught began with the colonization of this country by Europeans. We knew that wasn't true because we have been here for many thousands of years before Columbus. Indigenous stories go back to times when our ancestors were hunting the great woolly mammoths and buffalo of the last ice age. Perhaps we disliked history because the story of the Oregon Trail didn't include the story of the tribes displaced as a result of the western migration of European settlers. Perhaps we disliked history because we resented the fact that the great constitutional democracy this country was originally founded on didn't even include American Indians, African-Americans, or women. Many of our great grandfathers were not even citizens of this country until the Indian Citizenship Act of 1926.

To summarize the entire account of Indian-white relations and the telling of our story as entirely negative would also be wrong. John Neihardt beautifully captured the story of the Lakota way of being in Black Elk Speaks. Schoolcraft told a fraction of the truth in chronicling the history and culture of the Anishinabe. Densmore forever captured some of our old songs, where they will forever remain cataloged in the Smithsonian Museum. Warren left us with a written, albeit tainted, history. On the Fond du Lac Reservation, Sister Bernard Coleman, a Benedictine nun from the College of St. Scholastica, wrote a history of our community.

There are volumes upon volumes of written documents on the Fond du Lac Reservation, from initial European contact to the present. This collection could keep someone busy doing historical research for the rest of his or her life. This chapter is a sampling, a taste of all that is out there. Several locally written articles (Blueberry Stories and the Old Indian Hospital) are also included, as they tell another piece of our story.

References

Memmi, A. (1965). The colonizer and the colonized. New York: The Orion Press.

Fond du Lac on St. Louis River

Fond du Lac on St. Louis River

Spirit Island

Turd Island on the St. Louis River

Perch Lake

Mud Lake

Arnold Bassett

Donna Smith and Louise Smith

Lizzy Smith and Donna May Smith by government hospital.

Sawyer Church – 1909-1912

1912 – Sisters Zebence (Little Creek) and Wabiwewe (Snow Goose) holding baby Celia Goggle Eye, Maeh Kawbigwe (Squeezed in Chair). Zebence, Mike Shabaiash's grandmother died at the age of 128 in the Wagginogan (Poles That Are Bent) around 1926.

1914 – Aughquayaush wearing buffalo headdress given to him from East Lake by Sesakiwashi.

**Ben Bassett, Martha "Maita" Petite and Liz Smith,
hospital Autumn of 1949**

1911 – Deadfish Lake
Aushquayash - Mike Shabaiash's father, died April of 1923

**Liz Smith and
Isabella Savage**

St. Louis River

NEMHC Photo

NEMHC Photo

Mr. John LeGarde, 1807-2/27/11 – Old Fond du Lac (West Duluth)

St. Louis River

Part One:
A Book Review of Sr. Bernard Coleman's Where the Water Stops
– Bonita Sutliff

Sister Bernard Coleman's Where the Water Stops, published in 1967, is a concise history of Fond du Lac Reservation. The book, illustrated with old photographs and maps, takes its title from the English meaning of the Anishinabe word *Nagadjiwan*. It traces developments from the early fur trading days of the mid-1700s and early-1800s to the 1960s and offers such topics as religion, early reservation times, and leadership. Sister Coleman's work includes the results of about twenty-five years of field study and research in "customs, legends, and art designs of the Ojibwa" (Coleman 2).

Information found in the "Vita of Sr. Bernard Coleman" (St. Scholastica Monastery Archives) reveals that Sister Coleman (September 23, 1890 to September 26, 1974), an anthropologist, worked out of St. Scholastica Priory. During her career, she wrote or co-authored, six books or publications relating to the Ojibwe. Born and raised in Little Falls, Minnesota, she graduated from local schools; in 1910, from St. Cloud (MN) Normal School; in 1919, (B.A.) from St. Benedict's College (St. Joseph, MN); in 1929, (M.A.) from Catholic University (Washington, D.C.), and, in 1947, (Ph.D.) from Catholic University (Washington, D.C.). During her lifetime, Sister Coleman taught many subjects at several elementary and high schools and the College of St. Scholastica (CSS); she served as well in many other educational capacities, including principal of Cathedral Junior High (Duluth, MN) and Director of Adult Education at CSS [1-2].

According to a Duluth Herald (February 21, 1966) article, Sister Coleman's interest in Ojibwe culture and tradition was initiated by one of her college professors. Her first contact with reservation residents at Grand Portage, Fond du Lac, Mille Lacs, White Earth, and Leech Lake was founded on providing religious instruction. She soon became friendly with many of the Ojibwe people and "interviewed old timers and recorded stories which had been passed down orally from generation to generation" [9]. Where the Water Stops describes much of what she learned.

The 38 page book begins with an overview of the fur trade and its impact on the people of the Fond du Lac region. Evidence shows that this area, a choice location for fish, game, and wild rice, was once inhabited by mound-building people, who were replaced by the Dakotas. Reconnaissance records of fur traders Radisson and Groseilliers made between 1654 and 1660 report Dakotas living along the mouth of the *Wah-nit-ay-guay-oh* ("crooked" or "circular") or, as it is now known, the St. Louis River[3].

In the first part of the seventeenth century, fur trading Ojibwe journeyed from their Detroit home base to Quebec and Montreal trading posts. Weapons, ammunition, alcohol, blankets and other sundry goods were acquired in this manner. While it is true that they were being pushed from their eastern homes along the St. Lawrence by the Iroquois, it is also true that fur trading pulled them into the area. To lessen the long distance to the trading posts, the Ojibwe people settled in Mackinaw, then Sault Ste. Marie, and finally on Madeline Island[3].

From Madeline Island, the Ojibwe, in constant search of rich beaver fields, eventually fanned into Minnesota, Wisconsin, Canada, and beyond. This movement forced inhabitants of these areas to move or fight for their homelands. Wa-me-gie-ug-o, of the Marten family, was the first Ojibwe to pitch his wigwam at *Wi-a-qua-ke-che-gume-eng* (Head of the Lake or *Fond du Lac*). Other Ojibwe families settled on the islands of the St. Louis River, probably Big Island and Spirit Island. From this strategic point, they fought off attacks from the Dakotas, who were at that time living at Sandy Lake and Mille Lacs[4].

The book goes on to describe the first Ojibwe times in this area. From about 1745 to the mid-1800s the Dakotas struggled to retain their homelands, before survivors finally succumbed and moved westward. In 1750, Bi-aus-wah, an Ojibwe war chief, is reported to have led a large group of warriors to battle at Sandy Lake. "It is said that the trail of warriors was so long that a person on the hill could not see from one extremity of the lines to the other"[4].

The arrival of the fur trading era disrupted the Ojibwe hunting and gathering culture. Over time, heavy emphasis on hunting skills (beaver trapping) and growing dependence on trade goods, guns, and alcohol caused some loss of woodland living skills. The French established fur trading posts throughout the area and began marrying Ojibwe people, which further changed the culture. These marriages produced a new race of people, many of whom were "Voyageurs." Dressed in their brightly colored sashes and caps, they paddled the canoes of explorers and fur-trading companies, causing the wilderness to resound with their joyous songs"[4]. Voyageurs also transported trade goods and/or furs on portages[4].

In 1763, after the French and Indian War, the French ceded the

Minnesota country east of the Mississippi to Great Britain. Along with the British came Scotch and colonial traders. Jean Baptiste Cadotte, Jean Baptiste Perrault, and Alexander Henry, the Elder established separate posts and furthered exploration and documentation of the region. They penetrated into such areas as the Red River, Rainy Lake, and Grand Portage. Fond du Lac served as a fur collection point during this time. In 1793, Perrault oversaw the construction of Fort St. Louis, which was situated on the Superior Bayfront. The Northwest Company operated the fort until shortly after the War of 1812, when it was forced to withdraw. This fort became the distributing point (along with Grand Portage) for the Fond du Lac area, with traders coming from the upper St. Louis, Nemadji, Crow Wing, Red, and Pine rivers, as well as Leech, Sandy, and Cass lakes [5].

In 1816, John Jacob Astor built a post about twenty miles up the St. Louis River where Fond du Lac Reservation, as we know it today, is situated. From this site, he established the American Fur Company and, with the help of an Act of Congress, a complete monopoly. In 1826, Governor Lewis Cass and Thomas L. McKenny, of the Department of Indian Affairs, held treaty negotiations there. "Six hundred chiefs and their families gathered for the occasion" [5]. Beyond stating that "many of the half-breeds and native wives of the white men were named recipients of large tracts of land," Sister Coleman offers little information as to what happened at this gathering [5]. Shortly after this, the fur trade began to falter as beaver became more scarce. In 1834, Fond du Lac evolved into a fishery station [6].

The next topic that Sister Coleman's work presents is "Religion of The Chippewa." As might be expected, she concentrates on the Christian aspects. She does include an opening statement discussing animism:

> By nature, the Chippewa were deeply religious. Although they believed in Kijie manito, the creator of all things animate (i.e. having spirit power), they also believed in other manitos (spirits), such as the dream spirit. Each natural phenomena, each with its own spirit, some of them benevolent, like the sun, the moon, the lakes and streams; others, evil, as queer-shaped stones, or snakes. All that appeared to them evil or injurious, they made objects of worship to whom they offered sacrifices, such as tobacco or food, to prevent evil from happening to them [6].

In June, 1832, Reverend William H. Boutwell delivered the first documented Christian service held at Fond du Lac. Most missionaries of that time required the aid of an interpreter in their ministering and assimilation efforts. Where the Water Stops identifies some of the early missionaries who worked in the region, including Mr. Edmund F. Ely, William A. Aitkin, Father Frederic Baraga, Father Roussain, Father Skolla, and Reverent John H. Pitezal [6].

Many of the first missionaries were hunters and fishermen. Missionaries usually traveled appointed rounds by canoe, team, or on foot and held services at camp sites or private homes. Over time, their efforts saw churches and, often, mission schools built. Sister Coleman describes some of the hardships that people of those days faced. Rev. John H. Pitezal reported a tragedy that came with the transfer of the Indian payment from LaPointe to Sandy Lake in 1851. The delay in paying the annuity to the Indians resulted in nearly 200 deaths at Sandy Lake and along the trails. Fire, they were told, destroyed the new Indian Agency building, consuming their goods, money, and rations. This not only delayed the distribution of food, but increased the lack of it, especially since game had become scarce in the area. The Government issued rations of deteriorated flour and unwholesome meat. Most of the deaths were from food poisoning and exposure [7].

Sister Coleman summarizes Father Simon Lampe's account of the Cloquet-Moose Lake fire of 1918:

> A sixty-mile wind picked up several small forest fires and sent them sweeping over Brookston and Pupore with its enormous stand of hemlocks .... The Indian Reservation was set ablaze, and the wind swept the fire towards Cloquet and through it .... Realizing the fruitlessness of fighting such a fire, the missionary, carrying two satchels, started from an open spot along the railroad tracks between the priest's house and the St. Louis River. Finding the two satchels too heavy to carry, he abandoned them .... He was soon surrounded by absolute darkness and a dense suffocating smoke accompanied by a hurricane of wind and fire sweeping about him. Throwing off the burning particles that were raining upon him from the air, he anxiously awaited the morning ..... With the early dawn the fires seemed to have somewhat spent themselves. He made his way down the

tracks a mile and a half to Cloquet where he found the town of 8,000 burned to the ground .... back to his house he saw several Indians who were venturing out and from them learned that all the Indian homes in the Holy Family Mission had been destroyed except those of Antoine de Perry and Frank Dufault. Only one Indian perished in the fire. That was a little girl who fell from a wagon in which she and her family were fleeing from the flames [8].

Working out of Duluth, Father Simon began fund raising, and in 1919, a church, costing about $12,000, and a "commodious house" [8], costing about $4,000 were built. In 1923, Father Simon was replaced by Father Thomas Borgerding. An allotment given by Joe Petite was used for a cemetery [8].

Father Francis Bernick, O.S.B., installed in 1938, was pastor of Holy Family Mission until the mid-forties, when he was replaced by Father Benno Watrin. Father Watrin also provided religious instruction for Sawyer public schools, Holy Family Church, and Brookston children. The next pastor, Father Augustine, (Father Gus), established a clothing depot and saw electricity installed in the church buildings. In 1952, Father Jude Koll completed the parsonage, repaired the church and cemetery, built an addition onto the Big Lake Church and was in residence when Coleman's book was published [8].

A third section of the book deals with "Early Reservation Chippewa" and begins with a discussion of treaties. The first non-Indian explorers had reported this region as rich in metal. The Treaty of 1826 ceded metals and minerals. There was, however, no mining activity after the treaty signing. The Treaty of 1854 ceded land "north of the lake, extending westward to the line of the St. Louis and Vermilion rivers. This cession embraced nearly three million acres" [9]. The following is a description of the land set aside for the Fond du Lac Reservation:

> Beginning at an island in the St. Louis River, above Knife Portage, called by the Indians *Paw-paw-sco-me-me-tig*, running thence west to the boundary-line heretofore described, thence north along said boundary-line to the mouth of the Savannah River, thence down the St. Louis River to the place of beginning. And if said tract shall contain less than one hundred thousand acres, a strip of land shall be added on the south side there-

of, large enough to equal such deficiency [9].

First Chief Shingoop's signature is on this treaty, as well as those of two second chiefs: Mawn-gosit (Loon's Foot) and Naw-gaw-nub, (Foremost Sitter). The following headmen also signed: May-quaw-me-we-ge-zhick, Keesh-kawk, Caw-taw-waw-be-day, Ke-che-aw-ke-wain-ze, Ain-ne-maw-sung, Naw-aw-bun-way, Wain-ge-maw-tub, Aw-ke-wain-zeence, Shay-way-be-nay-se, Paw-pe-oh, and O-saw-gee. This tract held ninety-six thousand acres. In 1967, Sister Coleman wrote, "The boundaries of the Fond du Lac Reservation as determined by the treaty are essentially the same as they are today" [9].

During 1855, another treaty ceded land, almost half the size of the state, bearing valuable minerals and timber. Ojibwe people continued to live in their home-places. Non-Indian settlers began moving into the area, resulting in some interracial marriages. The village of Fond du Lac was platted in 1856. It consisted of a post office and fourteen other buildings; many of them were homes, or used for fur packing or provisions. In 1863, the Ojibwe ceded most of the Minnesota Red River Valley [9].

Leadership is the next topic discussed in this section. Traditionally, leadership derived through hereditary claims. Bands usually consisted of groups of extended family members living together. "The authority of the chief was more that of the head of the family than that of any other social grouping. The chief might be a war leader as well but this was not always true" [10]. This structure changed with the arrival of treaties when "the functions of the chief were to preside at councils of his band, to make decisions affecting the general good, and to represent the band at the payment of annuities and other gatherings" [10]. About this time some controversy concerning band leadership developed.

Edmund F. Ely writes that after the death of the old Chief Shingoop, which occurred on June 20, 1835, Joseph Naganub arrived at the school and inquired about the Indians, their gardens, and sugar camps, stating that he was the chief...[10].

Band elders, however, stated that Shingoope and Mawngosit were hereditary chiefs and Naganub "was only a spokesman" [10].

> (A) certificate signed by government officials installed (Mawngosit) as chief of the band of Fond du Lac. It ran as follows: This is to certify that the chief Shingoop, the speaker

Naganop, the head man and warriors of the Fond du Lac band of Chippeways, have this day requested that Mangusid be hereafter recognized as their chief pacificator and they have solemnly promised to refer to him all difficulties that may arise hereafter between them, and to abide by his decision[10].

"First Chippewa Village On St. Louis River Near Cloquet" is the title of the next chapter. County tax records of 1873 place Fond du Lacer's on the banks of the St. Louis River. Sometime in the 1880s, government officials urged Ojibwe people who had been living in the region and around logging camps to move onto the reservation, which had been logged by Nelson Lumber Company. "The Indians called the area where they were to live, '*Papashkominitegong*' meaning 'treeless island'"[11].

Sometime in the 1960s

Susan Madwayosh, gave this description of the earliest settlement on the reservation.

The land extended along the wagon road on the west bank of the St. Louis River near Cloquet. To help visualize the location, she explained it as occupying several hills behind Mike Houle's present home site, which is several blocks east toward Cloquet from the main road leading to the Holy Family Church today. When Mrs. Madwayosh's family moved from Carlton, the edge of the reservation, she was eight years of age. Her mother set up their wigwam on the first hill behind Mike Houle's home. Already settled on the hill they found Joe Frank's family, Tony Dufault's family, and a full-blood dark complexioned elderly woman, whom they called "Old Lady Makodemaquoque," who occupied a wigwam near them. Behind them, on the second hill, Tony Dufault's father's family lived in a large frame house. On this hill were also the Laclintas, the Ojibweys, the LaGroons, the Joe Houles, and the Naganubs, who lived in a blue house. On the next hill were the LaPrairies of Moose Lake, the Chisholms, of Lac Court de Oreilles Reservation, Wisconsin, and the Bassetts of Carlton. Susan's father came from Michigan

37

and was a fast mail carrier from St. Paul to Ashland. "He walked and never slept until he arrived at his destination." Gradually about one hundred other families came to take up land there. Mrs. Higby says their family came later, about sixty years ago, when the Great Northern Railroad was being put through to Carlton and Cloquet. Moses Posey's father and mother and family lived in a large frame house below the hill across from Posey Island. Later, his sister, Susan M. Posey lived with her husband in the only house at the edge of Cloquet [12].

Church and government officials encouraged Fond du Lacer's to farm, but they "were not interested in this type of work. Soil was poor and the growing season short" [13]. People lived much as they had in earlier times by hunting, fishing, trapping and harvesting wild rice, garden produce, berries, and other fruits. "Tea was a common beverage for all" [13].

The Chippewa had no great amount of goods or equipment. In each house was a cast-iron stove, a bed or two, table, benches, chairs or stools, a few shelves or cupboard for dishes or wooden bowls for private or common use, tin cans or kettles for cooking, a few knives and spoons. In many homes the children sat on the floor. Boxes or trunks for clothes were placed under the beds or along the sides. Extra clothing hung on hooks along the walls [13].

Many of the people worked for logging companies, the railroad, or fisheries. Until 1939, the government provided small annuities [13].

Fond du Lac did not escape the effects of the Allotment Act of 1887. "In due time, 173 individual allotments, covering 17,702 acres, were made in Fond du Lac Reservation" [12]. Non-Indian settlers and logging companies quickly purchased the remaining land. "The Indians received only small amounts for their timber, and since land was taken on all reservations, before long there were many landless and impoverished Indians" [12]. Governmental pressure to move to White Earth Reservation was resisted by 3,225 Fond du Lacers out of 4,000. By 1895, the government ceased issuing allotments [13].

However, John Lemieux of Superior declared that he and others received no allotments due to the injustices practiced by land agents. Finally his case was appealed and taken to district court December 1, 1923 by ten men and women, members of the Fond du Lac band, who lived in Superior. The plaintiffs were Emma Skye, M. Naughton, Peter Morrisette, John and Peter Lemieux and their relatives. The last six entered the litigation as heirs of Isabelle Osawgee Lemieux, daughter of Chief Osawgee .... (Lemieux) testified that on January 1888, the Government paid them each a small sum of money and some merchandise. Then Shah Bah Yaust, another member of their tribe, filed on their property and it was set aside for him. The government called this a test case and declared that the Indians could not claim the land unless they had lived upon it [13].

"Many of the people who live on the Fond du Lac Reservation today (1960s) are descendants of those who chose to live there or were pressured to accept allotments" [13].

"Reorganized Fond du Lac Chippewa" is the fourth and briefest chapter of Sister Coleman's book. It looks primarily at the Indian Reorganization Act (IRA) of 1934 and its impact on Fond du Lac Reservation. This Act of Congress, in response to the impoverished reservation conditions described by the Meriam Report, sought to enable American Indians to operate to relieve this distress .... More than two hundred Fond du Lac Chippewa refused to accept the charter at a meeting and called upon voters ... to reject the proposal. Members ... who argued against the "Reorganization Act" included: David Savage, Frank Houle, France Cajune, Joseph LaPrairie, Jim Rogers, John Landry and Mrs. Albert Fairbanks; Fred Doolittle, chairman of the Fond du Lac Chippewa presided. The Fond du Lac speakers believed that the act would put the Chippewa back two or three hundred years instead of advancing them. Although the Fond du Lac Indians did not vote for the act, two-thirds of the Chippewa in the state voted for it, and so they were duly organized under this Act on June 18, 1934, having adopted a constitution and by-laws and later, at their petition, were granted a corporate charter [14].

This section also describes the Farmer-Labor Party, chaired by David Savage, which was active at the close of World War II. Mrs. Josephine Thompson served as secretary, and Rudy Roddeo, a Cloquet lawyer, provided legal advice. This group, according to Savage, functioned well for "five or six years" and then met opposition from council members [14]. No further information on this subject is given.

Sister Coleman devotes a longer chapter to "Development of Chippewa Leadership." She opens with a description of the health conditions and treatment on the Reservation. Little mention is made of natural practices or treatment by medicine men. The year 1914 brought Cloquet doctors and Duluth specialists to Fond du Lac and a 16-bed hospital built by the Department of Indian Affairs. Fond du Lac Reservation people began using the hospital for births and various illnesses. After a time, hospital services were available to Nett Lake, Grand Portage, Tower, and Mille Lac reservation residents [14].

> The out-patient department was also well received, and medicines have been made available for many years .... In 1955, public health service took over the control of the hospital .... Thus the Chippewa felt it keenly when the hospital was closed March 12, 1958 [15].

> The closing of the Indian hospital was a historic occasion, making another milestone on the long road toward equality for the Fond du Lac Reservation's first citizens. It meant that concern for the health and physical welfare of the Chippewa was being lifted out of the "separate" category and classified with that of their neighbors [15].

The change in housing, from the "open wigwam and tepee, to crowded, poorly ventilated huts made Indians especially susceptible to infections from tuberculosis and trachoma"[15]. In 1911, a Reservation survey revealed that about one person out of every fifteen suffered from tuberculosis. A Walker, Minnesota. sanitarium received these patients [15].

According to the next section, it was in the 1920s, when American Indians became United States citizens, that living conditions began to change. Sister Coleman writes of interviews which she conducted:

> Second generation Indian youth tell me that their grandparents lived quite satisfactory lives. They engaged in hunting and fishing, ricing and some gardening, when they felt the need. It was later when game became scarce and the white man encroached on his domain that life for the Indian became deploringly restricted. During treaty-making periods, payments for land were made by the federal government in money, then in goods and services. Following the treaty-making period, Indians were confined to reservations and were the sole concern of the feder-

40

al government .... Most of the money .... came from Indian funds and not from tax money [16].

Federal aid was minimized and eventually stopped in 1929. During the Depression years, Fond du Lacer's were eligible for government programs available to every citizen. Employment conditions improved somewhat during World War II. At the time Sister Coleman's book was published, "although Fond du Lac employment is greater than on other Minnesota reservations," the population had increased, unemployment was high, and the Bureau of Indian Affairs contributed nothing to Indian welfare [16].

Formal education began for Fond du Lacer's in 1834. A mission school instructed by Edmund Ely of the American Board of Foreign Missions focused on "reading, writing, geography, and numbers. He [Ely] even allowed the pupils to count the number of pelts brought in to the trading post .... Indian pupils were pleased to learn that their knowledge of arithmetic was of some value to them"[16]. On occasion, school was canceled when students were needed for harvesting purposes and could thus "learn how to do these important things"[16]. The school closed in 1839 after growing "opposition to the government's methods of dealing with the Indians grew, and famine and sickness became more frequent"[16]. A Methodist mission school operated for a few years after that [16].

Sister Coleman relates that "most of the older people on the reservation have attended Government contract or church schools during the 1880s and 1890s" [16]. In these schools, assimilation was the goal: students could not speak their home languages; students learned English, farming, and other mainstream trades and habits. Discipline was enforced. Fond du Lac pupils attended boarding schools in such distant places as Collegeville, White Earth, Pipestone, and Tower, MN.; Tomah and Red Cliff, WS.; Pennsylvania and Kansas [16].

Around 1894, Fond du Lacer's were encouraged to enroll in the local day school. Students of five to eighteen years of age attended by walking or canoeing to school. John, Henry, and Mary Beargrease were among these pupils. The early 1900s brought a government day school under the direction of Mr. Von Felden; another day school was established in the Big Lake village. In the 1960s, students from the Reservation attended school in Cloquet, Sawyer, Brookston, and Carlton and formed about three percent of the student population. Sister Coleman includes her opinion that:

41

The disadvantages of the Indian student, as a member of a small minority, are a lack of awareness by others that he is culturally different, often intellectually starving, and usually economically deprived. But the Indian student is fully aware of these differences and, as a consequence, feels a sense of isolation within his peer group. His passive-aggressive personality traits are reinforced by this situation. The drop-out rate in the Carlton-Cloquet school system indicates the prevalence of these disadvantages [17].

The final section of Where the Water Stops investigates the "New Frontier" (of the 1960s). A geographical description of the Reservation includes:

The area within the boundaries of the Fond du Lac Reservation consists of approximately 40,000 acres of which 21,634 are Indian owned. Of this total, individual Indian allotments consist of 17,702 acres and the remaining 3,932 acres are tribally owned. Tribal land consists of eighty acres reserved for home sites at Cloquet and forty acres reserved for home sites at Sawyer. A total of 280.5 acres are being leased; farm leases account for 260.5 acres of this land. There is approximately 1,300 acres of swampland which presently holds out little value for development. Red pine and spruce plantations, covering 634 acres, have been planted in the period 1962 through 1964 [17].

About 650 people lived on the Reservation, with about 200 Fond du Lacer's in its immediate area, while "the Sawyer group consists of forty families. Eighty-five families resided in the area to the west of Cloquet, while fourteen families live in and around the village of Brookston" [17]. Although Ojibwe was "spoken in a few of the homes" [17], English had become the dominant language.

In 1964-1966, the Fond du Lac Reservation Business Committee had "become an active and dynamic force under the leadership of its chairman, Sherman Smith and Peter Dufault, secretary-treasurer" [17]. They oversaw conversion of the old hospital building into a community center. A section of the building was torn down, and the rest of it remodeled and modernized with new windows, a heating unit, and updated plumbing and wiring. The building housed rooms for administration, educational, and social purposes [17].

Photographs and drawings from Cloquet and Duluth newspapers, the St. Louis County Historical Society, tribal and mission archives, Eastman

Johnson, and private collections illustrate <u>Where the Water Stops</u>. One photograph displays the remains of the John Jacob Astor fur trading post taken in about 1856. Several photographs of the Naganab family showing Joseph, Alex, and Sophie, as well as one of Alex Naganab's Big Lake home are included. Of special interest might be an 1854 group picture of the Chippewa Peace Commission which shows E. Roy, Vincent Roy, E. Roussain, Frank Roussain, Peter Roy, Joe Gournceau, and D. George Morrision taken in Washington, D.C. Chief Mongosit holds a pipe in one undated picture, while Ben Beargrease stands with his wife in another picture from about 1870. The Holy Family Parish of 1920 is represented in a photograph of a large group of unidentified people taken in front of the church. Undated pictures, which appear to be more recent, show unidentified members of the Golden Age Club of Fond du Lac Indian Reservation residents. Another undated picture is captioned with "Cooperative venture on Fond du Lac Reservation is novel experience for Indians and visiting teeners." Sister Coleman's book includes several other pictures of both early and more recent times.

The strength of <u>Where the Water Stops</u> lies in the time span and broad range of topics presented. Sister Coleman's twenty-five years of careful research and interviewing can be seen in some of the examples rounding out historical facts, which enable readers to relate present day events and activities to those of earlier times. Extensive contact and interactions with Fond du Lacer's allowed her to trace and report changes created by their immersion into mainstream culture and something of its impact. Sister Bernard Coleman's work stands today as one of the most complete histories of the Fond du Lac Reservation.

Part Two:
Fond du Lac Village on the St. Louis River
– Betty Dahl

The term "Fond du Lac" as used by early French traders and missionaries designated the region around the bottom or furthest end of Lake Superior.

Lakes and rivers in the Northland were created by the receding of the last glacial period about B.C. 12,000. The new growth of vegetation attracted large game animals, which were followed by small groups of people about B.C. 10,000.

The St. Louis River, which flows from Lake Superior through the Fond du Lac area, was a major waterway used to travel to the north by means of portages, including the Savanna, Prairie River, and Knife Falls Portages. Jesuit cartographers in 1670 showed the St. Louis River on a map of "Lac Tracy du Superieur."

Many groups of people inhabited the Fond du Lac region, the last being the Dakotas, before the recorded coming of the Ojibwe in the early part of the 17th century when *Wa- me-gis-ug-o* "pitched his wigwam permanently at Fond du Lac, or *Wi-a-quah-ke-che-gume-eng*. He belonged to the Marten Totem family, and the present [1885] respected chiefs of that now important village, *Shin-goob* and *Nug-aun-ub*, are his direct descendants."[1] Many of his people followed and erected their wigwams on the islands of the St. Louis River, near its outlet into the lake for greater security. They held out against numerous attacks of the Dakotas, whose villages were two days march to the south on the St. Croix River, and at Sandy Lake, to the west. Biauswah II led a war party against the Dakotas at Fond du Lac, pushing as far west as Sandy Lake where he established a village.

Trading with Indians for furs began in the mid-1600's and continued for two hundred years. The first documented trading post in the Fond du Lac area was established by the North West Company in present day Superior, Wisconsin, in 1793. On the Minnesota side of the St. Louis River, in present day Fond du Lac, the American Fur Company traded from 1814 until 1834, at a location on the shore of the river between what is now 133rd and 134th Avenues West. Behind the post were two burial grounds, one Christian and one older Indian site at the base of the hill. Several missions and a school were con-

44

ducted at Fond du Lac during the 1800s.

Lewis Cass held council with tribal representatives at the Fond du Lac village in 1826, seeking ratification of the 1825 Treaty of Prairie du Chien. In 1832 Lieutenant Allen, with the Schoolcraft Expedition, reported four hundred persons, Ojibway and mixed, occupying the village of Fond du Lac, and left this description of the trading post: "The buildings consist of a dwelling house, three or four stories high, a large house for the accommodation of clerks, and some other buildings, for Frenchmen. They are handsomely situated on the bank of the river, and directly in front is an island of about two miles circuit [*Nekuk*], of very rich soil, and a forest of large elms, where the Indians assembled in the lodges."[2]

An interesting observation of Fond du Lac was written by Mrs. John I. Post, on December 24, 1854, which said, "The difference between the temperature of the air out upon the lake and the inland, causes us to view objects through a denser and a rarer medium, and produces mirages, which are sometimes very striking. This phenomenon is so frequent here, that the Indians have given it the name of The Spirit Land or Enchanted Land. Sometimes in summer the head of the Bay will also appear so near to us, as to almost doubt our own sanity."

The Ojibwe continued to live in the village, including the islands, until the Treaty of La Pointe in 1854, which established the Fond du Lac Reservation near Cloquet, Minnesota.

In the latter days of the fur trade, the late 1800's, game was no longer very plentiful. The people of Fond du Lac were often hungry and suffered from the winter's cold. Government payments were made at La Pointe and required each person, young and old, to make the trip to sign for payment.

The village was platted in 1856, incorporated in 1857, and eventually annexed by the City of Duluth. In 1870, construction of the Lake Superior and Mississippi Railroad passed through the burial grounds of the Fond du Lac village. This prompted Eustache Roussain, son of an early French fur trader and an Ojibwe mother, to move many of the burials to land he owned up the hill in what is now Jay Cooke State Park. Spirit houses and white picket fencing were present until the 1950s. The last burial in Roussain's new cemetery was a Mrs. Durfee in 1914.

Timber was harvested in Fond du Lac, and red/brown sandstone was quarried to erect some of the buildings in Duluth and elsewhere. The village became a vacation spot for picnickers transported on trains and boats. It included an entertainment center on *Nekuk* Island. Homes were built and, in time, the once-busy village quieted down to its present state.

In the early days at Fond du Lac, wild rice was gathered in the St. Louis River, fish and game were abundant, ducks were hunted around *Nekuk* Island, and wild plum trees grew on the property known today as Chamber's Grove. It was described as a "romantic spot, nestled among the wooded hills, with beautiful islands in the river, and the woods teeming with wild game...."[3]

References:

History of the Ojibwe People. William W. Warren. Minnesota Historical Society Press. St. Paul. Original date 1885, new edition 1984. Pages 129, 130.

Duluth and St. Louis County. Volume I. Walter Van Brunt. The American Historical Society. Chicago and New York. 1921. Page 50.

Duluth and St. Louis County. op. cit., page 38. Remarks by the Hon. Wm. E. McEwen, in a paper read in 1915 at a gathering of the Old Settlers of the Head of Lake Superior.

Part Three:
A History of the Boundaries of the Fond du Lac Reservation
– Robert Peacock

Since the negotiation of the 1854 Treaty of LaPointe between the Ojibwe of Lake Superior and the United States, the location of the boundaries of the Fond du Lac Reservation has been of continuing concern to the people of the Fond du Lac Band. Many disagreements have arisen over this issue, both among members of the Band and in legal battles between the Band, Band members, the United States, and the State of Minnesota. On September 30, 1854, the Ojibwe of Lake Superior entered into a treaty with the United States at LaPointe, Wisconsin, on Madeline Island, which is the historical center of the Chippewa people (10 Stat. 1109). Under the Treaty of LaPointe, the Chippewa ceded northeastern Minnesota to the federal government as described:

> Beginning at a point, where the east branch of Snake River crosses the southern boundary line of the Chippewa country, running thence up the said branch to its source, thence nearly north, in a straight line, to the mouth of East Savannah River, thence up the St. Louis River to the mouth of East Swan River to its source thence in a straight line to the most westerly bend of Vermillion River, and thence down the Vermillion River to its mouth.

The treaty also reserved and set aside certain reservations, including a tract for the Fond du Lac band, which was described as follows:

> Beginning at an island in the St. Louis River, above Knife Portage, called by the Indians Paw-paw-sco-me-me-tig, running thence west to the boundary-line heretofore described, thence north along said boundary-line to the mouth of Savannah River, thence down the St. Louis River to the place of beginning. And if said tract shall contain less than one hundred thousand acres, a strip of land shall be added on the South side thereof, large enough to equal such deficiency.

The first survey of the Fond du Lac Reservation was conducted by Peter Bradshaw in the summer of 1858. He concluded that the reservation contained 125,294 acres. He also discovered that the reservation, as surveyed, did not include the Band's primary settlement in the Perch Lake area, approximately four miles south of the Reservation's southern boundary line.

The above description describes the original boundary of the Fond du Lac Reservation.

> The southern boundary obviously depends on the location of the specified island in the St. Louis River called Paw-paw-sco-me-me-tig. However, this landmark cannot be clearly identified today, and its identification was already a concern when the land was first being surveyed because it was believed that the island would erode away. Because of this concern, an unnamed spring, which drained into the river across from the island on the river shore, was used to further identify the island. Today even this location is disputed. These details are important because the location marks the point of the beginning point of the southern boundary of the Reservation, and later it would mark the north-south line of the land added by executive order in 1858.

The 1858 Executive Order

By 1858, some problems with the treaty description of the boundaries of the Fond du Lac Reservation were emerging. After a survey of the exterior boundary of the Reservation had been made in conformance with the 1854 treaty description, it was found that the southern boundary, as surveyed by Bradshaw, was three or four miles north of the principal Band settlement at Perch Lake. Complaints by the Fond du Lac Band to the Commissioner of Indian Affairs and the Secretary of the Interior were submitted to the President of the United States so that lands around Perch Lake could be withdrawn from sale and appropriate steps could be taken by the President to settle the existing problems with the boundary by changing the lines of the established treaty boundary:

> The estimated area of the Reservation embraces 125,294 acres, being about 25,000 acres more than was contemplated by the

stipulations of the treaty, therefore, I would suggest that the Government as well as the Indians would be benefited by extending the southern boundary so as to include the Indian settlements, and by reducing the aggregate area in order that the reserve may embrace as nearly as possible 100,000 acres.

(Letter from J.W. Denver, Commissioner of Indian Affairs to J. Thompson, Secretary of the Interior, November 16, 1858.)

The Secretary of the Interior then requested the Commissioner to identify the specific tracts which he recommended to be withdrawn from public sale in order to establish new boundaries. In compliance, the Commissioner identified Townships 48 North, 12, 17, 18 and 19 West; Township 49 North, 12, 16 West, West of St. Louis River; and Township 49 North, 12, 17 18, and 19 West of the fourth principal meridian. The Secretary recommended that these tracts be withdrawn from sale for the purposes specified in the November 16, 1858 letter. President James Buchanan did so, in an Executive Order dated December 21, 1858, which simply stated: "Let the tracts specified be withdrawn, as requested by the Secretary of the Interior."   [U.S. Dept. of the Interior, Executive Orders Relating to Indian Reservations From May 14, 1855 to July 1, 1912 84-54 (Washington, D.C.: Government Printing Office, 1912)]. Another interesting issue is that the ranges numbered "12" may be misprints. Unfortunately, these misprints have created controversy in the years following the second boundary change. This Executive Order was the last formal action in regard to establishing the boundaries of the Fond du Lac Reservation.

In November 1859, President Buchanan authorized a new survey to implement the 1858 Executive Order. The new survey was conducted by S.A. Forbes in 1860, and added 41,280 acres to the south of the original Reservation, while reducing the western portion of the Reservation by 66,453 acres. The Forbes Survey thus reduced the Reservation to 100,121 acres – a net loss of 25,173 acres from the reservation as surveyed by Bradshaw in 1858. The Commissioner of Indian Affairs approved the Forbes Survey by letter to the Northern Superintendent of Indian Affairs on August 7, 1860, directing the

Superintendent to

> take measures ... to establish the exterior lines of the same, and when completed ... to report to this office a description of said exterior lines to the end that the same may be incorporated in articles of agreement ... to be concluded with the Fond du Lac Band with the view of securing to them the land embracing their improvements in lieu of that designated in the treaty.

(Letter of Commissioner A.B. Greenwood to Superintendent William J. Cullen, August 7, 1860.)

The Fond du Lac Band never entered into an agreement with the United States as recommended by the Commissioner's letter and there is no record that the Band knew of or approved the reduction of the western Reservation. The new Reservation boundaries were never formalized by congressional action. When the Band brought the matter before the United States Court of Claims years later, the Court stated that the Forbes Survey had been undertaken at the Band's request in order to include the Perch Lake settlements in the Reservation, and that the Band had made no objection to the western diminishment until the Nelson Act negotiations some 25 years later. Fond du Lac Band v. United States, 34 Ct. Cl. 426, 429 (1899). The result was that the Forbes survey constitutes the present day boundaries of the Fond du Lac Reservation (Figure 2).

The Nelson Act of 1889

The Nelson Act became effective on March 4, 1890, when agreements between the United States and each of the bands comprising the present Minnesota Chippewa Tribe (Bois Forte, Grand Portage, Fond du Lac, Leech Lake, Mille Lacs and White Earth) and the Red Lake Band, were approved by the President of the United States (25 Stat. 642).

Under the terms of the Nelson Act, each of the bands ceded in trust their land not needed for allotments. The United States promised to appraise the land, classify it as "pine or agricultural," and sell it for the Chippewa. The Nelson Act provided that the proceeds of the land and timber sold were to be deposited in a permanent fund, earning interest at a rate of five percent per annum. Three-fourths of the interest earned on the fund was to be distributed in per capita payments, and the remaining one-fourth was to be spent on education for the Chippewa. The permanent fund was to be distributed per capita 50 years after the allotments were completed.

Following the Nelson Act, allotments were made. On the Fond du Lac Reservation, some Chippewa had received allotments prior to the Nelson Act. Much of the land not allotted was classified as pine or agricultural, and sold. Passage of the Indian Reorganization Act of 1934 suspended all further sales of land, and the land not sold was restored to each of the Chippewa bands (25 U.S.C. § 461 et seq.).

The proceeds from the sales of land and timber were credited to an interest bearing fund, but, within 40 years of the effective date of the Nelson Act, the United States spent almost all money in both the principal (permanent) and interest funds.

The Nelson Act authorized the President to appoint commissioners to negotiate with the various bands and tribes of Ojibway in Minnesota for the cession and relinquishment of all title and interest in their reservations, except portions of the White Earth and Red Lake reservations. During these negotiations, the chiefs and headmen of the Fond du Lac Band communicated to the Commission their claim that the reservation boundaries were not in accordance with the treaty lines. The commissioners promised that the government would speedily remedy this error. Congress responded by authorizing the Fond du Lac Band, as part of an 1897 appropriations act, to sue the United States in the Court of Claims:

> That the claim of the Fond du Lac Band of Chippewa Indians
> of Lake Superior for compensation arising from the alleged dif-
> ference in area of the reservation as actually set apart to them
> and that provided to be set apart, under the [Treaty of LaPointe]
> is hereby, referred to the Court of Claims; and jurisdiction is
> hereby conferred on said court, with right of appeal as in other
> cases, to hear and determine the difference, if any, between the
> area of the reservation actually set apart to said Indians and that
> provided to be set apart in said treaty, if any, the said action to
> be brought by the said Fond du Lac Band of Chippewa Indians
> against the United States by petition, verified under oath by any
> duly authorized attorney for said Indians, within thirty days

from the passage of this Act; and in hearing and determining the said matter, the court shall take into consideration and determine whether since the date of said treaty there has been any equitable adjustment made to said Indians in whole or in part for the alleged difference in area, and the court shall also take into consideration and make due allowance for the fact that said Indians were given a share in the proceeds of the lands sold and disposed of under and pursuant to the provisions of [the Nelson Act] ... [S]aid action shall have precedence in said court and when completed, the court shall make a full report to Congress.

(30 Stat. 88-89).

The 1899 Court of Claims Decisiom

In its petition to the Court of Claims, the Band stated that it understood that the extension south to include Perch Lake was an addition to the reservation established by the 1854 treaty, that the southern addition was not made with an intent to cut off land on the west, and that the Band never consented to the diminishment proposed by the Forbes survey. The Band contended that the Reservation included all land in the Bradshaw survey plus the southern extension added by the Forbes Survey.

The Band took a different position when it submitted its Request for Findings of Fact to the Court. The Band proposed that "the only equitable adjustment allowed to said Indians for this land taken off the western part of the reservation was the addition made to the southern part of the reservation." The Band contended that the net loss was 25,814 acres, and that their share of proceeds from land sales under the Nelson Act did not apply to this loss. [Fond du Lac Band v. United States, 34 Ct. Cl. 426, 434 (1899)].

Following testimony, the Court of Claims found that the difference between the current reservation and the reservation as set apart by the 1854 treaty was 25,173 acres. The court also found that the land excluded on the west was "swampy and unfit for cultivation," while most of the territory added to the south included high, rolling, arable lands and was very productive. The court held:

That the lands on the west, excluded by the last survey, were of no greater value than the lands added on the south, so that in respect to the value of the original and diminished reservation there was little, if any difference.

[Fond du Lac Band v. United States, 34 Ct. Cl. 426, 434 (1899)].

The court also held that the Fond du Lac Band's share of the proceeds from the sale of land under the Nelson Act greatly exceeded the difference between the area of the original and diminished reservation. The court concluded that since the date of the Treaty of 1854, under which the reservation was originally set apart to the claimants, there had been an equitable adjustment made to said Indians in whole "for alleged difference in area," and that therefore the claimants were not entitled to recover compensation.

In 1988, Band members Marvin Eno and Judie Victrelli challenged state income tax assessments in state court on the grounds that they were exempt from state income tax because they worked on the reservation. Their argument was rejected by the Minnesota Tax Court. The court held that the [Cloquet] post office is not located within the boundaries of the Fond du Lac Reservation, and that their income was subject to taxation by the State. Eno v. Commissioner of Revenue, Nos. 4818 and 4832 (Minn. Tax Ct. Oct. 22, 1987).

The case was appealed to Federal District Court. In their complaint, Eno and Victrelli asked the court to declare the boundaries of the Fond du Lac Reservation to be those set out in the 1854 Treaty, and to include the land withheld by the 1858 Executive Order. They contended that the reservation contained over 230,000 acres. The Band also sought monetary damages for the exclusion of the disputed area from the recognized boundaries. Eno and Victrelli sought the return of state income tax collected on income earned in the disputed area. The defendants, the State of Minnesota and the United States moved to dismiss based on the preclusive effect of 1899 decision of the Court of Claims.

The decision by the United States District Court in the above case was that Congress provided a forum for the instant suit when it created the Indian Claims Commission. That this court does not have jurisdiction to hear a claim which, by express Congressional direction, was forever barred if not presented to the Commission.

In spite of this holding, the court addressed the issues raised by the dismissal motions. The court accepted the factual allegations of the plaintiffs' complaint which did not conflict with the findings of the Court of Claims. The Band attempted to avoid the preclusive effect of that decision by seeking a remedy – restoration of boundaries – which was not available from the Court of Claims. Unfortunately, that remedy was not available from the Federal District Court either. Consequently, the Court of Claims findings on compensation is binding.

The Court also found that the Band did not present to the Court of Claims its current claim for the land originally withheld by the 1858 Executive Order and then released after confirmation of the Forbes survey. Contrary to the Band's contention that the jurisdictional act precluded it from presenting this claim, the Federal District Court concluded that the Band did not claim any entitlement to this land in its earlier court action. The doctrine of res judicata which stated that the Band can't re-litigate a boundary dispute that was adjudicated by the Court of Claims, barred the Band from litigating the claim because it could have been presented in the earlier proceeding.

The Federal District Court found that the facts which provided the basis for the earlier court case were the same facts underlying the current claim. It determined that the Band had its day in court, and the arguments presented by the Band to avoid the preclusive effect of that earlier opinion were not availing, accordingly, the defendants' motion for dismissal was granted on March 16, 1989.

[Fond du Lac Band of Lake Superior Chippewa v. State of Minnesota, No. 5-87-0300 (D. Minn. 1989)].

So that is how our Reservation's boundaries were established. Are they the correct boundaries? There will always be disagreement because the location of the island called Paw-paw-sco-me-me-tig cannot be determined. If the island's location was further to the south, as many have claimed, then the cities of Cloquet and Scanlon would lie within the Reservation's boundaries, but some say that Forbes was influenced to avoid this area and run the boundary line west of the city of Cloquet. Because of this, the island which is today identified as Posey Island was at one time supposed to have been called Paw-paw-sco-me-me-tig.

It should also be noted that, in addition to the land reserved by the Fond

54

du Lac Band under the Treaty of LaPointe, the Band has added to the historical Reservation land base through various acquisitions, including the present sites of two Band casinos — the Fond-du-Luth Casino in downtown Duluth, Minnesota, and the Black Bear Casino & Hotel in Carlton County, Minnesota. Also, the federal courts have upheld the hunting, fishing and gathering rights reserved by the Band under Article 5 of the Treaty of July 29, 1837 (7 Stat. 536) and Article 11 of the Treaty of LaPointe. Fond du Lac Band of Lake Superior Chippewa v. Carlson, No. 5-92- 159 (D. Minn. March 18, 1996), aff'd, 124 F.3d 904 (8th Cir. 1997) (Figure 3).

As of this writing, the Reservation Business Committee is undertaking a thorough re-examination and legal evaluation of the entire Reservation boundary issue. Whether this inquiry will have any beneficial effect on the Band's land base remains to be seen. At the very least, however, we believe that it is our obligation to never let go of this matter, regardless of what the courts say.

Assistance in preparing this article was provided by Sonosky, Chambers, Sachse & Endreson Law Firm, Washington, D.C., Doug Endreson Atty., and Dennis J. Peterson, Atty. Fond du Lac Band of Lake Superior Chippewa.

Part Four:
Prairie Island: An Interview With Vernon Butcher
–Betty Dahl

[Interview with Vernon Butcher regarding possible burial ground on an island in Prairie Lake, located along Highway 73 between Cromwell and Floodwood, Minnesota. – Betty Dahl]

Mr. Butcher stated that some people thought he owned Prairie Island, but he did not. He cautioned that the information he gave in the interview was all hearsay, what he had heard.

Mr. Butcher said that on the west bay of Prairie Lake, where cabins are located, are below-ground burials. Indians who lived in that location were: John Foot, Blackcutter or Blacketter, and O'Day.

John Ukola (sp) told Mr. Butcher that, in 1910, he was a livery stable worker and was hired by the Lake Superior and Mississippi Railroad to hook up a team and go across the lake (ice) to bring in Mrs. John Foot and then witnessed her "X" to property transfer.

1875   Somehow the island was left off the Survey of 1875.

1911   Reapplied for Survey in 1911 but it did not go through.

1917   Prairie Lake Indians moved to Nett Lake.

1950's Mr. Butcher found a Land Law Book stating unpatented lands revoked to the government.

A surveyor from Denver had mapped and surveyed the island, but Mr. Butcher could not remember his name.

Pino's (sp) Resort on the north side of Prairie Lake – standing there you look right out at the island with the burial ground.

There are two other islands on the map: Sunken Island and one other for which Mr. Butcher could not recall the name. There is also Blackwood Lake at the southeat corner of Prairie Lake. Mr. Butcher noted a cemetery of Indians at Brookston Cemetery, and he wanted someone to take a look at strange pits in Brevator Township near the railroad tracks. He wondered if they were left by meteorites.

Mr. Butcher advised anyone going to the island in Prairie Lake to wear boots and long-sleeved shirts as the island is covered with poison ivy.

Vernon Butcher was correct in his belief that burials were present on

Prairie Island. A letter sent in 1912 by C. F. Hauke, Second Assistant Commissioner, to the Secretary of the Interior requested a survey of the island on Prairie Lake on behalf of the Northern Pacific Railway, after receiving citizen protests of possible disturbance of an old burial ground on the island still in use by Ojibwe. Mr. Hauke had requested the Superintendent of the Fond du Lac School to investigate and submit a report.

G. W. Cross, superintendent of the school, reported to the Commissioner of Indian Affairs in 1912 that Indians were living around the lake and that he had found a burial ground on the island. It contained about 25 graves, though Indians living there told him there were about 75 burials. The island had been in use as a burial ground for 50 to 75 years, he said. The Indians who had relatives buried there requested the island be retained by the federal government so the burials would not be disturbed. Cross found that the island had never been surveyed and was still in possession of the Federal Government.

F. H. Abbott, Assistant Commissioner, wrote to the Secretary of the Interior in 1912 recommending the application of the Northern Pacific Railway not be approved, and that his office "be instructed to prepare a bill for submission to Congress to reserve said island as a burial ground for the Chippewa Indians of Minnesota."[1]

Letters were submitted to the Northern Pacific Railway in 1915 informing of a decision by the Department of the Interior for a Denial of Application. However, after a number of letters requesting the island be withdrawn by Executive Order and reserved as a burial ground, Mr. Bo Sweeney, Assistant. Secretary, Department of the Interior, wrote to the Commissioner of the General Land Office, May 15, 1915, denying the request. He cited the fee vested in the Northern Pacific Railroad Company under a grant made to it by the act of July 2, 1904, (13 Stat., 365) had removed the island from government ownership. "In my opinion the reservation should not and cannot be made. Not only is such a reservation unnecessary but it does not appear that this island can be lawfully reserved for any purpose whatever."[2] The land was not, therefore, "public land" as referred to in 36 Stat. 847, which authorized withdrawals for public and other purposes.

Cross received an answer from Hauke, that the island could not be withdrawn and held as an Indian burying ground, as the title to the land had already passed to the Northern Pacific Railroad Company, subject to a dominant easement in the Indians for cemetery purposes.

In an address entitled "Indian Relics, Mounds and Remembrances of Floodwood," at the October 24, 1929 meeting of the St. Louis County Historical Society, he stated,

> At the time of my arrival (1888) Prairie Lake had an Indian settlement of 250 or more. The main part of the village was located where the Nordness home now stands. The Island in Prairie Lake was used as a cemetery, a good many Indians buried there."[3]

Another early Floodwood settler, Garfield Blackwood, in "Reminiscences" recalled, "in 1890 John Mckay was the first white settler at Prairie Lake, the site of his homestead was later known as 'Nordness Location.'"[4]

The Plat Book for the State of Minnesota for 1915 shows the "Nordness Location" (Norelius) in Section 20, T 50N R20W, which described the 1888 Indian village.

Interviews recorded by Rachael Ewoldsen in 1981 found seven people who reported Indian burials on Prairie Island. Ewoldsen conducted the interview as part of a project for Archaeological Research and included a walkover survey of the island. She reported several possible mounds and numerous impacted pits which she concluded had been burials, having found bone fragments and stone artifacts.

The site of the former Indian village on the northwest side of the lake coincides with the early Prairie Portage Trail from the St. Louis River near Gowan, Minnesota to Prairie Island, a distance of about six miles. The trail, known as the "Old Portage," was preferred by Indians over the Savanna Portage when carrying light loads and using light canoes. From Prairie Lake, travel was by canoe via the Prairie River on the western end of the lake, to Sandy Lake, and then to the Mississippi River. The Prairie River courses in a southerly direction to Prairie Lake, offering an alternative to the Portage Trail.

John Fritzen described the Prairie Portage in writing about the Savanna Portage which was much more difficult. Another reference to travel via Prairie

Prairie Island, Prairie Lake, and Prairie River were important to early travelers, as well as Indians who lived in the area, walked the portages, and canoed the waters.

Another reference to travel via the Prairie River was given by Jean Baptiste Perrault in his "Narrative....," which describes the wintering house built at Prairie Lake in 1784.[6] This information has been the subject of much controversy as to whether Perrault meant the Savanna River rather than the Prairie River.

During 1991 and 1992, two persons reported finding bone fragments and blue beads in the soil at the base of a tree on the island in Prairie Lake. Information from people living and vacationing in the area told of cows being put to pasture on the island.

A place such as Prairie Island should be remembered. Vernon Butcher remembered it and wanted us to know about it, too. We thank him and his wife for sharing their information.

References

5)   Letter: F. H. Abbott, Assistant Commissioner, General Land Office to Secretary of the Interior. June 28, 1912.

5)   Letter: Bo Sweeney, Assist.ant Secretary, Department of the Interior, to the Commissioner of the General Land office. May 15, 1915.

The two above letters, as well as others regarding Prairie Island that were reviewed, were by courtesy of the Fond du Lac Reservation Education Office.

"Indian Relics, Mounds and Remembrances of Floodwood." J. W. New. October 24,1929. p. 6. St. Louis County Historical Society.

"Reminiscences." Garfield Blackwood. Unpublished, Floodwood File 1, Northeast Minnesota Historical Center, UMD.

Other references:

Plat Book of the State of Minnesota. W. W. Hixon Co., Rockford, Illinois. 1915. p. 35.

"Preliminary Archaeological Report: St. Louis County's Prairie Lake,

Minnesota." Rachael Ewoldsen. Anthropology 8950, Advanced Research. Dr. Elden Johnson. SS I - 1981.

The History of Fond du Lac and Jay Cooke Park. John Fritzen. St. Louis County Historical Society. 1978. P. 2.

Ibid. P. 2.

Part Five: Old Indian Hospital
– Isabelle Whelan

I graduated in 1948 from Cloquet High School and that summer I was hired at the Indian Hospital as a nurses aide. I roomed upstairs in one of the rooms. Stella Morrissette was my roommate. This is where I learned many things. At that time, there were two big wards, a couple of private rooms, nursery, surgery and Pediatrics. We did everything. We cleaned equipment, made surgery packs and helped out in surgery. I remember once giving ether for a tonsil surgery. Doctors from Raiter's (a clinic in Cloquet) took turns coming out. We were always busy.

Miss Komosie, head nurse, lived in the nurses cottage. Ben and Arnold Bassett Sr. were the driver and janitor. Scoup Petite, Adeline Bassett, Martha Petite and Lizzy Smith were the cooks. We had many good times with the people who worked there at the time, including Louise and Donna Smith, Bernie Smith, Stella Bergland, Flora Whitebird and many nurses. I was sad when the hospital closed. I thought it was one of the nicest kept places.

Part Six: Blueberry Stories

— Isabelle Whelan and Thomas Peacock

<u>My Heart</u>
A bear
eating
blueberries
(Unknown author)

<u>The Order of Things</u>

Our ancestors recognized that everything was made by a Creator, and that each part of creation was dependent on what was created before it. The traditional Ojibwe story of the creation of the universe closely parallels the book of Revelation of the Bible. First to be created were the heavens, earth and the rocks, water and gasses. The Creator then made the plants (fruits, vegetables, trees, grasses and flowers) and put them on this earth. Every living thing was created for a purpose and has a reason for being. Later, the Creator made animals, and finally, humans. Everything is dependent upon the other to live. Plants need water, earth and sky for sustenance. The Creator gave plants the ability to live independently of humans and animals, but in turn made both humans and animals dependent on plants for sustenance (Johnston, 1976). This dependence is shown in our need for plants to serve as medicines, shelter, food, and for our psychological and spiritual well-being. Who could imagine an earth without plants? Even forces of nature like wind, without trees and grasses singing and bowing in its wake, would have little reason to blow. A spring without flowers and budding leaves would be a season without purpose.

Our ancestors also believed that all things had spirit., from the simplest of single-celled life forms to rocks, trees, wind and water. Moreover, they believed that plants could be co-joined in a wondrous and more powerful way with others of its own species to form a corporate spirit (Johnston, 1976, p. 33):

Each valley or any other life form– a meadow, a bay, a grove, a hill – possesses a mood which reflects the state of being of that place. Whatever the mood, happy, peaceful, turbulent, or melancholy, it is the tone of that soul-spirit. As proof, destroy or alter or remove a portion of the plant beings, and the mood and tone of that valley will not be what it was before.

Traditional blueberries

Everything has a purpose and reason for being. Even blueberries.

We may never know when our ancestors came to use blueberries for sustenance, but reason would tell us they came to recognize it as food by observing animals. We can only imagine them watching a bear from a safe distance as it moved from bush to bush, grunting and chortling in delight at the deep sweet taste of the berries. Later, as the bear moved on, our ancestors probably went into the berry patch and tasted the fruit for the first time. In time, they would also observe how other animals, like squirrels, dried and stored their food in the ground and trees for the long winters, and in that way learned how to dry and store their own food (Hilger, 1992):

> Berries of many varieties were eaten both fresh and dried. Informants and interpreters on all reservations were sun-drying blueberries, June berries and chokecherries on pieces of birchbark, on roofs, or on pieces of cloth. After two or three days' drying they were stored [in birchbark containers] and later cooked with wild rice and venison. Food supplies that were not needed during a season were usually stored in caches built near the home wigwam.

Many years ago on a visit to Ft. Frances, Ontario, I, Thomas Peacock, was served a traditional meal of venison and boiled potatoes. For dessert, the server brought me a bowl of blueberries and wild rice.

Blueberry Stories

There are many thousands of blueberry picking stories that could be told by the Ojibwe people. Here are two of them.

Isabelle Whelan: The Dave Savage family lived near the railroad tracks which is now called Houle Road (at the corner of Reservation and Jarvi Roads just west of Cloquet, Minnesota). Uncle Simon lived close by and Uncle Lyzeme and his family lived on top of the hill.

We would pick blueberries in the summer. Dad had made what we called a blueberry box made of wood and (with) leather straps. He carried it on his back. We went clear to Danielson's (about 3 miles west from our residence) to gather the berries. Mom would make a lunch, and I remember she would make tea in a bottle. Sometimes we would stop at Squaw Creek spring for fresh water. Then in 1943, we moved back out to Jarvi's old farm which the BIA (Bureau of Indian Affairs), had bought. This farm was 80 acres and the berries were plentiful. I remember many people coming out to pick. Dad would only let some in. We picked and mom would can them for the winter. When she had enough canned, we could sell the rest. I remember my cousins and I sent for some school clothes with the dollars (we made) from berries. A green dress and fancy shoes out of the Bell Hess catalog. When they came, they were not as pretty as we expected. There were a lot of deer on the farm. One day I was picking blueberries and singing away (and I) almost stepped on a little fawn. Scared me to death. We spent many happy hours out in the woods with the family. To this day, I go picking berries and making jellies.

Thomas Peacock: In my childhood eyes I remember the places my family would go out in the woods to pick blueberries. I remember an old abandoned farm up in Brevator (now the Mahnomen housing project just off Belich Road west of Cloquet). We would drive down an old road so far, then walk a trail which led to a large field. There, at the edge of the woods and field, was the berry patch. I remember wondering as I picked berries of the people who had lived in that old unpainted house that stood in the field. A house without windows; an empty barn and other outbuildings. I would wonder of their dreams. Sometimes I would sit in the tall grass and eat my berries one by one.

Another blueberry picking place was just north of the Catholic church, on the hill overlooking the river that flows through Nahgahchiwanong (Fond du Lac). This was before the road was built across Squaw Creek to Brevator Road, and long before Ridge Road. Along an old wagon trail that had been used by our ancestors as the main road up the river, there was a path that led through a small spruce swamp, then into a clearing where another old homestead had been. By then all that remained were a few grizzled apple trees and a stone foundation. Rusted kettles. Again, near the cleave of field and woods, were blueberry bushes. Today, that area has become the housing project on Ridge Road.

My grandmother, Emma Morrissette, made wonderful pies with the berries. Some she canned for winter. Always she made blueberry wine. I remember my first taste of blueberry wine. Sweet and mysterious. Once I remember awakening after an evening of drinking blueberry wine with a bright purple tongue and a blueberry smile.

But there were other times my family needed money to live; to survive in this place. At times like that, we picked blueberries and sold them at Jaskari's Store in Sawyer. During those hard times, the whole family picked berries. We, as children, never complained because our work was necessary to our family's well-being. We never expected a share of what money was made by selling berries. I remember taking the crates of berries into the store to be weighed. I remember how little we were paid for all that work.

A continuing story?

Times change. The post-forest fire, clear-cut habitat that supported the lush blueberry picking areas no longer exists. Most of us now buy blueberries in the supermarket. Does that mean there will be no new blueberry-picking stories? Will our relationship to a plant our ancestors used as sustenance somehow become lost in the blueberry muffins sold in deli's or the individually wrapped fried pies sold in convenience stores? Have we become too distant from our relationship with this earth to remember the sweet dance of wind, rain, sunshine and earth in the making of these things? Have we forgotten that all things have reason and purpose, and spirit?

We think not.

Our relationship with all of these things goes back many thousands of years. Our ancestors saw bears eating blueberries. Our grandchildren will do the same. We are a part of a story that goes on forever.

We know change is inevitable. Once this area was all woods, but it eventually became crossed by the trails we walked as children to our favorite berry patches. Some of these trails became roads. Fields of tall grasses and willow trees have been individually plotted into neat rows of streets and houses. We wonder what all of these changes have done to the collective spirit of these places.

We wonder.

References

Hilger, M. (1992). Chippewa child life and its cultural backgrounds. St. Paul: Minnesota Historical Society.

Johnston, B. (1976). Ojibwe heritage. Lincoln: University of Nebraska Press.

Chapter Three: The Great Fire of 1918

All around where I live are the foundations of houses that probably burned in the Great Fire of 1918 that swept the area. Just down the hill is an old stone foundation, its entryway still intact. Slowly, the Earth is reclaiming it, recycling it with the passing of each season. The unsuspecting eye wouldn't even see it hidden in the trees and brush along side the old river road that runs along the hills. The people who lived in the house must have had a beautiful view of the St. Louis River, winding its way through the city of Cloquet on its way to Lake Superior.

In the pasture that now serves as a raspberry patch are the remains of two other houses. The first must have had a timber foundation, or someone may have taken its foundation stones for other uses. All that remains is a mound of earth, a depression near the center, where the home stood (probably a root cellar), and an old overgrown hand-dug well, now filled with rocks. The entire area is covered with wild raspberries.

The second foundation was of concrete, and the people who lived there certainly chose a beautiful place in which to live. Into what must have been a shade tree for the people who lived there, "Coon" (LaVern) Shotley carved his name. It is now a dying birch tree (1961), but his name still proclaims itself to anyone with a discerning eye. It is one of my own sacred places, recorded in my personal journal:

> On another occasion I took a particularly vivid walk and sat on an old stone foundation in the pasture. It is one of my magic places because I remember sitting there as a child with my grandpa and grandma. The foundation is from a settler's home which probably burned in the Cloquet fire of 1918. It sits in the middle of a meadow and the foundation is surrounded by maple, burley oak and a dying white birch. These are trees old and wise in their age and they have had many sit in reflection in their shadows.
>
> – T. Peacock, Editor

Part One:
Milepost 62 and the Fires in Brookston and Fond du Lac

[Excerpts from the book, <u>The Fires of Autumn</u>. Permission to reprint given by the Minnesota Historical Society. The chapter describes the Cloquet Fire of 1918, with particular emphasis on the Fond du Lac Reservation.

     The St. Louis River is relatively placid above Cloquet, its smooth water only occasionally broken by shallow rapids and rocks in midstream. The steep banks, between 70 and 150 feet high, covered by birches, maples and aspens, give the St. Louis a picturesque tranquility that is particularly beautiful in the autumn. For a millennium, Indian people made this river a main artery to the western Great Lakes. For more than two hundred years explorers, fur traders and missionaries used the St. Louis River as the northern gateway to the Mississippi and as the highway to Rainy River, Lake of the Woods, and the Canadian West. For lumbermen, the St. Louis watershed was one of the richest pine lands in the upper Midwest. Every spring the river carried logs down to the great mills at Cloquet and Scanlon. And when the Duluth and Winnipeg Railroad pushed west from Cloquet in the late 1880's, it went up the St. Louis River valley along the narrow flood plain on the south bank of the river, until at Floodwood it struck out almost straight for the northwest. The railroad, acquired by James J. Hill in 1896 for his Great Northern, made this stretch of the St. Louis River a vital transportation corridor once again, with iron ore from the famous Mahoning mine moving down to the docks at Superior, Wisconsin. Ore trains, logging trains, passenger trains, and mixed freight labored up and down the double track along this part of the St. Louis valley, picking up cars, dropping off passengers taking on water at now-forgotten stations and sidings – Nagonab, Draco, and Brevator between Cloquet and Brookston; Congo, Paupores, and Mirbat between Brookston and Floodwood. Among these small railroad junctions, on the south bank of the St. Louis River, the great Cloquet-Moose Lake fires started.

     Almost all of the south bank of the St. Louis River, from just east of Paupores to Cloquet itself, is the northern border of the Fond du Lac Indian Reservation. This reservation was created through the Treaty of LaPointe in 1854, in which the Lake Superior Ojibway (or Chippewa) in the region ceded to the United States government most of the present day   "Arrowhead

Country" in exchange for reservations at Fond du Lac, Grand Portage, and Nett Lake (Bois Fort) and for cash annuities and various government services. The Fond du Lac Ojibway bands had traditionally enjoyed seasonal migrations up and down the lower St. Louis River valley. The new reservation of about 100,000 acres included their sugar bush camps and the wintering, ricing, and hunting grounds, and under government policy they were encouraged to settle down there.

The Fond du Lac Ojibway prospered in number, at least; in 1918 the population of the reservation was just more than one thousand, almost three times larger than the band had been in 1843. In 1887, however, Congress had passed the Dawes Allotment Act, allowing land on reservations to be allotted to individual Indians. Often these allotments were sold to white settlers or, especially at Fond du Lac, to lumbermen. In either case, a portion of reservation land passed out of the hands of the native people themselves. This was particularly true of Fond du Lac's northern border along the St. Louis River, where the railroad had been built, the timber cut, and the land settled by Finnish immigrants. The first placed burned by the great fires, long before they reached Cloquet or Duluth, were the immigrant farmsteads and the Ojibway allotments on the Fond du Lac Reservation.

Fires were burning north and west of Cloquet throughout the autumn of 1918. Brush fires, clearing fires, and railroad fires were smoldering all along the Great Northern line from Brevator, just upriver from Cloquet, to Floodwood. All of these fires contributed to both the atmospheric conditions and the staggering intensity of the great fires of October 12, 1918. Of the several fires identified, however, one stood out in public opinion as being of such magnitude as to be clearly the source of the disaster. The great fire that destroyed Cloquet and Brookston was the railroad fire along the Great Northern tracks at Milepost 62, four miles west of Brookston on the south bank of the St. Louis River, and fifteen miles northwest of Cloquet. Milepost 62 may be almost forgotten today, but it's name haunted a whole generation.

On Thursday, October 10, at about 4:30 p.m., a passenger train from Duluth to Hibbing, known locally as the "Wooden Shoe" after the conductor's wooden leg, stopped at Milepost 62 and a siding called O'Brien's Spur. For years, private contractors had used the siding, about two thousand feet long, as a loading station for various wood products. It contained large amounts (perhaps ten thousand cords) of pulpwood, cordwood, railroad ties, fence posts and telephone poles in piles on both sides of the track. Furthermore, the ground was strewn with bark and chips, making the siding a tinderbox in the autumn conditions.

Steve Koskela, who owned a farm a half-mile away, was working with John Sundstrom, a neighbor, culling ties at the siding for use in Koskela's barn. "Big Steve" and Sundstrom watched the train stop at the siding, and after it left they saw a small column of smoke rise at the western end of the siding. They rushed over, to find a fire about twenty feet across burning through the tall, dry grass near the piles of wood. Having no tools with them, they attempted to put out the fire by trampling it with their boots. "I tried to put it out," Koskela said, "but I ain't got anything in my hand, you know. . . I used to tramp it down with my feet, and I couldn't put it out." The grass was too dry, and the fire quickly spread under one of the several piles of cordwood at the siding.

Koskela went to get pails and shovels from home and, together with several other neighbors, began working to dismantle the rows of cordwood in order to make a firebreak. By 6:00 p.m., a Great Northern section foreman came down the track; when his crew arrived an hour and a half later the wind had stirred up the fire. A small railroad speeder came out from Brookston about 8:00 p.m., bringing Charles DeWitt, a Great Northern employee and the Brookston village president, who also had some logs at the landing; J.M. ("Matt") Miettunen, a store owner; Ray Paukka, his bookkeeper; and several others. They joined the section crew in working late into the night fighting the fire but were unable to put it out. The following day, Friday, October 11, the wind moderated; the fire, while still not out, seemed less dangerous.

When Koskela went back to the siding early in the morning three crews were there, but they soon left to work in Brookston and did not return. Even so, the smoke was sufficiently threatening that Anton LaFave, who had a small farm down the tracks near Milepost 61, decided to collect his tools from a small shed he had at the east end of O'Brien's Spur, lest they burn up. Koskela worked on the fire again later that day, although alone, he was unable to confine it to the siding.

On Saturday morning, October 12, Koskela went into Brookston to do some shopping, getting a lift on a railroad speeder with the section crew. The fire was quiet. Returning at 11:30 on the Wooden Shoe, he found the siding now in flames, with lots of black smoke being driven by a strong northwest wind. The environmental conditions favorable to generating the blowup of a major fire - what Haines and Sando described years later - had been met. Several years of dry weather had created the favorable climatic conditions - *"the shell is loaded into the rifle chamber."* Small fires were burning throughout the region - *"the hammer is pulled back."*

The passage of a cold front the previous day brought with it dry northwest winds and a record- breaking fall in humidity, which created a favorable synoptic weather pattern over the region - *"the trigger is pulled and the bullet is on its way.*

Koskela saw clearly that with the enormous amount of dried wood at the siding, the heat generated by the flames would soon drive the fire out of control. He returned to his farm knowing that it was directly in line with the fire and that he would have to protect his property. "I guess we have to make ready fighting that fire now," Koskela told his family, and sent his sons to pump water and fill pails. He wetted down his buildings, set his animals free, and got his money from the house. By 1:40 p.m. the fire reached the farm from across the pasture. Koskela was able to save his house and family, but lost numerous outbuildings, some of his stock, and his timber. The worst of the fire passed in less than an hour, during which time it also overran Koskela's neighbors. The first refugees of the fire were members of Henry Knutt's household. The Knutts, who lived about half a mile east of Koskela, kept boarders, mostly trainmen. After the fire burned them out, they all made their way to Koskela's house for assistance. It was the beginning of a long and tragic day....

The Great Northern RR had no patrols in this region, and the section crews that had fought the Milepost 62 fire on Thursday were pulled off to work elsewhere on Friday and Saturday. Theodore Kunelius, a fourteen-year-old section hand on the Great Northern, worked out of Congo. Within the past two days, he had fought fire at both Milepost 64 and Milepost 62. On Saturday morning, Kunelius was sent into Brookston to assist in straightening track. By lunch time, however, he was sent up the tracks with a crew on a speeder to investigate the smoke coming into town. About two miles west of Brookston, shortly after 1:30, they ran into fire burning along both sides of the tracks. The fact that even the railroad ties were on fire made them worry that the gasoline tank for the engine might explode. Nevertheless, they carried on through the fire to Milepost 62, where the wood piled at the siding was burning with great intensity. The foreman concluded that the passenger train, which was due in from Floodwood and farther north, could not safely pass by, and sent the speeder on to stop the train. The crew found fire burning on the south side of the track all the way to Congo and between Paupores and Mirbat."

Meanwhile, in Brookston, then a town of about five hundred people, Charles DeWitt, the village president, who had worked all night for the railroad, was awakened by his wife at 2:00 p.m. because things were looking ominous. The air was smoky, the sun was red, and the wind was rising. During the next two hours the smoke and the wind increased in intensity, coming right down the tracks from the west. Fire first swept by the town just to the south. As DeWitt said, "Well, it seemed – it just seemed like a long roll of smoke going right up and leaning over, just traveling across the country at probably about, oh, six or eight, maybe ten miles an hour."

In the great heat, houses along the streets in the town began to burst into flames even before the fire actually emerged from the woods to the west. There was a freight train in Brookston, ordered to serve as a relief train by George S. Stewart of Superior, the general superintendent of the Great Northern's Lake District. Many of the townspeople made their way to the rail yard and climbed on board. DeWitt recorded that at 4:10 p.m., with the town burning, the relief train pulled out of Brookston with about two hundred people aboard. Remarkably, much of the Great Northern property in Brookston was saved by a section foreman who stayed in the town, working the pumps along the river and hosing down the buildings in the railroad yard.

The relief train escaped from Brookston, but it was not yet out of danger. About a mile down the tracks, where both the river and the tracks turned south, the train encountered fierce flames at Flint pit. The fire that had swept past Brookston had burned east to the St. Louis River, and a great swirl of flame momentarily engulfed the refugees in the open gondola cars of the relief train, scorching many, including DeWitt and his wife and three small children, before they could cover themselves.

71

As the fire swept past Brookston, it trapped people attempting to flee by automobile. Matt Miettunen ran a store in Brookston; on Saturdays, Earl Miettunen, a sixteen year-old high-school student, helped his father and Ray Paukka, the bookkeeper and assistant, at the store. Matt Miettunen and Paukka had been out to help at the fire on Friday at Milepost 62, so they knew the dangerous potential of all that burning wood. When Brookston filled with smoke around 3:00 p.m., they decided to leave. Young Earl drove the Overland 80 south toward Cloquet along the Duff road. Five or ten minutes out of Brookston, a great cloud of smoke, sparks, and surface fire blew across the road. The automobile struck a tree blown onto the road and crashed into the ditch. Matt Miettunen, his wife, and Paukka were thrown out into the burning bush. Matt was badly cut and burned from crashing through the windshield and landing in the fire. Earl looked for his mother among the blankets thrown from the automobile and then ran searching for her in the burning woods, but she was never seen alive again. Forced away by the smoke and flames, Earl and Paukka helped Matt up and back onto the road. All three fled east through the woods, across the tracks near Flint pit, down the bank, and into the St. Louis River.

They made their way out onto a logjam some distance from shore, about a quarter of a mile below where the Cloquet River enters the St. Louis River. A few minutes later, the surface fire burned right down to the water's edge. That was followed shortly by dense smoke and the great roar of the main fire, which showered sparks and firebrands down on them.

"Now she is coming. Better we look for a place where we can duck," Matt Miettunen shouted, as they plunged into the water among the now burning logs. "I see some chunks of the fire flying right over us across the river right up in the air."

The flames spanned the river, igniting the trees on the opposite side. Shortly afterwards, the men heard the Brookston relief train, itself passing through the flames at that point. The Miettunens and Paukka stayed in the river until after dark, attempting periodically to warm themselves by moving as close as possible to the burning logs. Later in the night, they made their way to shore, where they huddled behind a large rock to keep out of the wind, unable to walk very far in either direction because of the fires still burning. At some point early the next morning, when they heard a train whistle in Brookston, they walked along the now passable track back toward the town for aid and were taken by the train to the north end of Cloquet.

The Milepost 62 fire was also traveling even more rapidly inland from the river in a southeasterly direction across the Fond du Lac Reservation. Ojibway people south of Brookston had no railroad to deliver them to safety. Grace Sheehy lived on a farm on the Duff road, about three miles due south of Brookston. She was looking after her five children, who were between the ages of twelve years and eleven months, while her husband, Paul, worked in the shipyards in Duluth. In the early afternoon, noticing the smoke and wind, she walked up the road to consult with her neighbors, the Christensens. They were packing up and told her to go home and get her children. The wind was so strong it was blowing down trees, so when she got home she did not think she could make it back with all of the children. Sheehy decided to try to save the farm herself. She put the two babies in bed so that they would not interrupt her, donned old shoes, got a shovel, and started to make a fire break.

At about 3:30 p.m., the neighbors sent Mike Beargrease to help bring her back. Beargrease picked up the little boy, Sheehy wrapped the baby in a mosquito bar, and they and the older children started north up the Duff road toward the Christensen's place. Unfortunately, by that time the flames had crossed the road, so they turned around and walked a mile south toward Cress Lakes (also called Twin Lakes). When they reached a hill near one of the lakes at about 5:00 p.m., they could see fire burning heavily to the north and west of it. They found a boat on the edge of the western lake, and Beargrease paddled them out onto the water. With a great roaring noise, the fire swept past the east side of Cress Lakes. From the boat they could see fire all around them, particularly north and east toward Cloquet, but the fire at the lake did not burn all of the shoreline. They could see other people on land, so about 8:00 p.m. Beargrease brought the boat in to shore.

"We couldn't pull the boat up on the shore so we jumped out in the water and I handed him the children and we started to walk around there." Sheehy said later. Beargrease walked over to John and Charlie Cress's farm, assuring Sheehy, "If the fire happens to come there we will go down to the water." By about 9:00 p.m. they all went to the Cress farm, where they and several other people spent the night. Sheehy and her children stayed there until Monday, when they went into Cloquet and found her husband.

News of the fire burning through the Fond du Lac Reservation west of town filtered into Cloquet by late afternoon. "Why, I learned that there was a bunch of homesteader children that were up on the Brookston road that had to be gotten out of there or they would be liable to get burned," said Dr. M.D. Whittemore, a Cloquet dentist.

Sometime after 7:00 p.m., Whittemore drove out past the Indian Hospital and then north about a mile and a half on the Brookston road until he was stopped by fire. There he turned into the Bassett farm, about five and a half miles southeast of Cress Lakes. No one seemed to be around, but upon entering the house, Whittemore found a distraught Mrs. Bassett and her four small children. Her husband, Ben, was "out in the fire," she said in tears. "I think he was burned up."

Just then Mr. Bassett ran in through the smoke. "Come for God's sake," Whittemore said, "and get out of here." Mr. Bassett, however, insisted on saving his horses. Just then they heard the whistles blow in Cloquet, and Whittemore remembered, "at that time it seemed to me that there was a tongue of fire that swept around and it broke loose, I whirled and ran into the house and grabbed two of the children, and the oldest one followed right close behind, and the mother grabbed the baby, and I threw them into the car, and we got out of there and started south."

After they had gone about a mile and a half in the automobile, they came to the corner of the Cedar Lake Road. Mrs. Bassett said, "Oh, God, can you go up to a certain place and get my other two children?" Whittemore turned west on the Cedar Lake Road and let Mrs. Bassett off to pick up her children while he drove on a bit farther. When he was engulfed in smoke, he could hear the voices of the people in the woods.

"When I got up there I could hear hollering and screaming, but I saw that there was no use – well, the fact of the matter, I got scared; I didn't dare to go in there; I was afraid I could not get out." He turned back, picked up Mrs. Bassett and her children, and headed once again for Cloquet.

About two miles northeast of Bassetts' was Joseph Petite's farm. Petite had spent the whole day picking rutabagas, carrots, and beets, but by late afternoon, he began to get worried about the smoke in the northwest. At about 7:00 p.m. the smoke was very close, so he and his wife decided to leave. They made their way by the old road into the Indian Village (the largest of the Ojibway settlements on the Fond du Lac Reservation) and past the Holy Family Catholic church.

"We was going to stay in the Indian Village," Petite recounted, "when we see these sparks falling, so we keep on going to Cloquet." They continued along the road south, then down the riverbank to the Northern Lumber Company yards. The fire was right behind them.

"You could hear it crackling and sparks coming over us. Of course, I could get away all right but the woman [sic] couldn't and I don't want to leave them there. They couldn't run fast." Some of the firebrands were as "big as balls," and he could see "the fire flying all over us." Although it was not yet burning, Petite saw no one left in the village when he passed by.

Southeast of Petite's farm lived Frank Houle with his wife and one child. During the day, Houle had been busy pulling tree stumps, oblivious to any approaching danger. By about 5:30 p.m., his wife was sufficiently alarmed by the smoke to leave with their child for the Indian Village. After an hours time, Houle himself became concerned, loaded up their furniture on the farm wagon, turned loose his livestock, and by about 7:15 p.m. headed for the Indian Village. Just as he pulled away, his house burst into flames and sparks and firebrands fell all around. As Houle remembered later, there were "big chunks of fire falling all over, and on the horses and all along the road."

Houle found his wife at the church in the village with a large group of women and children. Houses in the village had started to burn, so Houle unloaded his furniture, leaving it to be consumed by the coming fire, and took the women and children in his wagon down the hill from the village into the Northern Lumber Company yards. Houle's wife and the other passengers got out of the wagon at the Great Northern water tower, and Houle took the wagon through the lumberyards to the bridges over Dunlap Island to the north side of the river. He left his rig and recrossed the river by the log boom to Posey's Island, met his wife, and took her back to the north side of the river.

William Wiselan lived on an 80-acre farm south of Brevator, just more than a mile from the Great Northern tracks below Draco. He returned to his farm at 2:00 p.m., after spending much of the day cutting trees for the Cloquet Tie and Post Company. From his property he could see quite a distance to the west, and by late afternoon he thought that "it looked as if the whole country was burning up" and that the fire was moving on a front of three to four miles wide.

Wiselan sent his wife and two children off to Cloquet at about 5:30, walking along the old tote road (or Indian portage) that twisted south from Brevator to the Indian Village– about nine miles. The family got a ride with a neighbor who had a team of horses. Wiselan followed about a half an hour later and caught up with the team. Throughout most of the trip, the fire kept just to the west of them, but when they crossed Squaw Creek the fire "kept crossing the road behind them." They, too, came down the road through the Indian Village, but about a mile and half beyond, the fire "crossed the road ahead of us. "Sparks and embers were flying everywhere when Wiselan turned down into the upper yards of the Northern Lumber Company. He saw then that the fire was entering the company property.

The fire burned through much of the northern half of the Fond du Lac Reservation, striking the farms and homes of Ojibways and settlers alike. Completely destroyed were the Indian Village and the Holy Family Church, located on the high bluff overlooking the St. Louis River just upriver from Cloquet. George W. Cross, the Fond du Lac Agency Superintendent, telegraphed his superiors at the United States Office of Indian Affairs (OIA), [Bureau of Indian Affairs], for help the following day:

Fond du Lac Reservation devastated by forest fire. City of Cloquet and adjacent towns destroyed. Office records and furniture burned.

Many Indians homeless. Loss of life not known. Wire Five Thousand Dollars care First National Bank Duluth Immediate Relief.

Cross later reported to the BIA that some 57 Ojibway homes and many more outbuildings were burned. Although sources vary, between 245 and 269 Ojibway suffered sufficient losses to file damage claims in the aftermath of the fires. A great deal of livestock was killed and much of the hay and feed crop was also lost, with the result that the surviving animals had to be looked after at the Indian Farm (part of the reservation). Cross lamented that many histori- cally valuable Ojibway craft items, such as arrowheads, bows, tomahawks, and beadwork had been destroyed. Of more commercial importance was the loss of a large supply of decorated blankets that, along with beadwork, were sold for souvenirs and produced a good income for the Ojibway at the reservation.

Fortunately, and perhaps remarkably, no Ojibway were killed in the fire. Both Cross and State Forester William Cox noted that the Ojibway were much more adept at coping with the hazards of woodland living, even dealing with forest fires, than were many of the European immigrants. The *Pine Knot* concluded that "their keen wits saved them from perishing." In practical terms this meant getting on the relief trains, finding shelter in one of the local lakes, or crossing onto one of the islands in the St. Louis River that did not burn.$^{)}$

As the afternoon wore on, people who lived near Cloquet began to get anxious. Peter M. Nelson owned a small farm about a mile and a half south of the Indian Village, overlooking the Northern Lumber Company (close to the present-day Cloquet Country Club). Nelson came home from Duluth by train about 5:00 p.m., and, because of the smoke, walked over to the Indian Village to see what was going on. Seeing nothing but smoke, he went back home to milk his cows and do the chores. During supper the wind increased to such a force that it shook the house. He thought he would fill some tubs with water in case he should need to put out any fire. He was filling the first pail from a neighbor's well at about 8:00 p.m. when "all at once I see a big blaze right over the tree top of the balsam grove, northwest of me. As soon as I saw this I heard a terrible roaring through the woods. The wind was getting awful strong in the pine trees, and pine trees going up by the roots, and some was breaking off. I went in the house and told the woman we had better get out of there quick, so I grabbed the youngest child in my arms, and we started on the run to get away from there."

They headed south, hoping to get to First Lake, about a half a mile away, but ran through some heavy fire before they got there. On the road they met Harry Ruff and his daughter, who had driven their Ford automobile into the ditch. Nelson, despite having burned his hands in the fire, attempted to help Ruff get the Ford out of the ditch, but the canvas top caught fire while they were pushing. They aban-doned the automobile and made for an open potato field nearby. While the fire was now burning in front of them to the south, they heard the whistle at the Northern Lumber Company. They spent much of the night in the field while the fire burned past them, after which they walked to Charlie Main's house near the Indian Hospital. The hospital, the Indian Farm, and several other houses did not burn, protected perhaps by the open area surrounding First Lake, although the fire burned on both the east and west of this area.

In Cloquet, Archie Campbell, the street commissioner and water-works superintendent, was called from his supper at about 6:00 p.m. to look after a substantial brush fire at the Spring Lake pumping station, southwest of town. There he found a fire of about twenty acres that was seriously threatening many of the local wood frame houses but was of little danger to the pumping station itself, which was built of brick and had a supply of garden hose. Indeed, as the buildings in the vicinity began to catch fire, people fled to the pumping station to spend the night. When Campbell returned to town at about 9:00 p.m. to get more garden hose, the great fire had already entered Cloquet.

Alicia Panger remembered years later her family's frightening experience in the late afternoon as the fire approached Spring Lake. Her father, Fred, had first planned to fight fire on the reservation. He then returned home to take his wife and their eight children to Duluth, but when the fire overtook them they fled to the brick pumping station. Everything seemed to go wrong: the horse would not go in the right direction, the wind was so strong they could not hear each other speak, the axle broke on the wagon, and "a flaming two-by-four flew over our heads and set a field afire." But they made it to the station, where "three families and parts of two others, including 12 children, were jammed into the cement aisles between the whirring engines pumping as though they knew they were saving lives." They prayed and fingered their rosary beads and watched through the windows as the red sky gradually turned black.

Reference

Carroll, L.M. & Raiter, F.R. (1990). <u>The</u> <u>Fires</u> <u>of</u> <u>Autum.</u> The Cloquet-Moose Lake Disaster of 1918. Minnesota Historical Society Press. St. Paul.

Part Two: Fond du Lac and the 1918 fire
– Dan Anderson

The most important historical event in the Cloquet area was the fire of October 12, 1918, also known as the "Fires of 1918." Much has been written about these fires, but little about their effect on the Fond du Lac Reservation. In researching the history of the Fond du Lac Reservation, we find that Joseph Petite lost his house, barn, wagon, sleighs, furniture, all clothing, all feed, two pigs, a coop and 50 chickens. In 1921, he testified about the fire in a suit filed against the United States Railway Administration:

"I was pulling 'bagas (rutabagas) and carrots and beets that day, all day. I got through a little after four somewhere. We had passed down by the church, by the Indian village, then sparks fell all over big as balls, some of them. You could see the fire flying all over us. The fire was right close to us, just about a half mile away from us... and the wind so strong that it caught up with us pretty near before we go down to the church. You could hear it crackling and sparks coming over us."

The fire was actually a series of forest fires which grew into a fire storm as winds picked up after a long hot summer. It eventually burned 1,500 square miles, moving through an area of 8,400 square miles. Thirty-six towns were partially or completely burned, 453 people burned to death (mostly around Moose Lake), with another 106 dying later from complications.

In the early afternoon of October 12, the winds had picked up and the smoke blocked out the sun. By 6:00 p.m., it was clear the town of Cloquet would not be saved. Trainloads of people from Brookston had arrived with word that they had been burned out and the fire was heading toward Cloquet. The fire was burning along the St. Louis River and had reached the church by the Indian village by 7:30 p.m. The church and fifteen buildings in the vicinity burned.

It was the following day that Indian Agent George W. Cross sent his telegram to the Indian Office in Washington D.C. requesting "immediate relief." According to Cross' report of October 18, 57 Indian homes were destroyed. "Most of the Indians on the Reservation got to trains in time to get out of the city. There was loss of life among the settlers but the Indians seemed more fortunate or better able to take care of themselves."

They were cared for in Duluth, Superior and at the Fond du Lac Hospital. Fifty-thousand feet of rough lumber was purchased for temporary shelters. The plan was to build small shacks of rough boards and tar paper. For example, Mike Diver, who lost his home, barn and implements, was issued lumber on October 30 for a 12´ x 16´ house and 16´ x 20´ barn.

On June 30, 1919 an Act of Congress authorized $60,000 for the Fond du Lac Reservation for those who lost homes. The cost for each house was not to exceed $1,000. The Fond du Lac Council stated that this amount would not replace all buildings lost or construct much of a house. Forty-five Indian homes were burned, with many others losing barns and other buildings as well as stock, implements and feed.

Over 250 claims were filed by Fond du Lac band members against the U.S. Railroad Administration for damages to their allotments. These claims took years to be settled. Payments were finally sent to allottees and heirs beginning in 1937 in amounts ranging from $1.39 to $4,000. Most claims averaged from $200 to $300.

In 12 hours the fire had displaced over 52,000 people and caused an estimated $30 million in damage, but the memories it evokes are a better measure of its effect. As survivor Betty Gurno recalled 60 years later:

"It was horrid. Fire and me don't see eye to eye. I respect fire, but that too is from that 1918 holocaust. My husband was nine years old when that happened. He couldn't remember anything. Maybe it was so bad that he wanted to wipe it out. It was awful. I wouldn't want my kids to go through that. Scarey."

The following records culled from the National Archives outline the aftermath of the fire as it related to the Fond du Lac Reservation.

Pur-Sup.   5-1104   *RECEIVED OCT 21 1919*

82417-19 E.E.E.

Superior, Wisc.

DEPARTMENT OF THE INTERIOR

WASHINGTON

ADDRESS ONLY

THE SECRETARY OF THE INTERIOR

Mr. Leo S. Bonnin,

Supt., Fond du Lac School.

Dear Mr. Bonnin:

Authority is hereby granted for you to expend the sum of $45,000.00 from the fund "Chippewas in Minnesota Fund (Homes for Indians), in the purchase and construction of homes for forty-five Indians whose homes were destroyed by fire during the year 1918. Under this authority not more than $1,000.00 may be expended for any one home.

The wishes of the individual Indians, as explained in your letter dated September 24, 1919, should be carried out as to the manner in which their homes are to be acquired, except as to building houses under contract. You may, therefore expend for such Indians as desire to assist in building their houses not to exceed $800.00 for material and $200.00 for labor. For such Indians as desire to purchase homes in the cities or towns in which they are living not to exceed $1,000.00 may be applied. Abstracts of title should be required in all instances. Should any of the homes selected be worth more than $1,000.00, the difference above that amount should be deposited with you by the individual Indian so that total payment can be made by you to the owner and clear title obtained.

Instead of building houses under contract for those Indians who wished the work done in that manner, you should have them constructed in open market. As these Indians do not wish to assist in building their houses, authority is granted for you to expend for either labor or material such part of the $1,000.00 for each house as may be necessary.

Authority is also granted for you to sell to Wm. House, for $500.00, the day school cottage located at Cloquet, Minnesota, and $500.00 may be expended in moving this cottage to the land owned by Mr. House, in excavating for a basement, building the foundation, and repairing the cottage after it is moved. Of the amount above authorized, not to exceed $1800.00 may be expended in the employment of one foreman of construction, at not to exceed $10.00 per day for a period not to exceed 120 days. He should assist you in preparing bills of material for all cottages, advise the Indians in the purchase of homes, and take charge of the construction work. Bids should be invited on the material purchased, and the accepted bids and abstracts should be attached to the vouchers on which payments are made. Skilled and unskilled labor may be employed at rates not exceeding those paid in your vicinity.

   Cordially yours,

   Assistant Secretary

            Fond du Lac Indian School,
            Federal Building,
            Superior, Wisconsin
            September 24, 1919.

The Commissioner of Indian Affairs,

Washington, D.C.

Dear Sir:

Referring to Office letter of August 20, 1919 relative to Indian homes provided for under the Act of June 30, 1920 (Public—No.3—66th Congress) making appropriations for the current and contingent expenses of the Indian Bureau etc., page 14, appropriation of $60,000, the Office instructs me to submit recommendation as to the method which should be followed in the expenditure of this money, showing whether or not the materials should be purchased, and labor employed by the Indian Service, or whether portable houses should be constructed, or should contracts be let for the erection of the houses, I have the honor to make the following report:

As far as I have been able to learn, there were forty-five Indians who lost their houses by fire during the year 1918. There were many others who lost other property, such as barns, and other buildings, stock, implements, and feed, but there seems to be no provisions in the Act providing for the replacement of these other losses. Therefore, I am only reporting on those who lost dwelling houses. The following list of Indians have signified their desires, on account of the high cost of material and labor, to construct their own dwellings. They desire that the Government purchase for them about $800. worth of material, and expend about $200 in hiring help for them to do their own construction, hauling of material, etc., viz:

1. Bellair, Peter
2. Bellair, Mike
3. Bellair, Mrs. Joe
4. Beargrease, Mike G.
5. Couture, Antoine
6. Barney, Frank
7. Diver, Charles
8. Diver, Mike
9. Dufault, Simon
10. Duquette, Mrs. Mary
11. Gurno, Gus
12. Houle, Louise
13. Houle, Cecilia

14. Houle, Margaret

15. Houle, George

16. La Prairie, Henry

17. La Prairie, Louis

18. Laduc, Frank

19. Lemieux, Frank

20. Morrisette, Ed

21. Martin, John

22. Petite, Joe

23. Rabideaux, John

24. Roy, Willie

25. Read, James Coffee

26. Sheehy, Paul

27. Sheehy, Joe

28. St. John, Mrs. Roda Kari

29. Thompson, Mrs. Josephine

30. Wood, Sam

31. Winters, Frank

32. Whitebird, Mrs. John

The following list wish to buy houses at the places or in the towns in which they are now living, and apply the $1,000, they will pay from their own funds. vis:

1. Arbuckle, Mrs. Joseph, residing in Superior, Wisconsin.

2. Couture, Henry, residing in Cloquet, Minnesota.

3. Defoe, Frank, Seattle, Washington.

4. Howes, William, Cloquet, Minnesota.

5. Houle, Frank, Cloquet, Minnesota.

6. [unreadable text], Mrs. Albert, Superior, Wisconsin.

7. Lemieux, John, Seattle, Washington.

8. Northrup, James, Bishop, Duluth, Minnesota.

In the case of William House—he desires to purchase the Day School cottage located at Cloquet; which is now being occupied by Father Simon, Catholic Missionary Priest among the Chippewa Indians, but who will soon vacate the house and move into a cottage which is being built for him, and is about completed. This cottage was appraised at $500 and offered to Father Simon for that money, and is fair valuation. Mr. House says that he would like to use the balance of the $500 for moving the cottage from its present location to his land, which is a short distance from this place, to excavate a basement, and build a foundation, and otherwise repair the house, after it is moved to its new location.

The following list of Indians wish to have their houses built under contract:

1. Beargrease, Joe
2. Church, Julius
3. Petite, Antoine
4. Sailor, Mary
5. Wendelling, George

There is no reason why the same contractor might not bid on all of these houses, and construct the same, as there is no special reason why one contractor could not handle as many houses as he pleased, providing he could get the help.

The following name, Couture Joseph, wishes to have a ready cut house purchased for him at $717, and the balance of the $1,000 allowed to be used for freight, foundation, and additional help to assist him in constructing the house. I would recommend that these Indians be allowed to construct their own homes, for they have expressed the desire to do so; that the Government purchase the material for such purpose, and deliver same to them at Cloquet; and I believe that it would be a very good idea to allow them not to exceed $800 worth of material, and to allow them each $200 for labor to help construct their homes; and in the case of those who wish to buy homes, if the homes they select are worth more than $1,000, I would recommend that they be required to secure an abstract of title, and to deposit the difference in this office so that after the title is placed open by the Office, payment could be made to the owner, thereby getting a clear title. In this connection I have the honor to recommend, that the Office send here, a Superintendent of Construction to supervise and have charge of the construction of these houses, so that the Government will be fully protected in its expenditure of the $60,000. I note that the bill provides for 5 per cent of the amount of the appropriation for administrative purposes, therefore, the Office could easily employ a

Superintendent of construction to oversee these different propositions. It will be impracticable for the Superintendent of this office to give such time as would be necessary to oversee all of the work of purchasing materials, construction, etc.

Most of these people are anxious to get their buildings started, and in fact, one or two have already started building with the hope that they will be allowed later on, to apply all, or a part of the $1,000 on the materials they are using in the construction of their houses.

It will only be a short time until cold weather sets in, therefore, I recommend that this matter be given special attention, and the funds made available for use.

Very respectfully,

L.S. Bonnin

Superintendent

LSB/BM

Rebuilding   Fond du Lac Agency,

Permanent Homes for Indians   Cloquet, Minn., Jan. 10, 1919

The Commissioner of Indian Affairs,

Washington D.C.

Sir:

I desire to call the attention of the Office to the matter of rebuilding permanent homes for the Indians of the Fond du Lac Reservation whose homes were destroyed by the forest fire of October 12, 1918. Fifty Indian homes were destroyed by the forest fire and it seems that some steps should be taken to render assistance to them in rebuilding their homes.

The Office appropriated $5000 from the fund entitled Relieving Distress and Prevention of Disease Among the Indians. This fund has been used for the purpose of rendering temporary relief in the way of food supplies, feed for stock, and temporary shacks. This fund has now been exhausted.

The average cost of the homes destroyed by fire would be about $1,000 each. Barns and other buildings destroyed by fire, $500 each. This would make the loss to the Indians whose homes were destroyed by fire about $75,000. I estimate that it would take, to rebuild the homes as they were before the fire, about $100.000.00.

The Executive Committee of the Chippewa Council of Minnesota passed a resolution to ask Congress to appropriate from the Tribal Fund, the sum of $100,000 for the purpose of rebuilding these homes. It is my opinion that, if the matter was properly presented to the Local Councils of the different reservations in Minnesota, the majority of the Indians would favor the donation of this amount of money for the purpose of rebuilding the homes of the Indians, destroyed by fire.

I do not know whether Congress would be willing to appropriate so large a sum of money from the Tribal Fund of the Indians without the consent and approval. I believe that some assistance could and should be rendered to these unfortunate Indians and suggest that the Office give due consideration to the matter and make such recommendations to Congress as the case demands.

Very respectfully,

Supt. & S.D.A.   GWC/RC

Fond du Lac Agency

Cloquet, Minn., Jan. 6, 1919

The Commissioner of Indian Affairs,

Washington D.C.

Sir:

In reply to Office letter dater December 27, 1918 relative to Bois Fort Indians residing in Brookston, who lost their property by fire October 12, will say that I have been looking after these Indians. We have been issuing rations and securing assistance through the Red Cross just the same as the Fond du Lac Indians. I will have sufficient funds, together with the assistance of the Red Cross, to give temporary relief to these Indians.

Arrangements should be made for permanent relief for these Indians when permanent relief is given to the Fond du Lac Band.

Very respectfully,

Supt. & S.D.A.

PROPERTY BURNED AND ON HAND

Ash quay aush

Lost: Barn, hay, harness, all hay, blankets.

On hand: One pony.

Bassett, Ben – seven miles NW on Brookston Road, 9 in family

Lost: Barn and all feed, two horses, harness, wagon and sled, three chicken coops.

On hand: two colts, three cows, three heifers, house.

Barney, Frank, Brookston, Minn., 6 in family

Lost: House, wagon, sleighs, 2 sets harness, all furniture, all provisions, and clothing.

On hand: Two horses.

Beargrease, Joe

Lost: House, furniture, all clothing, 2 stoves, all provisions, hen coop, 25 chickens, 80 bu. potatoes, canned fruit.

Beargrease, Ben

Lost: All furniture and clothing.

Bellair, Peter – Brookston, Minn., 4 in family

Lost: House, barn, coop and fowls, 1 cow, harness, sleighs, furniture and provisions.

Live stock: One horse and wagon.

Issue: Lumber for a house 12 x 16 and barn for 2 horses.

Blair, Mrs. Joe

Lost: House, all furniture, all clothing, all provisions, stoves, barn, harness, sleighs and wagon.

On hand: One mare.

Blair, Peter

Lost: House, barn, coop, chickens, 1 cow, harness, sleighs, furniture, all provisions.

On hand: 1 horse, 1 wagon.

Blair, George

Lost: House, provisions, furniture and hay.

Bishop, James

Lost: House, furniture, sleigh, tools, barn.

Couture, Antoine – 2 in family

Lost: House, barn, coop and wood shed, all furniture, clothes, wagon, harness and all farming implements.

On hand: 2 horse, 1 cow, buggy, harness.

Couture, Joe

Lost: House, barn, shed, 2 horses, 1 colt, 50 chickens, harness, wagon, sleighs, furniture, clothing, all feed and provisions.

On hand: 7 head of cattle.

Couture, Henry

Lost: House, furniture, clothing and provisions.

Caldwell, Joe

Lost: Barn, feed and hay.

On hand: 2 horses

Coffey, James

Lost: House, barn, coop, wagon, 2 sleighs, 2 sets harness, buggy, furniture and provisions.

On hand: 2 mares and one colt.

Defoe, Frank

Lost: House, furniture, barn and all tools.

Diver, Mike – 3 in family

Lost: House, furniture, clothing and provisions, barn, 1 set harness, single buggy and harness, all feed, all farming tools, 2 sleighs, 1 cutter.

On hand: 2 mares, 1 cow, 4 chickens.

Issue: Oct. 30, lumber for house 12 x 16 and barn 16 x 20.

Diver, Charlie – 7 in family

Lost: House, furniture, provisions and clothing, barn and harness.

On hand: one mare.

Issue: Oct. 30, lumber for house 16 x 20 and barn 8 x 12.

Dufault, Simon

Lost: House, barn, sleighs and buggy.

Gurno, Gus

Lost: House, furniture, clothing, provisions, barn, tools, sleigh, feed and hay.

On hand: three cattle.

Grasshopper, John

Lost: Hay and feed.

Floodwood, Thos.

Lost: House, clothing, furniture and provisions.

Houle, Gus – 7 in family

Lost: Two houses and all furniture, eatables, axes, saws, and sewing machine.

Houle, Frank – 3 in family

Lost: House, furniture, sleighs, wagon, buggy, harness and all feed.

Live stock: two mares, one cow.

Houle, George

Lost: House, furniture, provisions, clothing, barn & all tools.

Houle, Celia

Lost: House.

Houle, Louisa

Lost: House, furniture, clothing and provisions, barn, feed and hay.

On hand: one mare and 2 cows.

Houle, Margaret

Lost: House and furniture, clothing and provisions.

No stock.

Howes, Wm.

Lost: House, furniture, clothing, provisions, barn, tools, and chicken coop.

Jackson, Charlie

Lost: Hay and feed.

Lemieux, Frank

Lost: House, furniture, clothing, provisions, barn, feed, oats, hay, tool shed, all tools, gasoline engine.

Lemieux, John

Lost: House, furniture, clothing and tools.

LaPrairie, Henry – 8 in family

Lost: House, furniture, provisions, clothing, barn, tools, feed, hay, wagons and sleighs, 1 cow.

On hand: 2 mares and 2 cows.

Issue: Lumber for house 16 x 20 and barn 12 x 16.

LaPrairie, Louis

Lost: House, furniture, clothing, provisions, barn, hay, feed.

On hand: 1 horse, 1 heifer, buggy.

Laundry, Joseph

Lost: All hay and feed.

On hand: 7 head of stock.

Mains, Frank – 8 in family

Lost: All hay.

On hand: 2 horses, 1 cow, 2 heifers, 1 calf. All buildings.

Martin, John – Brookston, Minn., 5 in family

Lost: House, furniture, clothing, provisions, barn, feed, sleighs, wagon.

Stock: 2 horses, 5 cows.

Issue: Lumber for house 16 x 20 & barn for 7 head of stock, shipped to Brookston.

Morrisette, Ed

Lost: House, furniture, clothing, provisions, barn & tools.

Northrup, Chas.

Lost: 2 tons hay, 1 store house, blankets, washtubs, pails, quilt.

On hand: 1 horse.

Ojibway, John

Lost: All hay.

On hand: 1 cow.

Petite, Joe

Lost: House, barn, wagon, sleighs, furniture, all clothing, all feed, 2 pigs, coop & 50 chickens.

On hand: 2 horses, harness, 1 cow.

Petite, Antoine

Lost: House, furniture, clothing, provisions.

Roy, Willie

Lost: House, clothing, furniture, provisions.

Rabideux, John Jr.

Lost: House, furniture, clothing, provisions, feed, hay, barn, tools, sleighs and harness.

On hand: 2 horses.

Rabideux, John Sr.

Lost: All hay.

On hand: 2 horses.

Simon, M.A.

Lost: House, barn, tool shed.

Sailor, Mary

Lost: House, furniture, clothing, provisions, barn and tools.

Smith, Joe

Lost: Two houses, furniture, provisions, clothing, barn, feed, hay, harness, tool shed and tools, 2 horses.

On hand: Two ponies.

Sheehy, Paul

Lost: House, furniture, clothing, provisions, barn, harness, feed, ice-house, tool shed, all implements.

On hand: 1 colt, 1 calf, 3 cows, 2 horses.

Sheehy, George

Lost: Barn, 12 tons hay, oats, farm implements, team and colt, wagon, buggy, sleigh, 2 sets harness, clothing.

Sheehy, Joe

Lost: House, barn, all tools, bed clothing.

St. John, Joe

Lost: Barn, tools, hay and feed.

On hand: 2 mares.

St. John, Rhoda

Lost: House, clothing, furniture, provisions.

Thompson, Josephine

Lost: House, furniture, clothing, provisions.

Trotterchaud, Frank

Lost: All hay.

Whitebird, John

Lost: House, furniture, clothing, provisions, barn, feed, 11 tons hay, chicken coop.

On hand: 2 horses, 2 cows, 40 chickens.

Issue: Lumber for house and barn.

Woods, Wm.

Lost: All hay

On hand: 3 head of stock.

Wood, Sam

Lost: House, all furniture, clothing, provisions, barn, feed, hay, harness, tools and sleighs.

On hand: 2 mares and 2 cows.

Wood, Arthur

Lost: House, furniture, clothing, provisions.

Winters, Frank

Lost: House, furniture, barn provisions, clothing, tools.

Wendling, George

Lost: Two houses, furniture, clothing, provisions, barn, tools and auto.

Abino, John

Lost: All hay.

Conners, Pat

Lost: All hay

On hand: One horse.

Church, Julius

Lost: House and furniture.

References

Martinson, David

1977   A Long Time Ago is Just Like Today. Duluth: Duluth Indian Education Advisory Committee

Testimony of Joseph Petite, Record: 1:901-10, *Philip Hall v. James C. Davis,* 150 Minn. 35 and 184 N.W. 25.

Testimony of Frank Houle, Record: 1:923-31, *Hall v. Davis.*

Records of the Bureau of Indian Affairs, National Archives Record Group 75 (Kansas City Branch), Correspondence Relating To 1918 Fire Claims, 1918-1939.

Holy Family Rectory - date of photo unknown

Remains of "Father Simon's" Catholic Church destroyed in the Great Fire on October 12, 1918

**October 15, 1918 – Father Simon's Rectory
Reverends Schiltz and Raymond**

Sawyer School

Chapter Four: The Written Record

The story of people as recorded by government documents is always incomplete because the human story invariably gets lost in the reports of government bureaucrats. Nevertheless, these documents contain much useful information on the business of people, the institutions which serve communities, and other useful data of the times. Government officials kept copious records on reservation people, and these records fill libraries all over this country. As a researcher, I brought back thousands of pages (on microfiche) of central office files of Bureau of Indian Affairs documents pertaining to Fond du Lac Reservation. In the process, I learned not only a good deal about the reservation, but about myself (Cleary and Peacock, 1998, p. 59):

> Several years ago, I spent the good part of a summer doing research at the National Archives in Washington, DC. I, Thomas Peacock, have always been a history buff, with a particular interest in the history of my home reservation of Fond du Lac in northern Minnesota and of the continuing impact of that history on the people today. Early into the research, I reviewed the education files of the reservation, looking for information on the old Bureau of Indian Affairs day schools and files indicating where the children of that period were sent to boarding and mission schools. The second file folder I opened contained a letter to the Commissioner of Indian Affairs in Washington. It was written by a mother requesting that she be allowed to keep her eldest son home from Pipestone Boarding School that school year, because she was ill and needed his assistance in the home. It read, in part, "I respectfully request that my eldest son, Harry..."
>
> I quickly went to the end of the letter and saw that it was signed by my great grandmother, and that her eldest son was my grandfather. A reply letter was attached from the Commissioner informing my great grandmother that her son must report to the boarding school as directed. Later, in reviewing other files, I was to find out my great grandmother died that winter from a flu epidemic that swept the reservation. I remember being overcome by a flood of emotions ranging from anger and disgust to grief. Anger and disgust for a government which felt it was in their right to overlord the personal lives of the people whose

nations they had possessed. Grief for a great-grandmother I had never known, who was no longer just a tombstone in the old Catholic cemetery up the road from where I live, but a person to whom I suddenly felt a strong emotional connection. I asked myself over and over again if history would have played itself out differently if my grandfather had been allowed to stay home that winter. Would it have made a difference in my great grandmother living through the winter and going on to live a full life, or would my grandfather also become a victim of the epidemic? Who would think a bureaucratic decision made by some long dead Commissioner of Indian Affairs would have such an impact on me.

A sampling of some of the documents I brought back to the reservation is included. They deal with land issues, schooling, health, and tribal government (including early tribal disputes). Of particular interest for many will be the documents relating to the Indians of Wisconsin Point, and the story of their removal, and the removal of the Indian burial ground. These letters and documents are part of our history, our story.

References
Cleary, L. Miller, and Peacock, T. (1998). Collected wisdom: American Indian education. Needham Heights, MA: Allyn and Bacon.

Document #1

List of scholars in Fond du Lac Methodist Mission School, 1843

No:	Names	Age:Entered:Left	Studies
1.	John McKender	Nov. 17, 1843	Spelling
2.	Mary McKender	March 14, ″	″
3.	Amaden McKender	″ 12, ″	″
4.	Eliza Gazoner	″ 10, ″	″
5.	George Bellenger	″ 11, ″	″ Reading, writing
6.	John B. Bellenger	″ 18, ″	″ ″ ″
7.	Paul Bellenger	″ 8, ″	″ ″ ″
8.	John Shegobe	″ 16, ″	″ ″ ″
9.	Antoine Shegobe	″ 10, ″	″ ″ ″
10.	Greten Shegobe	″ 15, ″	″ ″ ″
11.	Mary Shegobe	″ 11, ″	″ ″ ″
12.	Mary Shalow	″ 8, ″	″ ″ ″
13.	Joseph Mishlow	″ 11, ″	″ ″ ″
14.	Michael Mishlow	″ 9, ″	″ ″ ″
15.	Israel Mishlow	″ 12, ″	″ ″ ″
16.	Issac Thomas	″ 11, ″	″ ″ ″
17.	Ann Thomas	″ 20, ″	″ ″ ″
18.	Nega no se qua	Apr. 10, ″	″ ″ ″
19.	Wa o zhe go low	April 8, 1842	Spelling, reading, writing
20.	Pe Tah wah na go qua	″ 9, ″	
21.	Ta ga ma che wa shik	″ 19, ″	″ ″
22.	Yu qu koo sa	″ 15, ″	″ ″
23.	Ah de so heah	″ 11, ″	″ ″
24.	Nancy	″ 14, ″	″ ″
25.	John Na ga na be	May 10, ″	″ ″

Alfred Brunson

U.S.S. Ind. Agt.

La Pointe

Document # 2

Fond du Lac, Mina. Tery.
April 4, 1855

Mr. Gilbert,

Dear Sir,

We the undersigned take the opportunity of sending you a few lines to inform you with regard to our claims in Minnesota Territory.

According to the stipulations of the treaty made at La Pointe last fall with the Lake Indians, it was understood that each half breed family were entitled to 80 acres of good farming land etc.

In consequence of that stipulation all of us that had no homestead went to work after the treaty last fall and selected such land as we saw fit for us to have made and have made our improvements such as a comfortable Log House and cleared some of the land.

And now to our great surprise we find that we are encroached upon by the people, strangers coming from different parts of the world, and our claims are what is termed jumps and they tell us that we have no right to those claims whatsoever, and they are trying to take the advantage of our ignorance all they can.

Now for instance as this place, Fond du Lac, where all of us have been brought up, the improvements such as horses, fences, clearings, all of these have been made at the expense of our labor and means. It is our intention to keep possession of these place where our improvements are etc.

Sir. We look to you as our advisor and our protector with regard to our rights if we have any at all. It would be well to have notices sent to this place to make those people acquainted with our rights.

Dear Sir. We recommend our interests to you and we hope soon to hear from you and that you will give us your advice on the subject, and as before mentioned, it would be well to have notices sent through to us and have them posted at different places, etc. etc.

Very Truly Your
Obedient Servants
signed, F. Rucan
signed, Joseph Short
signed, Joseph (his (X) mark) Lagard

Document # 3

St. Paul, Minnesota
16th Oct. 1858

Charles S. Eniason. Esq.
Surveyor General, St. Paul, Minn.

Sir:

Agreeably to Instructions received from you dated 2nd to 29th April 1858, I started June 1858 from Superior, Wisconsin to survey the exterior boundary lines of the Chippewa Indian Reservation situated on the St. Louis River, Minnesota, and went thence as near as possible to the source of the East branch of Snake River, distant from Superior about 80 miles, then sending part of the party back to Fond-du-Lac for provisions, some seventy miles: I took 2 men and what provisions they could carry and followed down a stream on which we had camped to the first known point on Snake River which proved to be "Cheywatawna" distant about 100 miles. I then found that we had in the 1st place camped about 2 1/2 miles <u>West</u> of the true source of the River, proceeding immediately back to camp. I started a line in the middle of a large open Tamarack Swamp about 2 miles in diameter: the same being the true source of the East branch of Snake River, and run thence for the mouth of the Savannah River N. 11 degrees E. having reached the same, and having on hand just enough provisions for the purpose. I immediately ran and established the westerly boundary of the Reservation; length a little over 13 miles, thence proceeding back to the mouth of the Savannah River, ran the meander of the right bank of the St. Louis River down stream to a point opposite the center of an Island mentioned in the Treaty of Sept. 30th 1854 and called therein "pawpaw-su-mi-mi-tig," — as the Treaty does not designate any particular point or end of said Island I deemed right to take a point opposite the center thereof, particularly as said boundary lines would then include part of the clearings of the Indians on which they then had good standing crops, as well as Blacksmith Shop & houses which they had there built, and can thence West & Intersected Westerly boundary line.

I wish to call your attention to some of the difficulties under which this survey was made, viz., the range and indefinite nature and length of the boundary lines, as designated by Treaty, the country being a perfect wilderness—without even Indian Trails, as a means of transit, being mostly Tamarack and Cedar Swamps, rendering the operation of running the lines exceedingly difficult and tedious, being obliged to use "Burts Solar Compass" on the Survey, the uncommonly large amount of rainy and cloudy weather, (as shown by Journal accompanying notes) caused much lost time and was the principal reason of the survey being protracted through so long a period at so great expense; the nature of the Country rendered the obtaining of provisions for the party laborious, as well as expensive, all provisions having to be packed by the men at times from 12 to 70 miles, and as a pack of 50 lbs. carried 12 miles through that Country, not on line or trail is a good days work for a good packman, the difficulty of supplying the party can be at once seen.

I think it may not be inappropriate to mention some items of information obtained while making said survey. There are in this Section of Country three places at which the Indians have made clearings and improvements, to wit; one near Knife Portage and which the South boundary line in part embraces; there they have a Black Smith Shop, houses, and quite an extent of land cleared and under cultivation, though said clearing is mostly on an island referred to by above named Treaty, another small clearing is at "Pine Rapids."

The far most important one to them, is however, at "Perch Lake" situated in the S.E. corner of Township 49, R. 19 West, a Lake something over a mile across. There they have some log houses and quite an extent of land cleared and under cultivation, this is the only point in this Section of Country to my knowledge where the Indians if so disposed could maintain themselves the year round; — at this Lake the Indians obtain in abundance Field Rice & Fish—in its neighborhood they have good hunting and on the banks good sugar bushes, advantages which in my opinion they cannot obtain at any point within the boundary lines of their Reservation. Said Lake is 4 miles South of the boundary of the Reservation, and the Indians are very much dissatisfied with the location of said South boundary line—that it is not far enough South & that the Treaty of September 30, 1854 secured to them Perch Lake, and objecting to be moved from the same.

The land forming the Reservation is mostly 3rd rate and swampy with Tamarack and Cedar Timber—what good land there is being, as is generally the case throughout this Section of Country, composed of small islands as it were surrounded with Swamp or narrow ridges, and I think the Country too even to admit of thorough drainage of the Swamps if from their nature it ever becomes desirable.

I am Sir,

Very Respectfully

Your Obt. Servt. (signed)   Peter E. Bradshaw

Deputy Surveyor

Document # 4

Superior Wis. Nov. 3rd 1862

L.E. Webb Esq.

Indian Agent

Sir.

In accordance with instructions dated Oct. 16th. 1862 I, in company with Geo. E. Wheeler Indian Blacksmith, started on the 22nd day of October to explore the country adjacent to Big Lake and carry out your instructions. Big Lake I found to be about one and one half miles long, with an average width of one quarter of a mile. The land in the vicinity is very good, a rich sandy loam; the timber is Maple, Birch, Basswood and some Pine. There are several thousand acres of land surrounding the Lake which could be easily cleared at a cost not to exceed Fifteen Dollars per acre, which land would produce abundant crops of such grains and vegetables as are adapted to this climate. At this Lake there are now two families living who have, the past season cleared up about one acre which they planted potatoes, and have raised a good crop. The Lake abounds in fish, Perch Pike and Pickerel. While there I saw the Indians frequently raise their nets; they averaged a catch at each raise of from five to twenty fish. They say they can catch all the fish they need, both summer and winter. Wild Rice is abundant in the neighborhood at distances from the Lake varying from one half to two miles. There are extensive Hay Meadows from two to five miles from the Lake, from which at least Two Hundred Tons of Hay could be harvested in an ordinarily good season.

On leaving the Lake to look out a route for a road I found the country lying in an air line from the Lake to Twin Lakes to be swampy and otherwise impracticable; by keeping on the knolls and materially lengthening the distance, I was able to find a route over which a very good wagon road can be built, a portion of which, however, is low and swampy. Over this route I connected with the Military road at a point about one mile west from Twin Lakes, Twenty three miles from Superior. The distance between the Lake and the Military road by the route selected will be about Thirteen miles. The estimated cost is Three Hundred Dollars per mile. For this amount per mile a first rate wagon road can be built. One mile South of Big Lake is Perch Lake which I visited; I found there about twelve acres of land partially cleared and about thirty families of Indians. They have raised there this season 800 bushels of potatoes and gathered as near as I could estimate about 600 pounds of Wild Rice. Nine tenths of these Indians live on the West Side of the Lake; on the East Side I found three families who moved there last Spring. They have about two acres of land cleared up which they cultivated the past season. They harvested 250 bushels of Potatoes and 300 Cabbages; they have three Cows, four Pigs and two ponies. These three families have this year gathered 1200 pounds of Rice. The neighborhood of these Lakes is, in my estimation the most favorable portion of the Reserve to make improvements and permanently locate the Inds.

Signed   Very Respectfully
James Edwards

Document # 5

W.A. Mercer

U.S. Ind. Agt.

Ashland, Wis.

Sir:

I have the pleasure to transmit herewith by direction of the Indian Council of January 17, 1894. Copy of Resolutions adopted by Said Council protesting against the distribution of provisions, etc. among Said Indians instead of the moneys belonging to them, in order to enable them to meet engagements already contracted by them.

> Very Respectfully,
>
> Jas. I. Coffey
>
> Secretary of Council

Document #6

Reservation of the Fond du Lac Band of Chippewa Indians State of Minnesota
Cloquet, Minn. July 17, 1894

W.A. Mercer

U.S. A. Ind. Agt.

Ashland, Wis.

Sir,

Pursuant to the action of the Council I am authorized to inform you, that on the Tenth of July 1894, John Annimassung, Jr. was proclaimed head Chief of the entire band of Fond du Lac Chippewas by a regularly constituted Council. According to the custom of hereditary descent, to assume the office held by his father John Annimassung, Sr. deceased late Chief of the Fond du Lac Band of Chippewas. An executive body was also organized and proclaimed established on the same date to be known as the executive council. Composed of the head Chief, one Sub Chief, a Secretary and two advisory. The personnel of the present body is as follows:

John Annimassung, Jr.	Head Chief
Joe Obequat	Sub Chief
Jas. I Coffey	Secretary of Council
Joe Petite, Jr.	Advisor
D. (Dave) Ruttle	Advisor

I am respectfully,

Jos. J. Coffey

Secy. of Council

Document #7

UNITED STATES INDIAN SERVICE

La Pointe   Agency

Ashland, Wis., July 1894.

Mr. James I. Coffee,

Fond du Lac Band Chippewas,

Cloquet, Minnesota.

(Through Government Farmer Roger Patterson)

Sir:-

I return herewith a communication just received from you purporting to set forth the action of certain Indians in the election of head chief of the Fond du Lac Band, by a regularly constituted council, and that according to the custom of hereditary descent John Annimassung, Jr., was elected to said office, formerly held by John Annimassung, Sr., deceased; also that an executive body consisting of five members was organized and proclaimed established on the same day, Etc.

Any communications which you or any other Indian may have to forward to this office will hereafter be forwarded through the government farmer in charge of the reservation, and unless it is so sent will receive no notice from me. The farmer should have a chance to express his views on anything that pertains to the administration of the reservation under his charge.

Respectfully,

W.A. Mercer

Lieut. U.S.A.-U.S. Ind. Agt.

Document # 8

United States Indian Service
Cloquet, Minn.

Oct. 21, 1895

Lieut. W.A. Mercer, U.S. Ind. Agt.
Ashland Wis.

Sir:

Inclosed is a rude map of the Fond du Lac school grounds. The school is a little north of the center of the map, dimensions about 20 by 27 ft. with a shanty addition 10 by 10 ft. About 5 ft. west of the addition to the school house is the wood house, 15 by 30 ft. North of the school house about 15 ft. is a fence inclosing Coutcher's place: his house is about 30 ft. north of the school house. Seventy-five feet south of the school house is another house occupied by Indians. The travelled road is east of the school house about 95 ft. A few ft. east of the road the ground abruptly descends for 100 to 150 ft. to the narrow bottom bordering the St. Louis river.

The ground gradually slopes from the school house to the road, and also a very slight descent from the school house west some 70 or 80 ft. where there is a small swale, or low place. The natural drainage in the immediate vicinity of the school house is good. There is no system of sewage. Ventilation is obtained by means of the doors and windows and by an opening in the ceiling about a foot square. The height of the ceiling from the floor is about 8 ft. The windows are small, containing 6 lights or panes of glass to a sash. Since the school house was built it has settled, causing the floor to become uneven in some places. The school house is built of hewed pine logs and ceiled inside and an attic second story. The roof leaks some in rainy weather. Water for the school is obtained in the Summer and Fall from a spring, located about 1/4 of a mile from the school house, at the foot of the bluff, near the river. In the winter as the water in the spring freezes solid to the ground, water is obtained by cutting a hole in the ice in the St. Louis River. The spring does not afford water until June, and water is brought from the river until that time.

Conveying water from the river to the school house in winter is sometimes an arduous task, as the hillside is very steep and the path very slippery.

The facilities for industrial education are at present, not very good. The land in the immediate vicinity of the school house, not occupied by the Indian houses or yards, is of small extent, and badly covered with stone. The stone, which is in the form of boulders might be removed, and the land brought under cultivation. The soil is somewhat sandy and would require abundant fertilizer. West of the school house there is a strip of vacant land for a considerable distance but it is mostly covered with brush, shrubs and small trees and would require some drainage and clearing to render it fit for cultivation.

About 1/3 of the children attending school live north of the school house, and about 2/3 south of the school house. Mr. Diver lives farthest north about 1/2 mile from the school house and Mr. Cadot the farthest south, about the same distance. Mr. Coffy lives near Farmer's house and sends children to Cloquet.

The map, by Mr. Naganab, shows the location of the school house with the references to the Govt. Farmer's house. They are about 2 miles apart and by the only traveled road via planing mill, about 2 1/4 or 2 1/2 miles.

Very respectfully, W.C.B. Biddle

Document #9

Department of the Interior

U.S. Indian Service

Cloquet, Minn.

March 6, 1902

Honorable S.H. Campbell

U.S. Ind. Agent

Enclosed find completed papers etc.

I also inform you that I have disinfected and discharged small pox patients at the Indian village.

There exists (?) in Cloquet an epidemic of Scarlet fever and one hundred cases are reported. All schools, churches and all public places are closed. I have forbidden all our people to go to town except on important business and unless it is obeyed to the letter shall issue an order that none shall leave the reservation without a pass. The disease is very virulent and many are dying and it will be a serious matter if it gets started on the reservation.

Respectfully yours

John W. Morgan

Govt. Farmer

25309 Indian Office Incl. No. 3   1901

Facts relative to smallpox epidemic at Fond du Lac Reservation, Minnesota

Washington D.C.

Commissioner

Received at La Pointe Agent

52   Oct. 5 1901

Ashland, Wisconsin

Name	When quarantined	When Released	No.Days Quarant.
Joe Wenandy	Jan. 25th, 1901	Feb. 23rd, 1901	30 days
John Wenandy	″ 25th, ″	March 11th, ″	46 ″
Nancy Houle	″ 25th, ″	Feb. 23rd, ″	30 ″
Mrs. Pete Petite	Feb. 19th, ″	March 26th, ″	36 ″
Pete Petite	″ 19th, ″	″ 26th, ″	36 ″
Pete Petite's boy	″ 19th, ″ Died	March 17th, ″	27 ″
Pete Petite's girl	″ 9th, ″	″ 26th, ″	36 ″
Ella Connors	March 9th, ″	April 14th, ″	37 ″
Jim Coffie	″ 9th, ″	″ 14th, ″	37 ″
Lizzie Reed	″ 9th, ″	″ 14th, ″	37 ″
Annie Reed	″ 9th, ″	″ 14th, ″	37 ″
Mary Reed	″ 9th, ″	″ 14th, ″	37 ″
Philomine Reed	″ 9th, ″	″ 14th, ″	37 ″
Eddie Reed	″ 9th, ″	″ 14th, ″	37 ″
	Total number days		500
	″ ″	quarantined	14
	″ ″	having disease	7

Fond du Lac Res.

Total Expense Inc.

Expense per day $279.81

for one person—   .56

112

Document # 10

(COPY)

House of Representatives

U.S.

Committee on Rules
Washington, D.C.
19 March 1912.

Mr. John Lemieux
502 W. 7th. St.
Superior, Wis.

Dear Sir:

Replying to yours of March 15th will say that I have made an investigation of the Wisconsin Point description that you speak of and find that in 1854 one Joseph A. Bullen made an entry for lots 1 and 2 section 28, and lot 1 section 27, T. 49, R. 12, being the land described by you, thereafter there was an attempt upon the part of the Government to withdraw this land from entry for a military reservation. The right of the Government to do this was disputed by the grantees of Joseph A. Bullen, who it seems conveyed his interest in the land, and the matter was finally settled on November 23, 1891, by the issue of a patent to this Joseph A. Bullen. The records show that Jas. S. Ritchie and E. L. Johnson in 1893 made affidavit that they were then the owners of the land and that the original patent issued to Bullen on November 23, 1891 had been lost or mislaid and asking that a duplicate patent be issued to them. This the record shows was issued to them.

This compromises the record in the land office here at Washington. As to whether your family have any rights to the land will depend upon the laws of Wisconsin and the facts in connection with your father's possession of the land. The law of Wisconsin is that twenty years adverse possession under claim of ownership is sufficient to give a good title. It therefore, would become important to know whether your family's possession had been continuous and whether it was under a claim of ownership. The question would then arise as to whether or not, no patent having been issued until November, 1891, the matter being in controversy between the Government and Bullen, whether the adverse possession if there was such on the part of your father could date back

113

prior to November 23, 1891. It is my own judgement that it could, and that Bullen's equitable title ran clear back to 1854 when he made the cash payment for the land. Assuming, however, that this is not the case, the twenty years possible adverse possession if it could only begin with November 23, 1891, would expire on November 23rd last. As you will see the whole matter depends upon the laws of Wisconsin and the peculiar facts that may exist with reference to it. As you perhaps know I am not in the practice of law as I am devoting my entire time to my duties in Congress. Under the circumstances I would advise you to consult a lawyer in Superior and lay the facts before him and he will no doubt advise you correctly and if the facts are such as to warrant a reasonable chance of success, will no doubt take the case for you upon a reasonable basis. Of course, there are many good lawyers in Superior, W.R. Foley being one who would serve you well.

Assuring you of my readiness to aid you in any way possible, I remain,

Yours very sincerely,

I.L. Lenroot

Document # 11

[Editor's note: Contemporary Fond du Lac residents may feel unrest and dissent are something new to the reservation. The following letters are examples of past unrest.]

Reservation of the Fond du Lac Band of Chippewa
Indians, Cloquet, Minnesota, May 26, 1913

To The Hon. Commissioner
of Indian Affairs,
Washington D.C.

Dear Sir:

Thursday the 22nd, inst, three men, Mike Diver, Frank Pequette and Joe Northrup left here for your city, it is rumored here those men assume pretensions of being delegates or representatives from this reservation, and go to Washington relative to matters upon this reservation;

The writer is a member of the executive committee of the organized council of the Chippewas of Minnesota, elected to represent the people of the Fond du Lac Reservation in Minnesota, in all tribal matters. I write this letter in my official capacity, that you may possess some facts relative to the tribal status of the three men which I have named, in order that you may not be imposed upon by them;

They have not been authorized by the Chippewas of the Fond du Lac Reservation to go to Washington on their behalf for any purpose whatever, the Fond du Lac Reservation is represented in the general council of the organized Chippewas, through which its affairs will reach the Indian Office at Washington which is now the official channel; notwithstanding any papers they may present to your office.

I am told those men held a secret meeting and choose themselves to go to Washington, the meeting was not the regular council, and was secret, Mr. Frank Pequette seems to have furnished the motive, he is a methodist missionary among the Chippewas located at the village of Sawyer, Minn., on the Fond du Lac Reservation.

Mr. Pequette has been perniciously active among the Chippewas in their tribal matters to further his selfish motives, he is not a member of the Fond du Lac Band of Chippewas, nor is he a Minnesota Chippewa, this fact disqualifies him from participating in Chippewa matters in Minn., I am told that he is a colored man from Wisconsin and passes himself as a Chippewa, in ″THE TOMA-HAWK″ a publication of White Earth, Minnesota, under date of Thursday, May 15, 1913, the following item appears: (Head lines) ″ TRACKED TO FRANK PEQUETTE″

the protest which was made against the Fond du Lac delegates which attended the Cass Lake council has been traced to Frank Pequette, a member of the Michigan bands of Chippewas, according to a member of the delegation.

The delegation charges that Mr. Pequette has been unusually and conspicuous-ly active in his opposition to the organization of the general council of the Minnesota Chippewas, if this is true, it should be remembered that he is not a member of the Minnesota bands of Chippewas, and the criticisms by the Fond du Lac delegates are justified.

It is also charged that the methods of Mr. Pequette are decidedly questionable regarding Minnesota matters, and that he succeeded in having himself placed upon the rolls of the Chippewas of Minnesota and has taken an allotment of land. This could not have been accomplished otherwise than by fraud, and the matter should be thoroughly investigated to ascertain whether the report is true to the end that steps may be taken by the officers of the organization to have Mr. Pequette's name stricken from the rolls if he has been enrolled!

So far no investigations have been made into the report, the statement that Mr. Pequette is on the Chippewa Rolls in Minnesota may not be borne out by the facts, yet his activity in persuading the uneducated and incompetent members of our tribe to make journeys to Washington upon matters which they have lit-tle knowledge, encourages a useless expenditure of tribal funds.

The officers of the new organization will in the course of a little time, take up all Chippewa matters intelligently and in an orderly way. The principal officers of the organization, are men of education, lawyers and professional men, accustomed to and drilled into handling the details of business matters, suc-cessfully, intelligently and in an orderly way.

It will naturally follow that the relations between the Indian Office and the Chippewa's organization will soon get upon an intelligent basis, which may greatly relieve the arduous duties of the Indian Office as to Chippewa matters; Of the three men mentioned above, Mike Diver and Joe Northrup are members of the Fond du Lac Chippewas, but they have no official capacity in the tribe. Diver is an uneducated and incompetent Indian, Northrup has a little education, just sufficient to give him the spirit of a Robespierre, he was expelled from the Carlisle Indian School for rebellious conduct and taken back to his tribe in northern Minnesota in irons and turned loose, the easiest way the officers could get rid of him.

This description of those men are given here to enable you to deal with them intelligently when they make the request for assistance from the tribal funds for their expenses and return transportation.

The policy of the organized Chippewas of Minnesota is conservative in all matters, the needless waste of tribal funds for the assistance of self appointed delegates to Washington is discouraged, for the reason that tribal funds may become prey by scheming persons with bogus papers as credentials;.The three men herein named have gone to Washington of their own accord, presumably on a sporting trip, if aid is given them from tribal funds encouragement will be that means be given to self appointed delegates who in no way can benefit the tribe.

A delegation is being formed by the regular Chippewa organization to go to Washington in June, the date of which is not yet decided upon, it will be given credentials by the officers of the organized Chippewas of Minnesota.

Sincerely yours,

James I. Coffey

The Fond du Lac Member of the Executive Council.

Document # 12

DEPARTMENT OF THE INTERIOR

UNITED STATES INDIAN SERVICE

Report upon schools-

Cloquet, Minn.

Fond du Lac.

November 19, 1913.

The Honorable

Commissioner of Indian Affairs,

Washington, D.C.

Sir:-

I have the honor to report herewith upon the work of the Normantown Day School under the Fond du Lac Agency at Sawyer, Minnesota.

Teacher – Bertha Groth (Substitute)

Enrollment, 20 pupils – 10 boys & 10 girls

present,   15 pupils

Grades,

Primary...................4 boys & 2 girls

First Grade..............3 boys & 2 girls

Second Grade..........4 boys & 3 girls

Fourth...................................2 girls

I am assuming that Dr. Michael, the Supervisor, has taken up the matter of Buildings and equipment, so will not dwell at length upon the matter except to state that it is anticipated that the Office is to send a teacher (male) and his wife as housekeeper.

Commissioner

#2   The Farmer and his family are now living in the Teacher's cottage and the present teacher rooms and boards with the farmer. If a man and his wife are sent here as teacher and housekeeper new quarters will have to be furnished.

The school is suitable for a woman to teach, the attendance is not large and the greater number of the children are small. The school building needs paint inside and out and more blackboard is needed. There is now only about nine (9) square feet of blackboard.

The children have been attending the Public school at Sawyer formerly but owing to a change in the rates of tuition it was decided that it would be cheaper to open the Government Day School again. The pupils while attending irregularly have the free independent manner of the Public school child. All of the grades read twice a day.

The Daily Program is as follows:-

Primary Reading

First Grade Reading

Second Grade Reading

Fourth Grade Reading

Intermission

Primary numbers

First Grade numbers

Second Grade numbers

Fourth Grade Arithmetic

Writing

Noon Intermission

Primary Reading

First Grade Reading

Second Grade Reading

Fourth Grade Reading

Third Grade Language

Intermission

Fourth Grade Language

Second Grade Spelling

Fourth Grade Spelling

General Industrial Work

The pupils seem prompt and quite free in manner, they move quickly to and from classes. They raise their hands and ask questions of the teacher, they ask to have words pronounced and borrow pencils. Their voices were clear in the recitation. There is, however, need for drills in enunciation. While the children seem quite responsive compared with children in other schools I have seen in the north, they are lacking in power to apply themselves studiously for very long at a time.

The reading should be improved by more word drills, phonic work, drills in recognizing groups of words, phrases and short sentences.

There is need for training in attention: The teacher complains of having difficulty in holding the attention of the children in recitations. Their minds seem to wander and there is consequently a deficiency in memory.

The pupils are not so proficient in numbers as they might be. Drills in simple combinations should be placed upon the blackboard and a few minutes taken for learning correct answers each day. More thoroughness is needed in the work in numbers. More materials are needed for the concrete work in Arithmetic; cubes, inch, squares and other materials as listed in general suggestions.

The children need a course in ethical instruction. They are not as respectful in manner as they should be. The teacher has to spend much time and energy in correcting little outbreaks and infringements, which time would better be spent at the opening period in something which would strengthen the children for the Day's work.

The urgent needs of the school are more school supplies, Reading books, Arithmetics and Teacher's helps. (A list had been made to be handed in to the Office at Cloquet.), More blackboarding, oil or paint for the school-room floor, pictures framed to hang in the school-room, more attention to special drills and drills in simple number combinations, more phonic work and special drills for enunciation, a well-planned opening exercise and special attention to ethical training.

Fond du Lac Day School:
Jennie M. Rochford, Teacher
Elizabeth Rochford, Housekeeper
enrollment—23 pupils, boys and girls.
Grades
Primary. – 3 boys & 1 girl
  First Grade – 2 boys
  Second Grade. – 4 boys & 2 girls
  Third Grade. – 2 boys & 1 girl
  Fourth Grade – 2 boys

Buildings:

The Cottage is in good condition. The school building will be considerably improved if its walls are painted or kalsomined and the floor painted a lighter color. A yearly calendar is being prepared by the teacher. There is no written daily program but there are plans prepared and an attempt is made to follow them. School begins at 9 o'clock with an intermission for recreation and the noon hour. The class work closes at 3:30 when a half hour is taken for industrial work.

The pupils are better graded here than any school I have visited this year. The pupils are promoted when in the teacher's judgment they are ready to do more advanced work. They are carefully and intelligently questioned before and after the recital of each lesson and are made responsible for their lessons.

Methods of instruction are good. The manner of the teacher is quiet, easy, intense, her voice is low and controlled and she is quite well poised. Her influence over the pupils is good. The instruction given is practical and quite good in all of the grades. The number work was especially good. The reading was much better than that which one fails to hear at all in many day schools. The pupils read loud enough to be well understood. They were prepared to tell something of the lesson story in their own words. The singing was good. The teacher had her own song collection. The children were cleanly in appearance, clothing clean, hair combed, eyes, face and hands clean. There has been attention given to training in manners as the pupils were respectful and friendly toward strangers and the sympathetic connection between them and the teacher seemed strong.

Better results may be attained by a still higher grade of ethical instruction, more attention to the mechanical phase of reading, more progressive work in number with the necessary drill posted charts or on the blackboard. Suggestions were made to the teacher in both day schools, covering the needs of their respective schools and I have assurance that the suggestions will be followed.

The Normantown Day School has only recently been re-opened which accounts, in part, for the incompleteness of equipment. The children do not appear as well as to cleanliness, manner, habits of study, etc. as do the children in the Fond du Lac School but they can be improved in due time. Both Day

121

School communities are progressive and there is no reason why the schools cannot come up to a higher standard of work. The teachers have been advised to make collections of pictures for visual instruction. There are no other pictures than those in books and charts. The correlation with industrial work and life activities needs to be emphasized much more in both schools. The use of English also needs more attention in both schools, especially in Normantown, and there should be a period set aside for conversational exercises. Reviews are frequent; there is a tendency in the case of the new teacher to give lessons too long for review. Weekly outlines of instruction are prepared. They are as much in detail as the teacher has time to make them and while they are not so ideal in form or character as those made by teachers in Columbia Teacher's College, they are better than the average in plans made by Day School teachers.

The regular teacher, Miss Rochford, makes plans of her work. Miss Rochford also makes use of two educational publications. The course followed should conform as nearly as possible to the State course of study, as the time will not be long when Indian children in both Day School communities will enter the Public School.

As before stated, the equipment of both schools can be made more complete. The supply of books at the Fond du Lac School is quite complete and in good condition. Covers are used for the books and the teachers are making an effort to teach the children to be more careful in the use of books.

The equipment for Industrial instruction is not very extensive. The children are small and not very much industrial work is attempted. The children assist at Normantown with the sweeping, dusting, and other cleaning after 3:30. There is no noon-day lunch prepared. The children bring their lunches and a number of them live near enough to go home for lunch.

Methods of instruction in industries are good in so far as they go. There is no housekeeper at Normantown. The housekeeper at Fond du Lac has a class of the older girls in sewing. This class is learning the different kinds of stitches and how to embroider. While the girls do sewing under the direction of the housekeeper the boys are drawing or receiving special instruction to get to appreciate the resources on their own allotments. Not very much has yet been accomplished in this but it is my opinion that any interested teacher can bring the children in the Day schools into a lively appreciation of their own homes and take possibilities of the natural resources through the study of nature.

There should be more emphasis placed upon nature study in the little children's classes if they are to be interested in agriculture later on. This section of the country affords excellent opportunity for the study of nature. This is a lumbering country at the present time but eventually the land must be cleared and agriculture will be the leading industry. There are many lessons full of meaning that can be taught little children correlating industries and life activities. At this time a number of families are building new homes under the direction of the Superintendent and there is a beginning made in clearing the lands of tree stumps.

In the interest of health, games are played at recess at both schools. The teachers often join in these games with the children. There is no play-ground equipment. The Farmer at Normantown bought a baseball outfit for the boys. More time should be spent, however, in teaching active out-door games to the children.

As before stated, there should be more attention given to means for the culture and refinement of pupils as to ethical talks and stories, music, singing, games and actual experience in daily living up to the Golden Rule Standard. The moral conditions existing in the vicinity of the school are not of the best in every case but are better than in many other communities. At Cloquet the accessibility of the church is within a few rods and the opportunities for religious worship are frequent.

Employees:

The Misses Rochford, sisters, are in charge of the work of the Cloquet Day School, a substitute teacher, Miss Groth in charge of the Normantown School. Efficiency reports of the Former will be forwarded later.

I feel certain that all of the suggestions made will be carried out both by the teachers and the persons in charge.

      Very respectfully,
    (signed) Mary Johnson

MEJ/ADA   Normal Instructor.

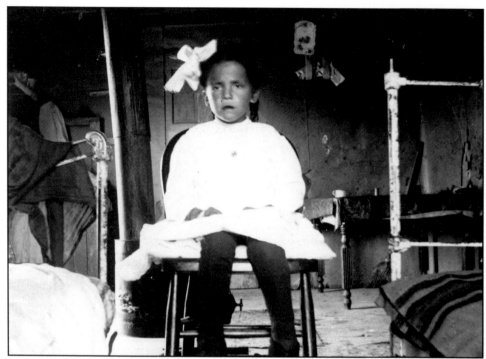

Girl at Sawyer c. 1910

Girls at Sawyer c. 1909

Sawyer School

MHS Photo

Sawyer Church congregation – 1909-1912

1854 Treaty Annuity Payment c. 1865

Document # 13

Letters Received
DEPARTMENT OF THE INTERIOR
UNITED STATES INDIAN SERVICE
HON.S.W.CAMPBELL, U.S. INDIAN AGENT
ASHLAND, WI.

I have your letter of the 22 with regard to children at Sawyer that are not attending school. In answer will say that I have known for two years that they were not doing what they should in that direction, and I have written you about it. I have tried every scheme I could think of to try to get them started. I got 7 to Tomah last fall and the promise of Peterson that his girls would go later. But when the time came the Mother, and an old grandfather set up a houl and prevented their going. I did get one little girl whom they had adopted to go to Tomah. Mrs. Porter sent one boy, and finally consented to allow a crazy girl to go to Canton Asylum. But she insisted on keeping one little girl at home to help care for the baby. There are two little girls at Petersons who are exceptionally bright that certainly ought to go to school. I do not recognize who the Waboz family are by that name. There are three nearly grown girls in the L Rose family who are the most abandoned prostitutes. Nevertheless I have tried to induce them to go to school. Knowing at the time they were not fit to be associated with young girls at school or anywhere else. Tom Kelley has been to school most of the time for 7 years. I took him to Tomah, 6 years ago. I have personally interviewed him twice at least this year but failed to get him started. There are two girls at Dead Fish helping Sam Martin who are very bright and about 16 or 17 years old that I have tried hard to get but have not succeeded, so you can see that I have not neglected these people. I have had Teachers from Morris, Pipestone, and other Gov't schools, over there trying to induce them to let the children go but all failed. In most cases the children want to go but the parents stand in the way. I have a letter from Mr. Compton of Tomah School saying he would come and get these scholars if it were possible to secure them. He says the lot I took there last fall are an exceptionally fine lot of pupils, and one boy that we were told we would have trouble keeping is now clerking in the office. I will go over there and make one more effort, before giving it up. They are exceptionally poor just now and it may have an influence in inducing them to send, there are several children of school age at Brookston, that should go to some school. I think there will be a public school there in the spring, perhaps if the Gov't would assist a little they could get it started sooner. I will report again in 3 or 4 days.

Here at this day school there are only a few scholars left, the sisters schools having taken many away, there is not over 15 in all and it is possible to get all out at one time, some will be sick and have other excuses. One or two men have gone away to work and taken the family with them. I don't believe any man on earth is more interested in this matter than I am. But at the same time I cannot force matters without some law to assist me. I think perhaps we could use the state compulsory law in case of day schools. But when it comes to compelling people to send their children to some outside school it becomes a different matter. If we had a day school in Sawyer, I think a fair attendance could be secured. I will make an effort to get them again and report the result.

Respectfully yours,

(signed)   John W.Morgan   Gov't Farmer

Document #14

November 16, 1913

Mayor S.W. Campbell,
Indian Agent. Ashland Wisc.
Dear Sir,

I will let you know that these Indians don't want this Reservation to be opened.

We had a council here amongst the Big Lake Indians, about the mill that you said would be put here and all those whose names are below, would like to see the mill start up but not to open the Reservation.

We did not have time to go to Cloquet to get the other names, but they are working on it there now.

Joe Naganub has gone to Washington with some man and we don't know what he has gone for.

Answer this letter what you are going to do and address it to John Peterson, Sawyer, Minn.

Document # 15

(COPY)

DEPARTMENT OF THE INTERIOR
UNITED STATES INDIAN SERVICE.
Fond du Lac Indian School
Cloquet, Minn., Oct. 10, 1914

Mr. E.C. Smith
510 Wieland Flats,
Duluth, Minn.

Dear Sir:

In reply to your letter of October 9th, beg leave to inform you that what you have heard about my circulating a petition among Indians is absolutely false. I was told by one of the Indians here a few days ago that Charley Drew is circulating a report to that effect.

Wish to say to you that I regret very much that it is necessary to remove the bodies from Wisconsin Point. I did all I could to get the cemetery made permanent. I recommended long ago to the Indian Office that the Government purchase the land from the Interstate Railway Company and establish a permanent cemetery on the Point. Also petition of Indians interested was forwarded to the Office but as you no doubt understand, the Indians ceded this land to the Government by the Treaty of 1854 and that the title of the land where the Indians are buried has long since passed from the Government to private parties. The Interstate Railway Company is the present owner of the land and they claim that they now wish to use the land for commercial purposes and have requested the Government to remove the bodies. Congress in August last passed a bill appropriating five thousand ($5,000.00) dollars for this purpose.

The Commissioner of Indian Affairs has requested me to take steps looking to the removal of the bodies. In compliance with this instruction from the Commissioner, I have secured bids for the removal of the bodies, purchase lots in Catholic and Protestant cemeteries in the city of Superior, and the purchase of tombstones. I am now waiting for the money to be deposited to my credit when the matter of the removal will be undertaken.

The only way to prevent the removal of the bodies is for the Government to purchase the land and I assure you that I would be very glad indeed to see this done because I know how the Indians feel about the matter. Steps should have been taken to establish a permanent cemetery on the Point before the Government lost the title to the land. The Government now proposes to purchase lots and remove the Indians to a permanent cemetery where the graves will be properly cared for.

It seems to me that the Indians ought to appreciate this since if the bodies are left on the Point the graves will be trampled over and desecrated by the Interstate Railway Company. You can readily see that there would be no object in my carrying a petition around to get the Indians to sign.

Charley Drew is circulating all kinds of reports in regard to this matter but I trust the Indians will be wise enough to investigate all reports that they may hear. Charley Drew is telling the Indians here that you have given fifteen dollars to prevent the removal of Indian bodies. I thought perhaps you were too wise to be caught that way.

Very respectfully.

(signed) *G.W. Cross*

GWC/ADA   Supt. & Spcl. Disb. Agt.

Document # 16

Clarence B. Miller   (copy)

Eighth District Minnesota

HOUSE OF REPRESENTATIVES, U.S.

Washington, D.C.

Nov. 12, 1914.

Mr. Edward C. Smith

Duluth, Minn.

Dear Mr. Smith:

I have your letter of the 6th. I have long been interested in the action of the Indian Office in the removal of the bodies. I have never understood where they got the authority to take the step. This matter is purely an Indian Office matter, and they have so far kept their motives and reasons well to themselves.

The money appropriated was not the Indians' money, but money out of the Treasury of the United States. At least, that is my recollection. I have not a copy of the bill here, but am quite certain the money was appropriated out of the United States Treasury.

The government has the legal right to appropriate and use for their benefit or alleged benefit, money belonging to Indians and in the hands of the government, independent of the consent of the Indians. I do not think they have a moral right to do so, however, against the wishes of the Indians, in any matter peculiarly within the sentiment or knowledge of the Indians.

Filed by J.M.S.

It was claimed, when the bill was in conference, that the Indians now consented to this removal of the bodies. I raised the question myself. There was no time to consult the Indians again, so I let it go. The Indian Office insisted upon it.

I favor making a cemetery where the bodies now are, and leaving them there, if that can be done.

Some time when you are in Duluth and I am at the Spalding where I stop, wish you would call to see me so we can talk Indian matters over.

With regards,

Sincerely,

C.B. Miller

Document # 17

Land-Sales   45920-1911   121298-1914   1-24691
   F I P

Deed for burial site in Superior, Wisconsin.

Mr. George W. Cross, Supt.,   *Nov 28 1914*

Fond du Lac School.

My dear Mr. Cross:

For your information there is enclosed a copy of a letter addressed to the Attorney General on November 20, 1914, asking that a report be made on the deed to a burial site in the Catholic cemetery in Superior, Wisconsin.

The Office was advised informally on November 23 that the deed was to be sent to the Assistant Attorney but that on its return examination in the Department of Justice would be made special. On November 16, 1914, the deed was returned from this Office to Rev. Eustice Vollmer, notation being made on the envelope for delivery to William J. Leader, Secretary of the Catholic Congregation, should Father Vollmer be absent from the city. They were requested to have inserted the words, "the United States of America," the words, "in trust for the Chippewa Indians in Minnesota." This addition in the granting clause was deemed proper for the reason that payment therefor is to be made out of Chippewa Indian funds. The matter was sent to Father Vollmer direct to avoid delay incident to separate transmissions of the papers. A copy of that letter is herewith.

Very truly yours,

E.B. Meritt

11-EVB-27   Assistant Commissioner

Office of Indian Affairs

133

Document # 18

Dec 7 1914 130365
DEPARTMENT OF THE INTERIOR
UNITED STATES INDIAN SERVICE

Land-Sales
45920-1911   Fond du Lac Indian School
12298-1914   Cloquet, Minn. Dec.4, 1914
  F I P
Deed for burial site in
Superior, Wisc.
The Honorable
Commissioner of Indian Affairs,
Washington, D.C.
Sir;

I have this date wired the Office to withhold approval of deed for parcel of land in the Catholic cemetery East End, Superior, Wisconsin, for the reason that I wish a little more time to discuss the matter with the Indians interested.

An Indian by the name of Charles Drew is making efforts to get a number of other Indians to join him in protest: First, Against the removal of the bodies, Second, Against their reinterment in the Catholic cemetery. He, Charles Drew, has opposed the removal of the bodies all along claiming that he is a spiritualist and has had communion with the spirits of the dead Indians buried on Wisconsin Point and that these spirits have advised him to oppose the removal of the bodies. He is now attempting to make it appear that the fifteen hundred ($1500.00) dollars to be paid for the parcel of ground in the Catholic cemetery in Superior could be used to purchase a much larger tract of land outside the limits of any established cemetery. While it may be true that fifteen hundred ($1500.00) dollars would purchase a larger tract of land outside of an established cemetery, it is true that most all of the Indians buried on the Point are Catholics and, so far as I have been able to discover, most all of these Indians prefer the dead bodies of their relatives to be interred in the Catholic cemetery.

134

Of course, a number of Indians who have relatives buried on the Point are non-residents and I have been unable to consult them. I am sure that only a few Indians can be induced to oppose the proposition to remove the bodies to the Catholic cemetery in Superior, but in order to suppress any future criticism that might arise I desire to discuss the matter a little further with the Indians interested. On these grounds I have requested the Office to defer the matter of the approval of the deed until further advised by me.

Very respectfully,

G.W. Cross
Supt. & Spcl. Disb. Agt.

GWC

Document # 19

DEPARTMENT OF THE INTERIOR

Land -Sales   UNITED STATES INDIAN SERVICE

45920-1911

12298-1914

F.I.P.   Cloquet, Minn., Dec. 15,1914.

Removal of Bodies

The Honorable Commissioner

Indian Affairs

Washington, D.C.

Dear Sir:

On December 4th, I wired the Office to withhold approval of deed to lots in Catholic Cemetery, Superior, Wisconsin. Same date I wrote the Office giving my reasons therefor.

I called a meeting at East End, Superior, December 12, 1914, for the purpose of discussing the matter of the removal of the bodies from Wisconsin Point Cemetery. There were about twenty-five persons present. I again, as I had done on two former occasions, explained to them why it was necessary for the bodies to be removed, viz: That the Indians ceded the land to the Government by Treaty; That the title to the land had long since passed from the Government, That said Interstate Railway Company wished to use the land for commercial purposes and had requested the Government to have the bodies removed.

I also explained to them that it was now proposed to purchase lots in the Catholic Cemetery, East End, Superior, Wisconsin and remove the bodies to that place; that we wished to be guided by the wishes of the Indians as to the place to which the bodies should be removed.

The Indians on this occasion as on the two former meetings refused to express their preference, stating that they did not believe that the bodies had to be removed. However, will state the Indians are most all Catholics and that the Catholic Cemetery is the logical place for the re-interment of the bodies. Besides, I have talked to the Indians privately and individually and am positive that when the Indians are convinced that the bodies have to be removed that they will want the bodies of their dead relatives re-interred in the Catholic Cemetery. The fact is that some have already removed their relatives to the Catholic Cemetery without waiting for the Government to do it.

The Indians believe they have title to the land on the grounds that Joe LaVierge, an Indian has lived on the land for the past sixty-seven years, and that before him an Indian by the name of Frank Lemieux had lived there for more than seventy years. They claim title through squatters rights. However, will state that Joe LaVierge was allotted on the Fond du Lac Reservation, Minn. but that he never lived on his allotment.

It is now most too late to remove the bodies this Winter. Next Spring or Summer will be more suitable time for the removal. Also would state that there seems to be no urgent reason why the matter of the removal should be rushed. It is my information that the Interstate Railway Company will not use this land for the next year or so.

I am very desirous that the Indians become reconciled to the necessity for the removal before the actual work begins. With this end in view, I have the honor to recommend that if possible the Honorable Commissioner of Indian Affairs, himself, visit these Indians and talk over these matters with them. They would be pleased to see the Commissioner and talk with him. If it is not possible for the Honorable Commissioner to visit this Reservation at this time, I recommend that a representative of the Office be sent to discuss the matter with the Indians.

Very respectfully,

G.W. Cross

Supt. & Spcl. Disb. Agent.

Document # 20

Wisconsin Point

45920-11 Fond du Lac 307.1

RECEIVED Dec. 19, 1914

To Indian Office

PETITION.

To our Beloved and Most Honored President Woodrow Wilson, and to Mr. Cato Sells, our Respected Father of Indians, both at Washington, D.C.:

Wisconsin Point, Superior, Wis. Dec. 14, 1914.

Dear President Wilson and Commissioner Sells:

Whereas, we respectfully and confidently approach the presence of President Wilson, whom we revere and love as a King Arthur, and Commissioner Sells, as a Sir Galahad, the first as a fighter of trusts, the second as one too good to be bought with liquor, gold, and,

Whereas, the United States Steel Corporation has laid claim to title to our Wisconsin Point owned for over seven generations by our O-sa-gie family of the Fond du Lac Reservation of the Chippewa Tribe of Indians, and,

Whereas, we feel outraged as to our property rights, secure, we thought, by right of squatters claim and by right of adverse possession on extending over a hundred and fifteen years, and also as to our hearts, insulted and wronged by the doings of traitor friends and conspirators, the Bardon Brothers, who have borrowed our papers which were given to Chief O-sa-gie of our Fond du Lac Band in the treaty of 1854 with the Ojibway and were destroyed and then our land was sold to various white men and then into the hands of the United States Steel Corporation, thereby repeating again, as is common in the Northwest the tale of Ramona of Southern California; and,

Whereas, we do with horror contemplate being torn from the property of our fathers on Wisconsin Point, our dear honored dead removed and the sacred cemetery desecrated; and,

Whereas, Agent Cross of Cloquet, supposed to be our protector, has stated that he very much regrets to remove bodies from Wisconsin Point and says he has tried to avert the event for years. He desires that the cemetery be made permanent, he says; he also states that he recommended years ago to the Indian Office that the Government purchase the land from the United States Steel Corporation and thereby establish a permanent cemetery on the Point, but, we,

138

the undersigned, do hereby register our remonstrance against the legality of the title to Wisconsin Point that the United States Steel Corporation holds.

We request that everything connected with the treaty of 1854 and since be looked into.

We wish to register a remonstrance against the proceedings of Mr. James Bardon, of Superior, who came to Congressman Lenroot in Washington last August, and stated that the Indians of Wisconsin Point consented to the removal, which was a pure untruth.
We urgently and respectfully ask that the claim advanced when the bill was in conference that the Indians consented to the removal of the bodies be confuted.

We quote from a letter from Congressman Clarence B. Miller to Captain Edward C. Smith, one of the leading Indians of our tribe and the respected Captain of The America, a large passenger steamboat plying between Duluth and Port Arthur and Duluth and Ashland this poignant sentence:

"The Government has the legal right to appropriate and use for their benefit money belonging to Indians and in the hands of the Government, independent of the consent of the Indians. I do not think they have a moral right to do so, however, against the wishes of the Indians in any matter peculiarly within the sentiment of knowledge of the Indians."

We do bitterly remonstrate against the legality of the title of the United States Steel Corporation. We do ask investigation of this so-called title. We do enter vigorous claim to the land of our Fathers and the graveyard of our Ancestors in the name of right of occupancy.

Our family is a branch of the Fond du Lac Band of Ojibway (or colloquially Chippewa) Indians. Seven generations and more lie buried in this cemetery, including Chief O-sa-gie or Chieftain Main Entry (named after the strait connecting Gi-Chig-a-mee) or (Lake Superior), three other Indian Chiefs and French Explorers and a few Irish colored and white bodies; in all, over two hundred bodies.

Therefore, Resolved, That we beg and beseech you, our two strong friends, filled with the best Spirit of the Age, to save for us our beautiful Wisconsin Point, our homes, our cemetery, and our lovely hunting ground of Wisconsin Point.

Wisconsin Point is unique, say those who have travelled much, in being a lovely strip of land about four and a half miles long and from three hundred feet to a quarter of a mile wide, lying between Allouez Bay which, with Duluth Bay, forms the largest fresh water bay in the world, on the south, and Gi-chig-a-mee, as we Ojibways call Lake Superior, on the north, a land covered with virgin Norway and white pines over two hundred years old, and with veteran white birches and soft maples and carpeted with blue berries, wild red raspberries, juniper and soft blue grass – the home of the moose, white-tailed deer, the black bear, the white rabbit and the partridge, which we hunt, and of the muskellunge, the pickerel, the pike, trout, white fish, sturgeon and lawyers and red horse – in other words, a noble hunting and fishing country within ten miles of the Twin Ports, as Duluth and Superior have been called, but sequestered in its solitude of wild beauty by its peculiarly picturesque situation and its being adjacent to the noble deer-hunting grounds of the Amnicon River country, to which come hunters from all over the United States.

We do grieve to contemplate the mere idea of this lovely nature nook, our beloved ancestral home, having warehouses and storehouses take the place of our homes, of cinders, covering our pure white sand, and our wild rose and harebell besprinkled grass, of groaning derricks and ore loaders, screeching like lost souls, taking the place of our wonderful Norway pines, sighing out their organ music in the Wa-bun-e-no-din, the East wind, of fire-eyed engine monsters supplanting the mild eyed deer, of cats and rats taking the place of our noble game, in a word we remonstrate against the spoilation of this natural park, dignified by so many unusual charms.

Whereas, Allouez is full of vacant lands available for the United States Steel Corporation's purposes, lands directly adjacent to their coal docks, but further inland and in no way beautiful or picturesque, and,

Whereas, we blame the people of Superior for inertia in letting another giant trust again (for the Northern-Pacific Railroad forty years ago preempted the bay front, promising to improve and beautify the dockage as well as do substantial things for Superior and have fulfilled not one promise) take undue advantage and destroy one of the loveliest natural parks in the world, one that Duluth, with her proud boast of noble, cascaded hillside parks, can in no way rival.

140

Therefore resolved finally that we recommend, advise, respectfully and confidently beseech that the Government of the United States at Washington, our Beloved President, and our Revered Friend, Commissioner Sells, bring it about that our unrivaled Wisconsin Point, our home and the burying ground of our ancestors, be secure to us without any question of title clear.

We would respectfully suggest that Wisconsin Point be purchased, if that be necessary; that the graveyard be made permanent by a picturesque stonewall around it, and we wish to state we shall in no wise discourage our white brothers, who are talking of making our Indian cemetery, with a bronze Indian monument, a permanent memorial to their red brothers and an honor to the Red Gods and the God of all Christians, one and the same All-Father.

We append hereto the list of names of Indians who own Wisconsin Point.

We the undersigned do approve of the foregoing and append our names.

X he'ss William Lemieux	*William Lemieux*
Peter Lemieux	*X Maggie Martineau*
John Lemieux	*Mary Martineau*
E.J. Lemieux	*Joe Martineau*
Peter Lemieux Jr.	*Leo Martineau*
Henry Martineau	*Ellen Moore*
John Laveirge	*Andrew McConnell*
Paul Lemieux	*Mrs. John Morisette*
Joseph St. John	*Mrs. Barney Klenzing*
Willie Durfee	*John Morissette*
Josette Durfee	*John Arden*
Peter Laveirge	*Frank Laveirge*
Charles Laveirge	*Gilbert Laveirge*

Document # 21

Land-Sales
45920-1911
130365-1914
  F I P
Removal of Chippewa bodies.

Mr. George W. Cross, Supt.,

Fond du Lac School.   *Dec 19 1914*

My dear Mr. Cross:

      I have your letter of December 4, 1914, setting out that objections have been raised by Charles Drew against the removal of the Chippewa Indian bodies from their present burial place and against their reinterment in the Catholic cemetery in Superior, Wisconsin.

      Mr. Drew should be informed that the present cemetery is on land belonging to the railway company and that the removal of the bodies is necessary. The provision made by Congress for the purchase of a new place of interment followed considerable correspondence, as you know. It is reasonably assumed that the interested Indians know the status of their cemetery. The tract to be purchased will be held in trust by the United States for the Chippewa Indians and will constitute a permanent burial ground.

      The abstract is still in the hands of the Department of Justice.

                    Very truly yours,

                    E.B. Meritt

12-EVB-16   Assistant Commissioner.

Document # 22

Office of Indian Affairs, Received FEB. 8 1915 14644

Sawyer, Minn.,   Dec. 21, 1914

To the Hon. Comm'r of Indian Affairs,

Washington D.C.

Dear Sir:

We the undersigned Indians of Sawyer, Minn., members of the Fond du Lac Band of Chippewas, desire to know if Mr. G.W. Cross, Supt. at Cloquet, Minn. has any authority to organize a business committee, composing of Indians of this reservation, and hold secret meetings behind closed doors, without notifying other members of this tribe regarding the nature of the meeting to be so held, or devulging the nature of such meetings.

Our Chief David Animasung and other head men here knew nothing of the selection of the Business Committee – seven in number and we would like to be informed if you the Indian Office at Washington D.C. gave Mr. Cross the authority to appoint such Committee. We would also request that a special agent be sent us at Sawyer to investigate the treatment we are receiving at the hands of the Indian Office at Cloquet, Minn., and that the Special Agt. see our Chief and head men here before appearing at the supts. office; also we be notified a few days before hand before the arrival of such Agt. so we can be prepared to meet him.

Very respectfully,

David Animasung – Chief

Joe Sha ba yash – Chairman

Peter Defauld – Clerk

Please write to any of the names above mentioned.

Document #23

Land Sales

4920-11

134996-14

 F I P

Title to Wisconsin Point lands.   *Dec 29, 1914*

Mr. G.W. Cross, Sup't.

    Cloquet, Minn.

My Dear Mr. Cross:

    The matters contained in your letters of December 15, 1914, are under consideration in this Office.

    It is claimed the Chief Osagie occupied Wisconsin Point long prior to the treaty of 1854, that he never removed therefrom but with his family continued to hold the land without claim or molestation from any quarter and that his descendants have likewise lived there, in undisturbed possession of a part of Lot 1, Sec. 27, and Lots 1 and 2, Sec. 28, T. 49 N., R.13 E., to the present time.

    It is stated also that Osagie who died in the early 70's, loaned to one, Thomas Bardon, now a resident of Ashland, Wisconsin, a paper or document delivered to him by the Indian Agent, which Osagie understood to be evidence of his title to the land, and that the paper was never returned to Osagie. The exact character and purpose of this paper has not been determined from any records in this Office. It is important that its contents and the circumstances of its possession and alleged retention by Mr. Bardon be learned.

    You are therefore directed to take up the matter with Mr. Bardon, and if the paper is not available for transmission to this Office, take a copy of it to which you will certify.

    In your meeting with the Indians living on the Point, you will get their statements and forward them with your report.

        Very truly yours,

                E.B. Meritt

12-NL-26   Assistant Commissioner.

Document #24

FEB 25 1915
Mr. David Animasung,
Sawyer, Minnesota
My friend:

In further reply to your letter of complaint dated Dec. 21, regarding the organization of a Business Committee among the Indians of the Fond du Lac Reservation and the holding of secret meetings, this Office has received a full report of the facts in the case from Supt. Cross of that reservation.

It appears that last fall a council of the Fond du Lac band of Indians was held at the village near Cloquet, Minn., and that a Business Committee was appointed with the consent and approval of the members of the council.

It also appears that there has been no secret meetings of this committee held and that all the matters discussed by the committee at the Superintendent's office have in turn been discussed in open council with the members of the Fond du Lac Band of Indians.

In view of this explanation, therefore, it appears that your complaint to this Office dated Dec.21 was evidently made without a proper understanding of the facts.

The Office will therefore take no further action in regard to this complaint. It is also suggested that whenever you have matters of complaint which you wish remedied that you talk the matter over first with the Superintendent of the Reservation, in accordance with my letter to you of Jan. 28, 1915.

Your friend,

E.B. Meritt
2-WWW-24   Assistant Commissioner.
Copy to Supt. Fond du Lac School
INITIALING COPY FOR FILE.

Document #25

(Reprinted from the Duluth News Tribune Nov. 18, 1946)

– submitted by Lawrence Murray

Chippewas Vote To Present Case Before State, UNO

Minnesota Chippewa Indians at a statewide meeting yesterday at Fond du Lac Reservation decided to appeal to the Minnesota Legislature and the UNO to seek redress for alleged infringements of their historic fishing and hunting rights established by treaty with the federal government.

SEEK RIGHTS

From the United Nations Organization they will seek recognition of certain sovereignty rights they claim the United States wrested from them in a series of aggressive wars.

The decision for action came at the "Pow-wow" called by William D. Savage, member of the Chippewa tribal council executive committee. Representatives from Leach [Leech] Lake, Grand Portage, Fond du Lac and East Lake Reservations were on hand for the meeting near Cloquet.

Delegate after delegate rose to the floor to protest "high handed action" in taking their game rights. Those not speaking English voiced their protests through Interpreter Ed Wilson, Ball Club, MN. All they wanted, they said, was the right to take away from reservations or other Indian properties pelts, game and fish they have caught in accordance with numerous treaties.

They cited numerous examples of game wardens seizing equipment and game of Indians attempting to take home deer legally shot on Indian reservations.

WANT DEER

"We merely want to take home deer along roads which in many cases were built by monies contributed directly by the Chippewa Tribal Council, but white man say 'no'."

They declared they have been refused that privilege on grounds that the Minnesota conservation department has ruled that no game or fish taken on Indian reservations may be transported on state roads. This ruling they plan to fight.

All properties owned by Indians come under special regulations which permit Indians or half-breeds to take any game during any season. But the Minnesota conservation commission has ruled that the game or fish cannot be taken from the area where it was killed over state owned roads, a representative of the commission, John F. Papaik, Cloquet, told the Chippewas at the meeting.

"So in effect," the Indians pointed out, "we can shoot and fish as much as we like but we can't bring it home to our families or sell it to make a little money to feed our children."

Attorney Clarence G. Lindquist, counsel for the Chippewas, told them they could either contest the ruling through the courts or appeal directly to the Minnesota conservation commission and legislature.

The attorney said that rights of Indians have been established by numerous treaties with Congress and that the Minnesota Legislature has no right to change those without specific permission of the federal government.

He urged the Indians to rise up and demand the government respect its treaties which, although written as a conquerer to the vanquished, still should be binding on both sides.

Indians, he declared, first agreed with the white man that he could have all land east of the Appalachian mountains. Gradually, by a series of 98 separate aggressive wars, the white man has wrested all the Indians' lands.

"Often times under fraudulent conditions the white man seized your lands."

"But," he added, "even if you have lost your timber and your mineral wealth, you still retain your hunting and fishing rights. And I feel certain you can get those rights back if you fight for them."

A grunt of approval came from Moose Skin, 90 year old hunter of the Fond du Lac tribe.

Two years ago, she single-handedly killed a 600-pound bear with an axe. She couldn't give bear meat to friends living off the reservation.

"That wasn't right," she said through an interpreter.

Then the session elected a committee to continue the battle for Indian rights. Named were Ed Wilson, Paul Lagard and Alton Bramer, Grand Portage, George Houle and Frank Whitebird, Fond du Lac; Charlie Abbott and George Abbott, East Lake. Delegates of Nett Lake will be named this week.

The committee was instructed to contact the Minnesota conservation commission and ask that body to "abide by Indian treaties" and give Indians the right to transport game.

The group was also instructed to explore the possibility of gaining redress from the UN as an oppressed nation. They declared they still hold sufficient sovereignty powers as a nation to claim protection of the UN.

United States authorities have always dealt with the Indians by treaty, they said, interpreting that as an admission they hold national status.

"But the United States has never given the Chippewas copies of those treaties. The United States has never respected its own signed words. We hold that the government has dealt with us in bad faith. We believe we have a case for the UN."

References

Document #1

National Archives RG 75, Microcopy No. 234

Letters Received by the Office of Indian Affairs, 1824-80. La Pointe Agency, 1855-59, Roll 388

Document # 2

National Archives RG 75, Microcopy No. 234, Roll 391.

Document # 3

National Archives RG 75, Microcopy No. 234, Roll 391

Document # 4

National Archives RG 75, Microcopy No. 234, Roll 392.

Document # 5

National Archives RG 75, Letters Received by the Office of Indian Affairs, Fond du Lac Reservation, 1894.

Document #6

National Archives RG 75, Letters Received, Fond du Lac Reservation, 1894.

Document #7

National Archives RG 75, Letters Received, Fond du Lac Reservation, 1894.

Document # 8

National Archives RG 75, Letters Received, Fond du Lac Reservation, 1895.

Document #9

National Archives RG 75, Letters Received, Fond du Lac Reservation, 1901.

Document # 10

National Archives RG 75, Letters Received, Fond du Lac Reservation, 1912.

Document # 11

National Archives RG 75, Letters Received, Fond du Lac Reservation, 1913.

Document # 12

National Archives RG 75, Letters Received, Fond du Lac Reservation, 1913.

Document # 13

National Archives RG 75, Letters Received, Fond du Lac Reservation, 1913.

Document #14

National Archives RG 75, Letters Received, Fond du Lac Reservation, 1913.

Document #15

National Archives RG 75, Letters Received, Fond du Lac Reservation, 1914.

Document #16

National Archives RG 75, Letters Received, Fond du Lac Reservation, 1914.

Document #17

National Archives RG 75, Letters Received, Fond du Lac Reservation, 1914.

Document #18

National Archives RG 75, Letters Received, Fond du Lac Reservation, 1914.

Document #19

National Archives RG 75, Letters Received, Fond du Lac Reservation, 1914.

Document #20

National Archives RG 75, Letters Received, Fond du Lac Reservation, 1914.

Document #21

National Archives RG 75, Letters Received, Fond du Lac Reservation, 1914.

Document #22

National Archives RG 75, Letters Received, Fond du Lac Reservation, 1914.

Document #23

National Archives RG 75, Letters Received, Fond du Lac Reservation, 1914.

Document #24

National Archives RG 75, Letters Received, Fond du Lac Reservation, 1914.

Document #25

Duluth News Tribune, Nov. 18, 1946

Chapter Five: Traditional and Contemporary Leadership
Leadership in Traditional Ojibwe Society

Traditional Ojibwe society was structured to fulfill five fundamental community needs: Leadership, protection, sustenance, learning, and physical well-being (Johnston, 1976). Most people were born into their roles, then given specialized training as children and young adults to fulfill their given purposes in life. A gifted few grew into their roles as a result of their ability. Each of these social functions was represented by a *dodaim* (totem), and membership in it had considerably more stature than community or tribal identity. The five original *dodaim* were represented by animals, themselves considered elder brothers because they were created and put on this earth by *Gitchi Manito* (the Great Mystery) before humankind. Of these, the crane represented leadership.

By its very nature, the crane symbolized leadership in traditional Ojibwe society. Cranes are echomakers whose call is so unique that when it sounds it causes others to cease what they are doing. Others listen when a crane speaks. Moreover, its speaks infrequently. Thus, leaders spoke infrequently and never for themselves, and when they did so it was important, something worthy of listening. In the fall and spring, cranes along with other birds flock together for migration under the influence of leaders. Leadership in a migrating flock is often temporary, with many assuming the role. As one leader tires, others take its place and the former leader assumes his/her place with the rest of the flock. There is no contesting for who will lead. Once migration is over, the flock disbands. There is no further need for leadership. So it was that leadership in traditional Ojibwe society was temporary, by example and action, not by proclamation or decree. Leadership was a burden, something not to be sought.

Young people born into leadership *dodaim* were given specialized training in history, tradition, grammar and speaking, all to promote the development of wisdom, eloquence, and generosity. Upon completion of the training, elders would hold a ceremony, offering the pipe to the person being trained, and its smoking would symbolize acceptance of the burden of leadership. Often the ceremony would be followed by the statement from the prospective leader: "You have made me a poor man, " because the person knew of the many hardships and burdens of being a leader (Johnston, 1976).

Leadership didn't always result from being born into it. If a person from another *dodaim* showed excellent promise, or if they were given life direction as a result of a vision, they would be given preference. Likewise, leaders who exercised poor judgement or ability lost their credibility and assumed other roles in their communities.

Decisions of leaders were not unilateral, but they relied upon seeking the guidance of a council of community leaders and elders, men and women.

The Evolution of Ojibwe Leadership

With colonization, age old ways of selecting leaders forever changed. Ojibwe leaders began to emerge as men who learned to communicate with the colonizers in French, and later in English. With the development of the reservation system, federally appointed Indian agents made most or all of the decisions for the Indian community. In the early part of the 20th century, modern tribal governments, as we know them today, began to emerge.

Federal laws soon forever changed the way Minnesota tribal communities chose their governmental leaders (Ebbott, 1985, p. 53-54):

> Present-day constitutions for Minnesota's other reservations [excluding Red Lake] came into being after the passage of the Indian Reorganization Act of 1934...The MCT [Minnesota Chippewa Tribe] Constitution was first adopted in 1936 and amended in 1963 and 1972 into its present constitution for the Bois Forte, Fond du Lac, Grand Portage, Leech Lake, and White Earth reservations and for the Nonremovable Mille Lacs band.

> Each of the six reservations elects at large a chairman and secretary-treasurer and one to three representatives by district, all by four-year terms. These officials form the Reservation Business Committee (RBC), the governing body of each reservation.

Traditional Ojibwe leadership was based on moral authority. Conditions of everyday reservation life have decapitated the upper levels of this intellectual, spiritual leadership. In the past, the community may have been able to draw on the perceived wisdom and knowledge of elders and other persons of knowledge. With the decline in the number of elders who practice traditional lifestyles and beliefs, and the acceptance of leadership styles based upon political power, many Ojibwe communities have seen a decline in the number of leaders who possess traditional leadership attributes. Nevertheless, to be accepted as leaders to the ordinary people on the reservation, a leader's moral authority still is basis for their influence over their constituency.

This transition from leaders based on heredity, and on moral authority, to contemporary leadership based on the political process — an elected, representative democracy, is shown in the leadership of our own reservation.

– T. Peacock, Editor

References

Ebbott, E. (1985). Indians in Minnesota (Fourth Edition). Minneapolis: University of Minnesota Press.

Johnston, B. (1976). Ojibway heritage. Lincoln, Nebraska: University of Nebraska Press.

Part One

FOND DU LAC CHIEFS AND HEADMEN 1690 -1890 (from <u>AN ANNO-</u><u>TATED LISTING OF OJIBWA CHIEFS 1690-1890.</u> John A. Ilko. The Whitston Publishing Company, Troy, New York. 1995, used by permission). [Brackets in text - E. Dahl]

AIN-NE-MAW-SUNG, possibly Strong Dog?
  Lesser chief of Fond du Lac, signing the 1854 Treaty

AN-NE-MAS-SUNG, possibly AIN-NE-MAW-SUNG
  Chief of Fond du Lac, signing the 1889 Treaty.

AW-KE-WAIN-ZEENCE or LITTLE OLD MAN
  Chief of [or] headman of Fond du Lac, signing 1854 Treaty.

BI-AUS-WA II, son of BI-AUS-WA I who was a great war chief
  of the Loon totem around Bayfield Peninsula in the late
  1600s and early 1700s. BI-AUS-WA II moved to Fond du Lac
  area. When middle-aged, he began his fearless war
  excursions against the Dakota at Sandy Lake, St. Croix and
  Mille Lacs. It was said that he was the first Ojibwa to
  camp at Sandy Lake after extinguishing the Dakota fires in
  that region ca. 1760s.

BIG WOLF or KEE-CHEE-MA-KEEN-GUN [KITCHI-MA-KIN-GUN, KITCHI MAIINGUN?]
  Chief at Fond du Lac, ca. 1840s.

CAW-TAW-WAW-BE-DAY or BROKEN TOOTH or MISSING TOOTH [Katawabaday]
  Headman of the Fond du Lac band, signing the 1854 Treaty.
  <u>Not</u> the BROKEN TOOTH of Sandy Lake.

DEAF MAN or GHIN-GWAU-BY [GIN-GWA-BI?]

Chief at Fond du Lac during the 1820s whose band consisted of over three hundred Ojibwa.

I-AU-WIND
Chief at Fond du Lac in the early 1800s.

KE-CHE-AW-KE-WAIN-ZE or GREAT OLD MAN   [KITCHI-AU-WAINCE?]
Headman of the Fond du Lac band signing the 1854 Treaty.

KEESH-KAWK
Headman of a Fond du Lac band signing the 1854 Treaty.

LOON'S FOOT or MON-GA-ZID   [MONGOZID]
One of the principal chiefs of Fond du Lac and the son of BROKEN TOOTH [of Sandy Lake].   Schoolcraft, a person of some questionable dealings, mentioned that LOON'S FOOT was also a jossakeed, a type of Ojibwa shaman. He signed the 1826, 1837, 1842, 1847, and 1854 Treaties.

MARKSMAN, PETER or GAH-GO-DAH-AH-QUAH
1815-1892. Chief born near Fond du Lac but residing at Ance, Michigan. He signed the 1847 and 1854 Treaties. Eventually he became a minister of Christianity.

MAY-QUAW-ME-WE-GE-ZHICK or ICE IN THE SKY
Fond du Lac headman, signing the 1854 Treaty.

NA-GAN-A-O or LEAVES HIM BEHIND
Fond du Lac chief signing the 1889 Treaty.

NAH-GAH-NUP and son ANTOINE NAH-GAH-NUP, SURPRISING OTHERS IN WALKING?   [NAGANUB, NAGANAB? same as Foremost Sitter?]

Chief of Fond du Lac signing the 1889 Treaty.

NAW-AW-BUN-WAY
Headman of a Fond du Lac band signing the 1854 Treaty.

O-SAW-GEE [OSAUGIE, of FDL and northern Wisconsin?]
Headman of Fond du Lac, signing the 1854 Treaty.
[Ancestor of Gus Lemieux of Superior, WI.]

SHAY-WAY-BE-NAY-SE or BLESSED or HONORED BIRD [ZHAWENBI-
NESI?]
Headman signing the 1854 Treaty. According to Winchell he was
from Fond du Lac and the 1854 Treaty implies he was from the Bois
Forte, Minnesota, region.

SHE-GOG or THE SKUNK [ZHIGAAG?]
Fond du Lac headman signing the 1854 Treaty.

SHIN-GOOB or BALSAM, possibly SPRUCE or SHING-GO-BE
Chief of Fond du Lac during the 1840s in league with other
chiefs, LOON'S FOOT, SITS AHEAD and BIG WOLF. He signed the
1826, 1837, 1842, 1847, and the 1854 Treaties.

SITS AHEAD, ONE WHO SITS AHEAD, or NA-GON-UB, NUG-AUN-UB
or
FOREMOST SITTER [same as NA-GAH-NUP? see above]
Following the death of LOON'S FOOT, SITS AHEAD assumed the
position of chief of Fond du Lac under THE BALSAM in 1863. He
signed the 1842, 1847, and 1854 Treaties.

SPIRIT MOON or MONETO-GEE-ZISOANS [MANIDO-GIIZIS?]
Chief of Fond du Lac signing the 1826 Treaty.

SPRUCE or SHING-GOBE, possibly the same as BALSAM or SHIN-GOOB

Winchell lists this Ojibwa as a chief of Fond du Lac, signing the
1837 and 1842 Treaties.

WAIN-GE-MAW-TUB

Headman of a Fond du Lac band signing the 1854 Treaty.

WA-ME-GIS-UG-O

Although not a chief, credit is due this great Ojibwa, being the
first Ojibwa to pitch his wigwam at Fond du Lac. Being a member
of the Marten totem, his descendants include SHIN-GOOP and
SITTING AHEAD.

YOK-WEAN-ISH   [YAUK-WI-NISH?]

Chief of one of three bands at Fond du Lac in 1843. The other
two bands were headed by SHIN-GOOP and NA-GAN-NAH. No treaties
were signed by this chief with this spelling.

Part Two:
Tribal Council Leaders 1894-Present
Brenda Pollak

FOND DU LAC COUNCIL MEMBERS

1894	John Annimassung, Jr.	Head Chief
	Joe Obequat	Sub Chief
	Mike Diver	Chairman
	James I. Coffey	Secretary of Council
	Joe Petite, Jr.	Advisor
	D. (Dave) Ruttle	Advisor
	Frank LaDuc	
	Pete Petite	
	John Connor	
	Frank Winters	
	Henry Martin	
	Joe Martin	
	Joe Smith	
	Joe Beargrease	
	Michael Petite	
	Joe Frank	
	Peter Annimassung	
	Joe Petite, Sr.	
	John Whitebird	
	Joe Whitebird	
	Frank Houle	
	John Martin	
	Joe Naganab	
1897	Joseph Frank	Chairman
	David Ruttle	Secretary
	Joe Martin	
	Antoine Couture	

	Frank Godfrey	
	George Couture	
	Frank Houle	
	Joseph Houle, Sr.	
	John Whitebird	
	Joseph Houle, Jr.	
	Wm. H. Lyons	
	John Cameron	
	Henry Martin	
	Jake Ruttle	
	James I. Coffey	
1904	Frank LeDuc	
	Joseph Naganab	
	Mike Diver	
1900	Thomas Jackson	
	John Martin	
	Mike Diver	
	Frank LeDuc	
	Paul Sheehy	
1912	Frank LeDuc	Chairman
	Simon DuFault	
	Joseph Smith	
1913	**Full Blood Council**	
	Be-tah-wash	
	Nah-bah-nay-aush	
1914	Mike Diver	Chairman
	Joseph Northrup	Secretary
	Frank LeDuc	
	Paul Winkleman	
	Benjamin Bassett	
	Thomas Jackson	
	David Ruttle	

1914 **Full Blood Council**

Joe Shabaiash	Chairman
Frank Whitebird	Secretary/Interpreter
David Aynemahsung	
James LaRose	
Frank LaRose	
John Albina Sr.	
Louis Blair	
John Grasshopper	
John Whitebird, Sr.	
Frank Whitebird	
John Albina, Jr.	
Sam Martin	

GENERAL COUNCIL OF CHIPPEWA INDIANS OF MINNESOTA

1917

Joseph I. Coffey	Delegate
Joseph Drew	Delegate
William Coffey, Jr.	Delegate
Frank LeDuc	Delegate
Frank Connors	Delegate
Frank LaRose	Delegate
John Laundry	Delegate
David Ruttle	Delegate
Joseph Diver	Delegate
William Howes	Delegate
William O. Coffey	Delegate
Joe Petite	Alternate
Henry LaPrairie	Alternate
John Connors	Alternate
John Ojibway	Alternate
Joe DeFoe	Alternate

1918 James I. Coffey   President

        William O. Coffey   Delegate

        John McCarthy   Delegate

1919 J. Francis Laundry

        Henry LaPrairie

        Chas Jackson

        John Arton

        Mike Diver

        Benjamin Bassett

        Joseph Defoe

        Frank Lemieux

        Antoine Couture

        Mike Smith

        Gus Houle

        Joseph Diver

        Louis LaPrairie, Sr.

        John Rabideaux

        Peter Petite

        William O. Coffey

        Charles Diver

        John Whitebird

        Joe Houle

        Peter J. Dufault

        John B. Ojibway

        William Wood

July 24, 1936: Reorganization

"The following members and officers of the Tribal Executive Committee appointed to lead the Tribe during the preparation of this constitution shall call and hold the first elections for tribal delegates, and shall serve until the first Tribal Executive Committee is formed under this constitution:"

TRIBAL EXECUTIVE COMMITTEE:

White Earth – John Broker

Leech Lake – Ed Wilson, Jacob J. Munnell

Fond du Lac – Henry LaPrairie, Joseph LaPrairie*

Bois Fort – Charles Bowness, Peter Smith

Grand Portage –James Scott, Mike Flatt

Mille Lacs – Fred Sam, William Nickaboine

TRIBAL OFFICERS:

John Broker Tribal President

Ed Wilson   Tribal Vice President

Henry LaPrairie*   Tribal Secretary

Jacob J. Munnell   Tribal Treasurer

TRIBAL EXECUTIVE COUNCIL (TEC) DELEGATES

1939   Ben Bassett

Ben Petite

1941   **Brookston**

Mary Higbee

George Houle

Cloquet

Lyzeme Savage

Louis Laundry

Sawyer

Joe Northrup

Henry Martineau

1953   **Fond du Lac**

William Dave Savage

Frank LaRose

January 7, 1939 Meeting at Fond du Lac Village

Majority vote decided to conduct meetings as a Tribal Council and not as a Farmer-Labor meeting.

CHAIRMAN:

1939   Ben Bassett

1940   Paul W. Sheehy

1941   William. David Savage

1942   ″   ″

1943   ″   ″

1944   William David Savage

1945	William David Savage
1946	William David Savage
1947	〃 〃
1955	Lois Laundry
1956	William David Savage
1958	William David Savage
	Russell Savage
1962	Sherman Dale Smith

VICE CHAIRMAN

1958	Josephine Thompson
1962	Mike Houle

SECRETARY

1939	Joseph LaPrairie
1944	Josephine Thompson
1945	Josephine Thompson
1946	Josephine Thompson
1947	Josephine Thompson
1948	Josephine Thompson
1955	Cecelia Robinson
1956	Joseph Thompson
1958	Joseph Thompson
1962	Joseph L. Thompson

DELEGATES

1939 **Sawyer**
Alex Naganub
Ben Petite
Cloquet
Ben Bassett
Lyzeme Savage
Brookston
Mary Higbee
Paul W. Sheehy
1940 **Brookston**
John Couture

Cloquet

Mrs. Josephine (Riley) Thompson

Frank Houle

David Savage

Mrs. John (Mary) LaFave

Sawyer

Alex Naganub

Mike Shabaiash

1944 **Duluth**

Mrs. Mary Landrie

Mrs. Kate Savage

Cloquet

George Houle

Ben Bassett

Sawyer

Frank LaRose

Henry Martineau

1945 **Brookston**

John Couture

Cloquet

George Houle

Ben Bassett

Sawyer

Frank LaRose

Simon Thompson

Peter Mesabe

Duluth

Mary Landrie

Mrs. Kate Savage

Louis Laundrie (alternate)

1946 **Cloquet**

George Houle

Ben Bassett

Brookston

    John Couture

Sawyer

    Frank LaRose

    Peter Mesabe

    John Martin

Duluth

    Mrs. Mary Landrie

    Mrs. Kate Savage

1947   **Fond du Lac**

    Cloquet

        George Houle

        Ben Bassett

    Duluth

        Mrs. Mary Landrie

        Mrs. Kate Savage

    Brookston

        John Couture

    Sawyer

        Frank LaRose

        James Martin

1955   **Duluth**

        Mary Laundrie

    Cloquet

        Josephine Thompson

        David Savage

    Sawyer

        Frank LaRose

        Peter DuFault

1957-1958   **Sawyer**

        Frank LaRose

        Joseph LaPrairie

SAWYER LOCAL COUNCIL

1956-1957   Chairman
                              Alex Naganub
                      Secretary
                              Cecelia Morrison

1957-1958

                      Chairman
                              Mervel Jones
                      Vice-Chairman
                              Eddie Aynemahsung
                      Secretary
                              Mike Morrison
                      Assistant Secretary
                              Ceceilia Morrison
                      Treasurer
                              Mike Shabiash

FOND DU LAC RESERVATION COUNCIL

1957-1958

                      Chairman
                              W. Dave Savage
                      Secretary
                              Joseph Thompson
                      Ben Bassett
                      Josephine Thompson
                      Alex Naganub
                      Russell Savage

1958

                      Chairman
                              Russell Savage
                      Vice-Chairman
                              Josephine Thompson
                      Secretary
                              Joseph Thompson
                      Ben Loons

	Ben Bassett
	Mike Shabiash
	Francis Albeino
1962	Theresa LaPrairie
	Joseph G. Thompson
	Alice Northrup
	Cecelia Morrison

Additional names mentioned in minutes: Edward Wilson, Alex Naganub, ? Heisler, Monroe Skinaway, Cecelia Robinson, Jesse Davis, Tom Stevenette, Joe LaPrairie, Mrs. Mike Shabiash, Florence Greensky, Adam Barney, John Tiessen, Stella Morrissette, John Rabideaux, Sam Thompson, Mike Beargrease, Antoine Barney, Riley Thompson, Simon Savage, Alex Houle, Charles Tiessen, Lucy LaRose, Evelyn Martineau, Lizy Misquadace, Adam Barney, Susan Shabiash, Florence Greensky, James Blacketter, Bill Moose, James Davis, Mary Porter, Mrs. Lyons, Isabelle Moose, Pat Albino, Sophy Naganub, Charlie Albino, Mrs. Julius Church, Jesse Davis, Henry Houle, Mrs. Joe Posey, David Couture, Josephine Martineau, Mrs. Harriet Sharlow, Mrs. Agnes Misquadace, Mrs. Evelyn Northrup, John LaFave, Joe Defoe, Charles Pequette, John Ojibway, Mary Porter, William Diver, Frank Jarvi, Susan Mudwayaush.

FDL Leaders 1960-64

1960	Chairman:	Sherman Dale Smith
	Vice-Chair:	Josephine Thompson
	Secretary:	Joseph Thompson
	Treasurer:	Peter DuFault, Sr.
	Committeemen:	Ben Bassett
		Vincent (Roy) Martineau
		James Northrup
		Theresa LaPrairie
1961	Chairman:	Sherman Dale Smith
	Vice-Chair:	Josephine Thompson
	Secretary:	Joseph Glen Thompson
	Treasurer:	Peter DuFault, Sr.

	Committeemen:	Ben Bassett
		Mike Houle
		Theresa LaPrairie
1962	Chairman:	Sherman Dale Smith
	Vice-Chair:	Mike Houle
	Secretary:	Joseph L. Thompson
	Treasurer:	Peter DuFault, Sr.
	Committeemen:	Theresa LaPrairie
		Mrs. Cecelia Morrison
		Mrs. Alice Northrup
1963	Chairman:	Sherman Dale Smith
	Vice-Chair:	Maurice Ojibway
	Secretary:	Joseph L. Thompson
	Treasurer:	Peter DuFault, Sr.
	Committeemen:	Darrell Blacketter
		John Tiessen
		Mrs. Margaret Ojibway

The Reservation Business Committee

The duly elected governing body of the Fond du Lac Reservation is the Reservation Business Committee (RBC). Under the Treaty of 1854, Public Law 93-638, and the Indian Self-Determination Act of 1975, the Reservation Business Committee has jurisdiction and authority to exercise regulatory control within reservation boundaries. The RBC authority is defined by the Charter of the Minnesota Chippewa Tribe given by the Department of the Interior under the Indian Reorganization Act of 1934 and the Minnesota Chippewa Tribe Constitution and By-laws.

The Reservation Business Committee is made up of one representative of each of the reservation districts of: Cloquet (District 1); Sawyer (District 2); and Brookston (District 3); a Chairman and Secretary/Treasurer who are elected at-large. Each term lasts for four years to encourage continuity, with members elected every two years in staggered elections. Following is a chronological list of Fond du Lac leaders from 1964 (under the revised tribal constitution) to the present.

(Note: Secretary/Treasurer and Sawyer District Representative election years are staggered from the positions of Chairman, Brookston and Cloquet District Representatives.)

* Special Election

CHAIRMAN:

1964-1968:	Sherman (Dale) Smith
1968-1972:	Sherman (Dale) Smith
1972-1974:	Warren Barney (resigned)
1974:	Harvey DeFoe (appointed in the Spring, until regular election)
1974-76:	William Houle
1976-1980:	William Houle
1980-1984:	William Houle
1984-1988:	William Houle
1988-1992:	Robert (Sonny) Peacock
1992-1996:	Robert (Sonny) Peacock
1996-	Robert (Sonny) Peacock

SECRETARY/TREASURER:

1964-1966:	Peter DuFault, Sr.

1966-1970:	Peter DuFault, Sr.
1970-1974:	Peter DuFault, Sr.
1974-1978:	Peter DuFault, Sr.
*1-23-1978:	Bernard Loons, Sr.
1978-1982:	Bernard Loons, Sr.
1982-1986:	Clarence "Chuck" Smith
1986-1990:	Peter Defoe, Jr.
1990-1994:	Peter Defoe, Jr.
1994-1998	Peter Defoe, Jr.
1998-	Peter Defore, Jr.

CLOQUET REPRESENTATIVE:
DISTRICT #1

1964-1968:	Joe L. Thompson, Joseph Glen Thompson (temporary appointment until reguar election)
1968-1972:	Raymond Smith
1972-1973:	Theresa Smith (resigned)
1973-1974:	Harvey DeFoe (appointed until reappointed to Chair)
1974-1976:	No appointment
1976-1978:	Robert (Sonny) Peacock (resigned)
*1978- 1980:	Ferdinand Martineau, Jr.
1980-1984:	Harvey DeFoe
1984-1988:	Ferdinand Martineau, Jr.
1988-1992:	Clifton Rabideaux
1992-1996:	Clifton Rabideaux
1996-	Clifton Rabideaux

SAWYER REPRESENTATIVE:
DISTRICT #2

1964-1966:	Darrell Blacketter
1966-1967:	Herman Wise
1967-1968:	Dennis St. John (temporary appointment until reguar election), James Northrup
1968-1970:	Cecelia Robinson
1970-1974:	Cecelia Robinson
1974-1978:	Darrell Blacketter

1978-1982:	Herman Wise
1982-1986:	Herman Wise
1986-1990:	Herman Wise
1990-1994:	Herman Wise

*1994: Daryold Blacketter appointed upon death of Herman Wise

1994-1998	Daryold Blacketter
1998-	Vincent "Butch" Martineau

BROOKSTON REPRESENTATIVE:

DISTRICT #3

1964-1966:	Maurice Ojibway
1966:	No eligible candidate filed
1967-1968:	Ed Pellerin, Jr. (appointed until regular election)
1968-1972:	William Houle
1972-1974:	William Houle
*1974-1976:	Richard Smith (resigned in Jan.)
1976-1980:	John Smith (appointed)
1980-1984:	John Smith
1984-1988:	Theresa LaPrairie
1988-1992:	George Dupuis
1992-1996:	George Dupuis
1996-	George Dupuis

Voting: Dave Savage, Ernie Diver, Frank Whitebird, Dorothy Savage and Tony Savage, Mrs. Dale Smith.

1939 – Ben Bassett at the door of the White House in Washington, D.C.

Chippewa Farmer-Labor Unit – May 15, 1938, Cloquet, Minnesota

"The first and only all American Indian unit, of the reigning political Farmer-Labor Party of Minnesota."

Front Row Sitting (Left to Right): Bert Shotley, unknown child, Naganab, Charlie Diver, Henry LaPrairie.

Row Two: Unknown child, Martha Naganab; Moses "Hambone" Posey, Joe Posey, unknown boy, unknown woman, Truman "Joe" Savage; Dave Savage, Francis "Mead" Defoe, Marie (Mrs. Billy) Diver, unknown child, Josephine Thompson, unknown child, unknown child, Art Woods mother, Art Woods.

Row Three... Willie Stevenette, Joe Diver, Buddy Benton, Marie (Diver) "Pee Wee" Benton, Mary Savage, Louisa Smith, Smith child, Delma LaPrairie, Betty Ann (Sheehy) Houle, Riley Thompson, Irene (Sheehy) Houle, unknown child, Henry "Sausage" Houle, Emma Diver, Mrs. Mary Laundry, Ollie Defoe.

Row Four: Henry "Pat" Martin, Ben Loons, George "Sandy" Diver, Paul Sheehy, Judge Diesen, Albert Fairbanks, Mrs. Albert Fairbanks, Julia (Mrs. Ben) Loons, Bill Sheehy, Bert Wendling, Bill Chisholm, John Laundry.

Mike Diver

Chapter Six: A People's Story

Nearly 30 years ago, I set out with James L. White, a dear friend who has since passed on, to interview elders of the reservation. Jim was a professional writer, a poet, who earned his living as a poet in residence for the Minnesota Poets in the Schools Program. I was then and still am your basic rez Indian. Over the span of a winter and early spring, we taped interviews of over 20 elders, hoping to weave a collective story of the history and people of Fond du Lac. Our book never materialized. Jim passed on and I moved up to the Leech Lake Reservation for a number of years. Eventually, two of our interviews with Betty Gurno and Jack and Mary LaFave were published in one of Eliot Wigginton's Fox Fire Collections. The rest of the tapes were forever lost with Jim's passing.

Most of the people we interviewed have long since passed on. I don't even remember all their names. But here are some of them – Bill Moose, Mike Shabiash, Cecilia Robinson, June Pellerin, Eliza Danielson, Bill and Frank Martineau, Adam and Jim Barney, Betty Gurno, and Jack and Mary LaFave.

There are particular moments from those interviews I will forever carry in my memory. I remember sitting at Eliza Danielson's home and asking her about dancing when she was young. In my mind was a picture of traditional dances, the ones before the advent of the modern-day pow-wow. But Eliza told me about square dancing. "We used to have big square dances all the time," she said.

I also remember Jack and Mary LaFave opening an old trunk and sharing hundreds of their family pictures with us. There was a particular look in their eyes, a level of understanding that what they were sharing with us was both intensely personal and important.

Finally, I remember bringing Betty Gurno a copy of Wigginton's book, which contained her interview, "Red is the East for the Sun." Just several days later she would have a stroke and pass on.

All of the days since then I have thought about how fortunate I was to know these people, and to be so blessed to have heard their stories. And in many ways, <u>A Forever Story</u> is the book that I never wrote 30 years ago. I was a young man then. My children were still babies. Maybe I needed to complete more of the circle of my time on this earth. Maybe I needed to listen to many more stories. Our elders knew intrinsically there was a time for everything, a season for everything, and reasons why certain things were to be done at certain times. Now that I am a grandfather, maybe I am beginning to understand these things.

– T. Peacock, Editor

The Nagahnub Family: An Interview With Esther Nagahnub

– T. Peacock, Editor

Antoine would be the oldest. I believe there were two, Antoines. At least that's what my aunt Delia said. He was the one that signed the treaty of '54 [the Treaty of 1854 which established the Fond du Lac Reservation]. He was Buffalo's [Chief Buffalo] war chief and I understand at that time that's what they called the other chiefs or sub chiefs. They used the war chief to sign a lot because who better to sign a treaty than a war chief? He signed as Buffalo's second.

My auntie, now 97 and living in a nursing home down in Odanah, Wisconsin told me that he was quite a strong minded man, and at one time he was attempting for some reason to raise his grandchildren. One of the grandchildren (allegedly) had nits or something, and someone became outraged and they sent somebody up here and took the kids without him knowing it and brought them down to Wisconsin, and my auntie said it was quite a sight.

MHS Photo

Nagahnub (The Foremost Sitter), orator and second chief of Ojibways – 1863

In her words, he made a spectacle of himself. He took the train down there and he came off the train holding on to that side bar with one hand and he had his rifle in the other hand and he had on some of his tribal regalia. She said he looked so fierce and so angry. She said that everybody was afraid of him and they ran. In my view, he was going to get his children that he felt had been stolen from him. And that's the way he was.

Let's go down to my grandfather. That would have been Alec. I believe he was one of ten children. He wasn't the oldest, I believe Joe was the oldest. Joe was in line for the chieftainship because it was heirship. He didn't want it, there was too much responsibility, too much. He just didn't want anything to do with it. And he wanted my grandfather to take it and my grandfather said that he would but he wouldn't do it unless it was signed over, lawfully and legally and everything. Joe did that and those papers, the originals are signed and hanging in the clinic [Min-no-aya-win Clinic in Cloquet, Minnesota]. I don't know how many chiefs we had here at Fond du Lac. I know that there was more than one. I know who the hereditary ones are, you know that signed the treaty, but I know that whites would grab Indians off the street practically and make them a chief so that they could get them to sign something. I think it was 1943-45 when the chieftainship was abolished. Grampa stayed on for awhile, but the one I remember after him was Frank LaRose.

Frank LaRose led Sawyer for a long time. I don't know if he led the whole Rez, I just remember Grandpa telling me that he was trying to get everybody together. Somebody from Brookston, somebody from Cloquet, so that they could have a council meeting. And they would have it right at his house or anyplace they could. But, you know they didn't have much to work with at that point.

I think back in those days that there was a bitterness, especially with men. I think they finally were realizing how they been betrayed. For example, the hunting and fishing and things. Grandpa went out to shoot a bear. He shot a bear and he had more than he could use and he decided because they didn't have money in those days, that he would sell some and, well. he ended up trying to sell it to the game warden. The game warden immediately arrested him, because he had shot something. Grandpa took the case to court and the court dismissed it, citing the 1854 treaty that you could hunt, fish and gather in ceded territory. Of course, that includes the rez. This was something which more people didn't use, the treaty was kind of forgotten. In fact, I remember in 1985-86 people didn't remember even that we had a treaty or that it was still in effect.

They didn't realize that we still had the rights because the game wardens and everyone had inflicted all these rules on us. For example, telling us, "Yes, you can go hunt anywhere you want but you have to eat it right there because you can't take it over a county road." I was told that personally. I was arrested, along with Bob Diver, for ricing by Floyd Jaros [a former Minnesota Department of Natural Resources game warden]. He wanted to cite me and

Bob for the canoe being a couple of inches too wide and it was a little bit too long and the knockers weren't right. So he took all our rice and we went to court and that was old [judge] Hugo Lane. I think he's dead now.

I hired Don Bye to defend Bob and I and Pete DeFoe Sr. came in with the treaty and the judge threw that one out. We all went out to eat afterwards, the judge and the attorney and me. As long as this has been dismissed now, I said, "I'd like to have my rice back." Hugo Lane said, "If I would have known that you were going to push, I would have never dismissed it."

I tried to get my rice back from Floyd and he wouldn't give it to me either. The thing was that we didn't have a state license to rice within the confines of the reservation. That was another thing we were doing wrong and we were ricing at the wrong time.

There was just an endless list of what we had done wrong. But Grandpa was always a treaty fighter and from the time that I can remember, I always was told, "The treaty will protect us, the treaty will protect us." I didn't even know what the treaty was but yet all through the years and that's why in 1988, when I heard all the stuff happening with the treaty rights, I went ballistic. But he was such a staunch defender of that because he knew the time would come that they would want (because it was happening even then) everything we have, except us.

And at that time, there was electricity going to be put in out here and he didn't want electricity and the people were mad at him. They said he was "a mean old man" and that he was just being backward and he was being mean. But he wasn't because his attitude was that all of the Indian people that lived around the lake would lose because as soon as electricity would be put in all the white people would come out here. And all the Indians would lose their land around the lake and as you can see, it's true. The people wanted the electricity and he okayed it because he had the authority to sign. Electricity was put in and here they came. And that's where we are today. At the same time, he couldn't understand why people would have their outhouse in the house. He thought it was unsanitary and never did understand that. He never understood that until the day he died.

One misconception is the Nagahnub name. My 97 year old auntie again said it to me Friday. She said to quit saying Naganub, your name is Neganub.

It means to sit in front. Neganub. That's one misconception and I've been saying it for more than half a century. So its a hard one to break and its a hard one to get other people to use.

In some books, I think one is Warren's [William Warren's History of the Ojibway Nation], he said we were the Marten clan and I don't know anything about the Marten clan. I grew up knowing Bear clan and when that popped up again I went to a certain type of gathering where I asked that question and was told from the higher up that I was Bear clan, there was no question and so that clears that up.

There's one other thing that is really kind of humorous, that somebody came to me and said that there's a rumor going around that I wasn't Esther Naganub, that I was somebody that had assumed her. I can't remember why or how this came about, but I had only assumed the name and assumed my relatives because something didn't jive. So in order to clear that up, I have to, it's really quite simple. When my mother went into labor, my family was living in Superior, Wisconsin. When she went into labor they took her, during a terrible, terrible blizzard, to St. Joseph's Hospital in Superior. They wouldn't let her in. They turned them back. So they took her home and she had me at home and then in those days, you were lucky to have a mid-wife and in a blizzard like that I don't know if there was one there or not, but it took several days for a doctor to come and stamp something and say "yes this child was born." My mother died nine days later. So that's where the misconception comes in. And I thought it was pretty funny but that's another one, those are one of the ones that get going around and its hard to fathom (sic) how they get started.

Tom: How would you like your family to be noted in history?

That we were always avid treaty supporters, that the treaty was important enough to put ourselves on the line for it, that the people would live, the people would have a place. Always have a place and always be able to hunt and fish and to gather. A place for their roots, for their children and their children. And if Pete Caches said, and although Pete Caches is not from our tribe. "The Black Hills are not for sale." And when he said that, I thought of Fond du Lac. Fond du Lac is not for sale, our treaty is not for sale, our land is not for sale. Nothing is for sale because it belongs to the people. That's the way I would like our family to be remembered.

Angeline January

–Betty Dahl

Angeline January was born in 1858 at the old village of Fond du Lac along the St. Louis River near present-day Duluth, Minnesota. She was married to Charles January and lived in the village, passing on in 1942 at the age of eighty-three years. Her parents, Mr. and Mrs. Joseph Charette and grandparents were all born at Fond du Lac. She had one child, Theresa, who died at twelve years of age, and a foster son, Joseph.

The Fond du Lac village area was the scene of conflicts between the Sioux and Ojibwe before the Sioux were driven west in the early 1700s. Angeline told how her grandmother related stories of the fighting and noise of the battles with the Sioux, in one of which her husband was killed, and how frightened she was, always expressing her fear of the Sioux.

Angeline's father had a small farm in the Fond du Lac village and hauled with a team of oxen. He also built canoes for sale, hunted and trapped, tanned hides and sold furs and deer, and worked as a carpenter to make a living for the family. A large stand of maple trees near the home provided maple syrup and wild rice was gathered from the St. Louis River. In 1934-35 the Works Progress Administration erected a replica of the Astor Fur Post of 1814-1834 in Fond du Lac, along the St. Louis River in a location known today as Chamber's Grove. Angeline was an honored guest and invited to be a speaker at the Pageant marking the opening of the fur post replica. She beaded a new dress for the occasion and, though shy and hesitant to speak in front of strangers, related some history of the area, of how her

**Angeline January and
Joseph January**

180

father traded furs at the old post, remembered early missionaries and told of attending the Fond du Lac School, completing the fifth grade, of her later job cleaning the school, and reminisced of her life as a young girl when the Indians gathered at the grove for dancing and games. In her childhood, she stated, the banks of the St. Louis River extended to the highway at some points and as far as the railroad tracks.

Angeline was described as a kind soul with keen black eyes and black hair just beginning to grey at the temples, and her constant companion and guardian in later years was "Buster," her dog, who allowed no one to come near the house after dark.

Mr. Joseph Charette, Angeline's father, lived with her in later years in their home located between 130th and 131st Avenues on the upper side of West Fifth Street. A lifelong resident of Fond du Lac, Mildred Rushenberg Behning, recalled spending many happy hours at their home. As a child, she helped Angeline gather wild rice from the river and went with her to tap and gather sap from the maple trees near the home. One time young Mildred accidentally tipped over a pail of sap with no reaction from Angeline other than her saying it was alright.

Angeline took Mildred with her occasionally to visit other Indian families of the area. "Wherever we went she would always hold onto my hand firmly while we walked, I remember that. She was quiet and shy, very kind, and always kept to herself. Oh, I just loved her, she was my friend."[1]

References

1)   Personal interviews with Mildred Behning, 1985-1997.
     General References: <u>Duluth Herald</u>, August 5, 1935.
     List of Allottees of Fond du Lac Reservation, n.d.
     Census (1865) of Town of Fond du Lac, St. Louis County, State of Minnesota.

Mrs. La Prairie (L), Angeline January (R)

Clement (Tim) Gurnoe

– Betty Dahl

Mr. Clement (Tim) Gurnoe was born November 12, 1911, at the hospital on the Fond du Lac Reservation, near Cloquet, Minnesota. His father was Gus Gurnoe, and his mother was Mary Rabideau from Red Cliff Reservation, near Bayfield, Wisconsin. The family lived on Reservation Road at the time of Tim's birth.

Gus Gurnoe, Tim's father, was a government Indian Agent and United States Marshal from 1918 until 1932 or 1933, quartered at Fond du Lac Reservation. Preceding him as Indian Agent were Guy Hauchon, who served in that capacity for thirty years before Gurnoe, and before Hauchon, the agent was Freeman Adams. According to Tim, Adams lived in a blue house about one block from the present-day site of Mash-ka-wisen Treatment Center at Big Lake.

Rations, including foodstuffs, were distributed to the Indian people by the agent, Tim said. These rations of food might have contained salt pork, flour, dried peas and beans, and other food. Rations were given out once per month and signed for by the recipients.

There were some reports of "ration breakdowns" or insufficient supplies and of some persons being shortchanged on their allotted amounts. The elderly, especially, were sometimes confused as to amounts and items due them, and Tim recalled the belief that these elderly persons were taken advantage of. The people hunted, trapped, and fished to help out with food and clothing, and other necessities, Tim said, recalling that credit at stores was not available to Indian people without money in a bank account.

In earlier days, the government agent lived at the government farm which was located where the Fond du Lac Housing Compound just west of Cloquet Center is today. Tim recalled the blacksmith's shop at the farm. The Gurnoe family lived at the farm while Gus Gurnoe was the government agent.

An interesting bit of history was related by Tim, concerning his father-in-law, Chief Animosin, who was also known as Louis Animosin, McCart(h)y or McCourtney. Tim said the name "Animosin" translates from the Ojibwe language as a word meaning "swamp" or "water," and that the name McCart(h)y or McCourtney was suggested by President Warren Harding as a more fitting name for a man who did much to help his people.

Tim related that Animosin negotiated and was responsible for obtaining direct payment to Indian people by the U. S. government, rather than the previous practice of dispensing requisitions for payments, which resulted in long waits and difficulties. This action greatly benefitted the people. Payments were made twice yearly, in the amount of $150 to $300. The Indian Agency was at Cass Lake, Minnesota, at this time, a distance of over 100 miles from Fond du Lac Reservation.

Animosin's concern for his people was demonstrated another time when he traveled to Washington D. C. to request that a school be moved to another location. The school was situated across from a railroad depot [possibly at Carlton, a few miles south of Cloquet], making it necessary for children to cross the railroad tracks to attend school classes.

Animosin lived on Mission Road near Big Lake, about 500 feet from the lake. He also had camps or property at Dead Fish Lake and at Rice Portage Lake, both of which are in the vicinity of Fond du Lac Reservation. An early burial ground exits on Mission Road in the Big Lake area, as well as an early log church which was built by Catholic priests, Indians, and loggers. Chief Animosin passed on in 1932, Tim said.

The early village at Fond du Lac Reservation was located on Reservation Road in the vicinity of where Holy Family Mission Church is located today. This early mission was established by Catholic priests, and though the building has been replaced several times due to fires, the congregation attends regular worship and other church-related activities today.

One of the early schools was operated by the priests of Holy Family Mission. Located about one and one-half blocks from the church, toward the Posey family property, the school offered classes in grades one through seven. Classes were taught by non-Indian teachers whom Tim remembers as being very helpful. Prejudice and discrimination were common in early days, Tim said. Non-Indian children were given first chance to attend school functions while Indian children were omitted unless there were extra invitations. Seating at tables was also segregated, with non-Indians apart from Indian children.

Other early village areas, in addition to the village on Reservation Road near the Holy Family Mission, were near Big Lake on Mission Road close to present-day Sawyer, Minnesota, and around the confluence of the St. Louis and Cloquet Rivers, near Brookston.

There were many other areas of habitation, but these were early gathering places for families and the start of communities which still exist today. Early burial grounds are noted in each of these locations. In times of sickness, there was little, if any, medication available for the people, making it necessary to rely on home remedies. There was a hospital on the Reservation for a time, which treated patients from the Indian community. Doctors who practiced at the hospital also had living quarters at the facility. The hospital building and land were later sold to a Mr. Hebert, for whom Tim drove a cab for a time. Mr. Hebert removed the building from the site and the property was later occupied by a horse farm.

Those patients needing further or more intensive treatment were sent by train to the hospital at Bemidji, Minnesota, accompanied by a traveling nurse. As Tim pointed out, this is a distance of about 125 miles. In early days, general hospitals were located at Cloquet, Onigum, and White Earth.

The Indian Agency at Cass Lake had a contract with Tom Murragh, of Cloquet, to provide mortuary services for Indians from the Fond du Lac Reservation region. Tim remembered Mr. Murragh's establishment was upstairs in a building in back of the lumber company.

The Posey family, early residents of the Cloquet area, lived on the Fond du Lac Reservation. Their property was on Reservation Road and along the river. An old foundation may still be seen at the end of the Jarvi Road, near the old railroad bed close to the river, indicating where a residence had been. Nord Albert Posey, as he was called by some, reportedly came down from Canada with his father, who was a fur trader, and his mother, who was from the Indian community. Tim suggested the route taken by Posey may have been from Fort Frances to International Falls to Kabetogama Lake and River, and then along smaller rivers and branches to the Nett Lake area of northern Minnesota, and down to the Duluth and Cloquet area.

Tim stated that Nord Albert had at least one brother, Moses, who never married. According to Tim, the name "Moses" would translate into Ojibwe language as "Mose" [e=a] or "Mosay." Moses Posey studied for the priesthood. In time, his sight failed and he became blind.

185

Through his Chippewa wife, Nord Albert and his children were related to the Martin, Whitebird, and Petite families of Fond du Lac Reservation. The Martin family lived about three and one-half blocks from the Posey property on Reservation Road, toward Holy Family Mission, until moving to the Sawyer area in 1916 or 1918. The Petite family home was about five-tenths of a mile up Reservation Road from the Jarvi Road, toward the Mission, on the right hand side of the road.

On the Posey property, near the railroad bed which ran close to the river, and about one and one-half blocks from the Posey home, was a warehouse. Some reports indicate that Nord Albert Posey may have been employed by the U. S. Government to distribute supplies to Indians from the warehouse. Other information may identify Nord Albert as a blacksmith employed by the government to teach the trade to the men at Fond du Lac Reservation. [Neither report has yet been authenticated].

The Posey family may have also lived on Posey Island, located in the river in the same area as the house and warehouse. Early surveyor George Stuntz wrote of canoeing up the river to Posey's to pick up Joe Posey and head north along the canoe route. [It appears that Nord Albert may have been called Joe by some people. His son was named Joseph. The reference appears to refer to Nord Albert, however.]

The canoe route referred to by Stuntz was accomplished after a portage from the St. Louis River, and would bring the traveler to northeastern Minnesota and to the Vermilion Lake area. This appears to have been an established route in the early days of written history and journals of the region, and undoubtedly was in use for centuries before Stuntz' notation.

The rivers were used by the timber and logging companies to float logs down to the mill. Tim recalled that the Johnson Wentworth Company operated a planing mill and box factory near the paper mill facility in Cloquet. Tim worked for the logging interests in the woods near Paupore's Siding, several miles west of Brookston, Minnesota, as a young man.

Following a period of working in the woods, Tim enlisted in the U. S. Army and later left with the Duluth based 125th Field Artillery Battalion on June 17, 1940. He later worked at setting up electrical generating plants for the government in various locations. Tim and his wife raised a family, but never returned to live in the Cloquet or Duluth area, he said.

Ricing

Tim Gurnoe recalled days of ricing and remembered these areas where people gathered wild rice:

Perch Lake and Rice Portage Lake near Sawyer, Minnesota

Lake Minnewawa north of McGregor, Minnesota

Big Sandy River near McGregor

Wild Rice Lake north of Duluth

East Lake near McGregor

Mud Lake east of Floodwood, Minnesota

Hunting

The people hunted anywhere on the Reservation, Tim recalled. The forest area around Meadowlands, Minnesota, was an especially good place to hunt deer, while the Gheen district, south of Orr, Minnesota, was a popular area in which to hunt deer and moose.

Fishing

A variety of fish was available to fishermen in earlier days, Tim remembers. Pickerel, pike, bluegills, sunfish, and catfish were abundant in the waters. Buffalo Fish, resembling suckers, were caught in East Lake. This fish averaged about three to four feet in length and swam in or on top of mud and consequently tasted muddy when prepared for eating.

Walleyes were caught at Big Lake and Perch Lake, where ice-fishing was also popular in the winter. Bullheads were scooped out from the water with a manure fork and filled a washtub in short time. Night-fishing was also popular.

Tim related how his grandmother preserved fish for later use by salting the fish down in a barrel. To reconstitute the fish for preparation for eating, his grandmother would soak the fish in water overnight to release the salt. Salting down meat and fish was a common procedure for preserving these foods in earlier days.

Berrypicking

Favorite places for picking blueberries were in the Long Hills, between Sawyer and Atkinson and at the "Rocks" near Carlton. The "Rocks" area is the area where the old dump for the City of Carlton was located on Carlton Road.

Raspberries were gathered along the Ditch Bank Road west of Cloquet and at other areas, especially where there had been fires. Raspberries often thrive on land that has been cut-over or burned.

A large cranberry bog was known about three and one-half miles from Sawyer on old Highway 2. Known as Corona Bog, the cranberry marsh was considered to be dangerous. Tim advised anyone going there to be very cautious of sinking in the swamp and recalled using snowshoes and four-foot skis to aid in gathering cranberries in the bog. One needed to kneel on skis to travel about and pick cranberries at Corona Bog.

Picking Cherries, Plums and Wild Grapes

Large quantities of high-bush cranberries, pincherries, and chokecherries were gathered for food from many areas around the Fond du Lac Reservation. Wild plums grew in some areas, and were picked from the trees at Lake Minnewawa, near McGregor. An island in East Lake yielded wild grapes. There was much food provided when conditions were right for growth and ripening.

Additional Information

Tim guided us to the "Big Cemetery" off Reservation Road, which is in the vicinity of the old village. Tim recalled the cemetery was started about 1914 or 1915. Reports of the Office of Indian Affairs, dated November 1883, record a "grave yard and church located in village." Perhaps this refers to the old cemetery near the Big Cemetery. Other burial grounds are near the churches on Reservation Road, Mission Road, and in the Brookston area.

August and Mildred LeMieux
– *Betty Dahl*
[The interview was recorded August 4,5 1997]

Gus LeMieux was 98 years old when this interview was recorded, having been born May 31, 1899, the child of Peter LeMieux and Elizabeth St. John Le Mieux. His wife, Mildred, was 91 years of age at the time of the interview.

Peter LeMieux was the son of Frank LeMieux and Isabelle Osagee, who were married May 27, 1847, in Bayfield, Wisconsin. Isabelle was the daughter of Chief Osagee and Margaret Nah-Gah-Nub. Other children were John, Frank William, Mary Ann, and Margaret. Peter Le Mieux and his wife, Elizabeth, had nine children: Peter, Eli, Belle, Maggie, Mary Ann, Frank, Paul, August, and Catherine.

August "Gus" Le Mieux (spelling changed to LeMieux) recalled being sent to a government boarding school in Tomah, Wisconsin, when he was older than seven years. He went to the school in the fall and stayed until spring and recalled it was a "nice place, a nice school."

**August (Gus) LeMieux
U.S. Navy, age 17 (1916)**

Gus recalled that, when he was about ten or eleven years old, the family went by boat up the St. Louis River to Fond du Lac, Minnesota, where they camped on the island to fish and harvest wild rice. Gus said, "Everybody went," including extended family members. When they camped, the girls slept in one tent and the boys slept wherever they could find a place, "under the stuff in canoes or under rowboats."

There was lots and lots of rice. "We'd be gone hardly an hour or two and then be back with a lot of rice. We'd be back with enough that the women would start parching, you know." Someone had a big rowboat there and they

189

loaded the rice into it, though Gus did not know why they put it all in one boat.

"Later we rode it all the way up from Fond du Lac clear around down to Cedar [?] Point and came down the Bay and then loaded that down there [Superior Bay]. We used to pack it in what was called 'Bean Bags' in those days." The round bags were sewn for them and stood more than three feet high. "The women and girls would ride a bus or something from Fond du Lac to Duluth and then came by ski-car all the way home to Superior. Wouldn't go in the canoes or rowboats. Gets pretty rough, you know, in the bay there."

Chief Osagee

Mildred remembered that Gus's mother said one time that going up in the canoe was all right, you only got a little bit wet, but coming back the water would be near the top of the boat, because of the loaded rice, and the men would paddle and paddle, and their arms would be wet all the way up.

Gus's sister, Belle, lived to adulthood, but took sick and died. "She was alright, walking around, going to school at night, but soon needed a crutch to walk, and died soon after." Gus did not known the cause of death, but recalled many cases of diphtheria, typhoid fever, and scarlet fever during the time. "I remember Pete being in bed," Gus said, "everybody thought he was going to die. I guess he had typhoid fever or something. Pa had pneumonia and I was in school and they sent for me to come home, they thought he was going to die," Gus said.

Gus joined the U. S. Navy when he was 17, during World War I, and served for almost three years during and after the war. He studied steam engineering, "and of course that went along with the Navy and they just kept moving me around wherever they needed me, you know. So, I wasn't in long and on four different ships in three different Navy yards, in two years time."

Gus served on two battleships, the Rhode Island and the Massachusetts, as well as the oil tanker, and a marine tender.

Gus was stationed on an oil tanker that was in the Gulf of Mexico when World War I ended. "And then I had to run a submarine tender and I had to go into England to get three submarines that the Germans turned over to the United States. They were in England at the time, so we had to go to England to get them back to New York. From New York, we took one of them up to Halifax, Nova Scotia, and from there we came down the St. Lawrence River to Chicago and they're still there. I've got pictures of it."

Gus came home to Superior after the war and continued to work in construction. "When I came home, my brother was driving pile for the Northern Pacific ore docks and he said, 'My kid brother's coming home on that train that's coming across the bridge there,' and my father said I got off the train down at the Depot and I walked home to see my mother, and there was a knock at the door, and a man was there who asked, 'Is Gus there? Tell him I want him to go to work right away.' So, I said I would be there in the morning, and he said, 'You'll be there at noon. I've got to get a steamboat ready by morning.' I got there right after dinner, but it was eight o'clock that night before we got that engine running so we could go home!"

What was it like for people back in those days? "Backbreaking work," both Gus and Mildred agreed. "They were building Superior at that time, you know. Ore docks, coal docks, grain elevators. I worked on all of them," Gus said.

Gus and Mildred (Larson) LeMieux (b. February 9, 1906) were married November 15, 1921, in Duluth, Minnesota, and established their home in Superior. They had two daughters, Eileen and Elizabeth. The house they still live in was built mostly by Gus and Mildred.

"We had two hammers, a hand-saw, and a bucket of rusty nails, a level and a square." Mildred remembered. "That was the sum total of our tools. And I've pounded and straightened and pounded as many rusty nails as anybody in this town! When we put a siding on here, he [Gus] and the girls got twenty-five dollars apiece from some government fund when they paid these Indians off. That was in 1930, '31, '32. He bought cedar siding for the house. That was seventy-five dollars and enough to cover the house. So, we bought a gallon of linseed oil and a gallon of turpentine, mixed it up and [on saw-horses] I painted every single board that went on this house, inside and out. We had enough old boards to build a scaffold on each side. I don't know why I didn't fall off and break my butt. We had this notched thing to measure where it went; so, we'd get up there and I'd pull up to get that end up and he'd hold up his end and I'd nail that end. We got siding on all right and painted.

Mildred told of the women who came regularly to visit with Gus's mother, all of whom smoked pipes. A rack hung on the wall from which they took their own pipes, some of them corn-cob pipes and some clay pipes. One woman had a habit of gesturing with her pipe, and on one day the hot ashes fell into her hand and lap. She calmly put them back into the pipe and continued as though nothing had happened.

Chippewa in the immediate area formed the "Zaagii Club," and husbands and wives held regular meetings every Saturday night. Mildred, as a non-Indian, recalled one woman member who treated her badly, keeping her from joining the club and doing everything to keep her out. Mildred helped with many of the Indians who were sick and while working at old St. Mary's Hospital, operated by the Poor Handmaidens, the hospital informed her one day that a member of the Lemieux family was a patient at the hospital. She went to see her and recognized the woman who had been so unfriendly and who then greeted her warmly, apologized for her past behavior, and from then on insisted that Mildred care for her during her amputation and follow-up care.

"When they made the reservation, this was all reservation, and the state line came in and cut it all up," Mildred said. Gus added, "The people, the chiefs of the Fond du Lac Tribe at that time, shouldn't have allowed the state line to interfere with their business. They'd been enrolling these people, but the State line cut it all off there. The State and the Federal Government let them do that. And they cut that all up and we all had property on the reservation.

We were still enrolled at Fond du Lac, but they cut the enrollment out. This enrollment that we're talking about was made here in Superior. And this one that we're talking about is the original, 1854, was made in Superior. They went from there to Minneapolis, I guess, and made a new one. They added a lot of names on that after they made the new rolls. But they gave the old one back to the guy that wrote it all out and told him to burn it, and instead of burning it he gave it to my father. And he kept it and that's how it came to be in Cloquet and on the reservation now."

Gus stated that his family was enrolled at Fond du Lac Reservation and that "... when the city was planned, the Indians were started to be allotted, or given their title. We were over here in Superior and we were never allotted. When they run the boundary line [Boundary line along the St. Louis River which separated Minnesota and Wisconsin], they left the Superior people out."

Gus's father, Peter Le Mieux, was always called chief. The family had an item that stated that Peter Le Mieux was chosen as Chief of the people that lived on the Superior side of the boundary line, but, unfortunately, someone from Fond du Lac Reservation had taken it. Peter knew everyone and everyone knew him. Gus recalled, "I don't know if there was any mention of him being on this side of the line. I don't think the line was mentioned there."

Mildred stated, "Well, it did say in that little notice that we got because I wrote and asked for it. But he was called Chief because he was on this side. He was Chief of the people on this end of the reservation."

Gus and Mildred kept the Annuity Rolls and other papers for Peter, after his death in the early 1930's, and "... as people would need them they would just come for them — things that he would have given to his people had he been here. Some of the things we could not give away. Some of them were stolen from us, well, just borrowed, we'll say. I won't say anybody stole them, they had as much right to them as we did, I guess," Mildred said.

Peter Le Mieux had entrusted the original 1889 Annuity Roll to Gus and Mildred, saying to Mildred, "I trust you. I'm not asking him (meaning Gus), to take care of it because he is too big-hearted. He would loan it to somebody and we would never see it again." This brought a chuckle from Gus.

Concerned for what might happen to the Annuity Roll after they had passed on, Gus and Mildred brought it to Fond du Lac Reservation a few years ago. Needless to say, it caused some excitement and they were told they had made many people happy. "I was glad that I had the courage and the tenacity to do something like that for him [Peter Le Mieux]. I would have done anything for him, anyway, he was such a good guy and Grandfather," Mildred said.

Gus' father, Peter Le Mieux in later years lost his eyesight and went to the hospital on the Fond du Lac Reservation. Gus and Mildred described the hospital as a big, old, weatherbeaten wooden building which was nice and clean with fairly good equipment for the time. It had two wings, one for men and one for women. Recalling that they and their children visited Peter there several times a week, Mildred described the trip from Superior.

"We went to Cloquet and out of Cloquet, up a hill, I remember. And that's when the scary part started. It wasn't a good road, it may have been gravel, but it was a very poor road. It wound around and I assume it was on the Reservation. And there was brush. And every here and there, in the bushes, you'd see a little house, most of them unpainted. Those people, I used to just cry going through there. They had so little, and our car would hardly run up a hill but we had one.

"The hospital had a big stone fireplace, sort of a hanging-out place, I think. It was staffed by Raiter Brothers in Cloquet, the doctors — Dr. Roy and I don't remember the name of the other one. He [Peter] was so happy to see the kids, you know, and he'd talk to them in Chippewa and English. He had no eyes and the man in the bed next to him had no leg control. So, they would put their arms around each other and go out and walk on the deck, the full length forth and back, two or three times. That was their exercise."

Peter Le Mieux lived there for six or seven years, suffered a fall and bad head injury. He was well-cared for until he passed on in the early 1930's.

Gus and Mildred offered a description of the reservation from that time, saying, "It was exactly the way it was written up. You know, unkempt, uncared for. They had no money, they had nothing. They were very poor and a lot of people around there were, but the Reservation was poorer than anyone. [The Depression] depressed those people a lot more than it did the people out around. They survived. They are survivors."

Gus said that Wisconsin Point had been a traditional home for Chippewa, and Chief Osagee had been given the right to reserve a square mile of land. The government retained the tip of the Point for a lighthouse. Gus stated that Osagee's family and others lived there and when the LeMieuxs' moved across the bay to the town of Superior, for work, they left family members who promised to stay there and watch the place. But the Steel Company desired to gain title to the land and offered $5,000 to the relative living on the land to leave.

"They took the money and moved off. Well, then the Steel Plant said they bought the land, but they didn't, they just paid them to move off." The burial ground was excavated and burials moved to the cemetery along the Nemadji River. "Well, but they couldn't sell the land because they didn't own it. After they won their case, and they got everything, they dropped it, as far as I know," Gus said, and maintains the land still belongs to the family.

In recent years, there has been interest by some in moving the Wisconsin Point burials again, this time back to the original burial ground on the Point. Gus and Mildred said that when the Steel Company claimed ownership to Wisconsin Point and proposed to move the burials to Nemadji Cemetery in 1918 or so, that two old Indians forecast trouble, and said that if the burial ground was disturbed that nation would rise up against nation and the country would burn up. Gus said that as soon as they started digging, in short time, World War I was underway and areas of Minnesota and Wisconsin experienced devastating forest fires.

A marker was installed on Wisconsin Point, several years ago, to remember the original burial ground, but Gus and Mildred said it was put in the wrong place. The burial ground was across the road. "They put it in a parking lot and the people don't know they're parking in the cemetery," said Gus. "You know," said Mildred, "the general run of people don't realize what a closeness the native people had with their God and the spiritual rulers of the world. Oh, I'd hate to see them move them, because something would happen. Leave them where they are. They're going down the hill, apparently. The cemetery itself is moving down the hill. Eventually, it'll get to the river. And eventually, it will flow back to the Point from where it came. And then they'll be home."

Gus asked if the interviewer would like to see the burial site at Nemadji Cemetery. We went to the cemetery where we visited his family burials in St. Francis Cemetery and viewed the burial site of the people moved from Wisconsin Point to what is called Nemadji Cemetery. The whole cemetery was originally called Nemadji Cemetery, Mildred thought, with a Protestant area and a Catholic part which became St. Francis Cemetery. The burials removed from Wisconsin Point were placed in a trench, a common grave, on a slope of the shoreline of the Nemadji River, in what appeared to be an unusual and least desirable location for burial. A sign was placed some years ago to mark the place. At the time of our visit to the site (1997), the burials seemed to be sliding down the short slope and approaching very close to the river.

Gus Lemieux believes the land chosen on Wisconsin Point by Chief Osagee may still be an allotment, and that the plans of the Steel Company were thwarted because of their inability to gain title to the land. To this date, the land remains unoccupied and is a popular recreation site.

John, Marce, Larry, Grandma Bassett, Grandma Martin.

Mrs. Houle (?)

**Mike and Maggie Smith
1913 wedding portrait**

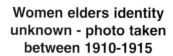

MHS Photo

**Women elders identity
unknown - photo taken
between 1910-1915**

CCHS Photo

The Lord Family of Solon Springs, Wisconsin

–Betty Dahl

(August 6, 1997)

An interview with local historian May Nightingale of the Solon Springs, Wisconsin area, in December of 1982, provided information regarding the Lord family, one of the oldest in the town of Solon Springs, as well as insights into the early history of the area. Mrs. Nightingale also shared news clippings and recalled names, places, and other interesting information about the area from her own personal experience.

According to Mrs. Nightingale, the town site of Solon Springs was originally an Indian village until settlers moved into the area in the late 1800s.

On the banks of the Brule River in 1831 stood the log home of Chief Joseph Osaw-gee, who was engaged in trapping and trading with the American Fur Company in an area within the valley of the Brule River, Lake Nebagamon, and along the shores of Lake Superior as far as the present locations of Duluth, Minnesota and Superior, Wisconsin.

It was during this time that the Osaw-gee's daughter, Catherine, was born. She grew up in northern Wisconsin and Minnesota. Small in stature, she learned the ways of her people and, in time, became expert in beadwork and capable of creating regulation size canoes to be used on lakes and rivers. She learned about medicinal uses of plants, weather signs, and how to harvest wild rice, and make maple sugar. By her teen-age years, she had learned to use a gun and carried a small hand gun in her pocket through her old age.

In the 1850s, Charles Lord, a fur trader for the American Fur Company, was in the area at the western end of Lake Superior called "Fond du Lac," a French term meaning end of the lake. He was of French and English ancestry and a member of one of the finest families of Montreal, Quebec, Canada. According to Charles Lord's reminiscing, he traveled from the Chippewa Agency at Crow Wing at the head of the Mississippi River and arrived at the end of Lake Superior [Fond du Lac] on March 26, 1854. He was sent by Lyons and Crittenden, Indian traders, and under the influence of David Herreman, Indian Agent, to take charge of the trading post on Minnesota Point and to protect the Indians from the abuse of liquor. Charles carried a letter of recommendation to George R. Stunt, government surveyors, who lived at the end of

Minnesota Point on the east side of Superior Bay. He became acquainted with the 20 or so Indian families residing at the end of the Point, and recalled as many as 200 Indians in the area at some times. He soon noted an influx of immigrants who settled on the south side of Superior Bay at the Town of Superior.

At this time, the Osaw-gee family was living in the Fond du Lac area, which included Minnesota Point. Charles, manager of the trading post at the end of the Point, became acquainted with the Osaw-gee family and their daughter Catherine, and became a frequent visitor at the Osaw-gee home. Charles made his intentions toward Catherine known on New Year's Day, 1855, by proposing marriage.

The marriage of Charles Lord and Catherine Osaw-gee took place the following April in Superior, Wisconsin, and was reported in an article in the Superior Evening Telegram along with other information about the family:

> Early in the spring of 1855, old timers danced at the first wedding in Superior, or the present Twin Ports. It was no common wedding either, for the bride was a princess and beautiful, the daughter of Chief Joseph Osaw-gee of the Chippewa nation, whose royal blood lines extended back into the dim days of tradition. Charles Lord was the bridegroom. He was a young fur trader and voyageur from Canada and he furnished the wherewithal to make merry for three days. R.B. McLean, discussing the event, said that no such marriage feasting has since been seen. The ceremony was performed by Father Corraine, an Indian missionary.

According to a news article [Welter], Charles and Catherine took a claim at Fond du Lac, Minnesota, and during the time they lived there, two daughters and a son were born to them. Hard times forced the family to move back to the Superior, Wisconsin area.

In a paper written by his daughter in 1881, Charles Lord stated that his affiliation with the trading post ended in 1855. In about 1870, Charles learned that a railroad was to be constructed from Chicago to Superior. He soon took a claim in the town of White Birch, Wisconsin, near the proposed route of the railroad.

Following the hard times of the 1870s which caused people to abandon their claims and move out of the area, he "settled in the school section in Douglas Co., Wis., where I remained for four years farming and trading."[2] He worked as a cook in a hotel, and later opened the first bakery in the city, being a baker by profession. Tiring of the bakery business, he opened a saloon and established the first billiard and pool hall in the city. When business slowed, Charles again began trading in furs, and traveled by dog sled, bundled in a buffalo coat, to the Dakotas and the Vermilion Lake area of northeastern Minnesota to trade for furs with the Indians living there.

Charles built a large home on his claim at White Birch. It also served as a boarding house, with extra bedrooms on the second floor, to accommodate travelers, missionaries, trappers, lumbermen, and surveyors. Missionaries always chose to stay with the Lords while traveling through the area. The kitchen of the house built by the Lords at the Town of White Birch contained a restaurant-sized cook stove, with a warming oven and reservoir. There was a large wood box in the corner and wooden cabinets and work tables.

A large room was added on, off the dining room, which was used as a chapel. The chapel was sanctioned by the Bishop of La Crosse and the Lords were given permission, by a document written in French, to hang the Stations of the Cross in the new chapel. Catherine had received a wooden cross from Father Frederic Baraga as a token of esteem and Charles and Catherine donated several acres of land to be used for a church and cemetery to be established on the hill overlooking the town.

Charles "was also a very accomplished violinist, named 'White Devil' by the Indians, because when he played his violin everyone around got up and danced."[3] Some of the Lord's nine children became musicians also, playing the piano or organ, violin and saxophone.

The Lords also owned a real estate company, sawmill, grocery store, and even operated the Post Office. Charles and his son Leo were often called upon to read letters for many who were unable to read, which was not uncommon in those days.

During the years of Charles' business ventures and financial losses, Catherine bore nine children who were educated in the schools of Duluth and Superior. Her days were very busy caring for the family. She taught her children the language of her ancestors and related stories which both taught and entertained them.

Not all of Charles' and Catherine's nine children survived; such losses were not uncommon among families in the early days of settlement in the area. Of those who did reach adulthood, "Philomena married Daniel Van Iderstien and they had no children. Isabel married Harrison Richards and they had one daughter, Margaret. Felix and his wife, Jane Baker, had four children – Belle, Maggie, Susan and Basil. Charles, Jr. and his wife, Sadie, had no children. Leo and his wife, Margaret Lucius, had thirteen children – Joseph, Andy, Carrie, Mae, Arthur, Dewy, Margaret, Catherine, Clarence, John, Miller, Gladys, and one child who died at an early age."[4]

A Democrat, Charles was elected to the office of Clerk of Circuit Court of Douglas County, Wisconsin, a position to which he was re-elected four times. He was also elected to the offices of Town Treasurer and Town Assessor. His son, Leo, was the first Postmaster [of Solon Springs] and also acted as County Surveyor. Leo was married to Margaret Lucius, member of another early family in the Solon Springs area.

Catherine Osaw-gee Lord died on November 22, 1893, at the age of 62, and Charles Lord on March 6, 1910. On the day of Mr. Lord's funeral, "the local school was closed and all the students marched to the church in a body to attend the services."[5] Both were buried in the cemetery on the hill, located on the land they had donated, in what is now the town of Solon Springs.

Some of Charles and Catherine's descendants still live on land held by the Lord family in the Solon Springs area. Their's is a great legacy handed down by two enterprising, family-oriented ancestors who left their mark in history, one a young fur trader from Montreal, Canada, and the other the daughter of a Chief of the Chippewa.

References

"The Story of Princess Catherine." Rachel Welter. Story in a newspaper, 7-7-1975, name of newspaper not available.

Paper written by a daughter of Charles Lord in 1883. Family resource.

"The Lord Family." Bicentennial 1976. Northwoods Shopper, Wednesday, n.d.

Ibid.

Ibid.

Taped interview with May Nightingale, December 2, 1982.

The Posey Family
– Betty Dahl

North Albert Posey came to this country from Canada in 1838 and to Duluth, Minnesota in the 1850s. Land records list him as "Nortalbut Pose"[1], citizenship files of 1871 show "Nortalbut Posey"[2], but he was also known as Joe and N. A. Posey.

Posey, his wife Margaret (Guay mah bequay), and their children, Susan, Joseph, Mary, and Leonora, lived in the old village at present-day Fond du Lac Reservation, along the St. Louis River, near Cloquet, Minnesota. Posey was a blacksmith and during the 1860s worked for the Bois Fort Band of Chippewa in northern Minnesota.[3]

The gold rush of the 1860's in northern Minnesota brought prospectors, among them George R. Stuntz, early resident and surveyor. The Chippewa brought rock from the Vermilion area to Posey to ask if it was gold. Recognizing it as hematite iron, Posey brought samples to Stuntz and Lewis Merritt, of the mining family, in 1863, but neither was very interested at the time.[4]

In 1865, Stuntz took samples of the rich ore of the Vermilion to Duluth for "... tests that proved the commercial value of what later was called the Lee and Breitung mines and Stuntz stated later that the first white man to know that iron existed on the Vermilion Range was a man named N.A. Posey."[5]

Stuntz told no one until 1874, and then George Stone went with the information to Charlemagne Tower, a mining investor, who sent a crew in 1875 with Stuntz as a guide, to check the Vermilion area. Geologist Arthur Chester said that his part of the exploring party went first by rail to the Northern Pacific Junction, and across the portage to Posey's, where they obtained two large canoes. "As we left Joe Posey's house, we left behind us the last signs of civilization on the St. Louis River, and we hailed it again with satisfaction on our return... [Posey's] wife was a good cook and housekeeper, and we could always get a square meal and a good bed."[6]

In 1875 the Legislature granted lands to the Duluth and Iron Range Railroad Company, later acquired by the Duluth & Winnipeg Railroad and Stuntz completed his last exploration for ore at Vermilion for Tower and associates in 1881.[7]

During this time, Posey was threatened by two men who came to his house demanding to know where the ore samples he had shown to Stuntz had been found. At his refusal to tell, they said <u>they would be back</u>.[8]

On the evening of January 9, 1882, Posey had come home about 5:00 p.m. from Knife Falls, and had called to Joseph Martin, a brother of Margaret, to give some rice and eggs for his sick boy. He wanted Susan to go with her mother to visit the sick child and asked if the two younger children would go also, but they did not want to go. After supper, Margaret, Susan, aged 19, and Joseph, aged 17, fixed a lantern and walked about a mile up the hill over the old wagon road to Martin's home, intending to stay all night. Susan testified later that as they left the home, "Leonora [seven years of age] was undressing and crying. Mary [13 years of age] was standing in the cupboard. They all looked through the window to see us go. This was about 7 p.m. [After we got to Martin's] little boy came in and said there was a fire somewhere." Went right out doors. Knew it was our home as soon as I went out. Went with my brother Joseph down to the house."[9] Fresh footprints were seen in the snow and an axe and shovel were found at the open back door. Joseph testified the axe was at the woodpile when he left for Martin's.[10]

The Duluth Tribune, January 12, 1882, reported that after Margaret, Susan, and Joseph arrived at the burning house, "... the son made an attempt to enter the front door, but the heat was too intense. With an axe he broke open the shutter and looking in saw the charred remains of his father on the floor. The bones of one of the children were found in the hall, as if she had attempted to escape through the door. She also was apparently suffocated."[11] Posey had accumulated a number of lots in the City of Duluth and had intended to complete a sale of the property the next day to the Duluth & Winnipeg Railroad.

A Coroner's Inquest was held at Knife Falls, on January 11-14, 1882. Among the witnesses who gave testimony was one who stated that two men had come into a dance hall on present-day Dunlap Island, down-river from Posey's, about eight o'clock on the evening of January 9, and she had "heard someone say that the man with the Mackinaw suit on was the one who set Joseph Posey's house on fire."[12] Other incriminating evidence was presented and the jury returned a verdict that North Albert, Mary, and Leonora had been killed by persons unknown and that a fire had been set to conceal the crime.[13]

In June, 1882, test-pitting began at what later became the Lee mine on the Vermilion Range and the Minnesota Mining Company was formed in December.[14] The first spike for the railroad was driven the same year.

George Stuntz died a "very poor man" in 1902 at the age of 82,[15] but he and Lewis Merritt always "...gave Posey the credit for the origin of their dreams."[16]

"... North Albert Posey, in his own small way, had a part in shaping the history of the Arrowhead region and the country."[17]

References

Register of Deeds. St. Louis County, Minnesota.

Citizenship Records for St. Louis County. Microfilm. Duluth Public Library Reference. Duluth, Minnesota.

"Outlook." Duluth News-Tribune. Duluth, Minnesota. Page 62. n.d.

Duluth and St. Louis County. Volume 1. Walter Van Brunt. The American Historical Society. Chicago and New York. 1921. Page 345.

Ibid. Page 345.

Ibid. Page 352.

Ibid. Page 360.

William "Dave" Savage. Personal interview. 1982.

Records of Coroner's Inquest, January 11-14, 1882. Testimony of Susan Posey. Carlton County, Minnesota.

Ibid. Testimony of Joseph Posey.

Duluth Tribune, January 12, 1882.

Records of Coroner's Inquest, January 11-14, 1882. Testimony of Carrie Winchell. Carlton County, Minnesota.

Ibid. Verdict of Jury.

Duluth and St. Louis County. Volume I. Walter Van Brunt. op. cit. Page 360, 361.

Ibid. Page 354.

"Outlook." Duluth News Tribune. op. cit. Page 62. n.d.

Ibid.

Mr. and Mrs. Joe Petite, sitting
Joe Posey, standing

Ricing: Simon Savage, Carrie Savage, Susan Posey
Savage, Mary Agnes Savage, Truman Savage, Eugene
Savage. In background, Mary Ellen Savage and Dave
Savage

**Sawyer 1912 – Joseph Northrup and family; wife Angeline Peterson
Northrup, daughter Juna, dog Danger.**

Dave Savage

– Isabelle Whalen

Dave was born July 31, 1888, in Carlton County. His schooling was at Odanah, Wisconsin (boarding school) and Pipestone, Minnesota. He went to [the] eighth grade. He always said, "In one door and out the other."

He lived an exciting life. He worked in the lumber camps as a cook, hoboed across many states, went to the homestead in Canada where his father's relatives lived. He then came back to Cloquet and met Mary Murray. They were married in November, 1923. Mary was 18 and Dave was 35. "I remember as a young person, Dad working W.P.A. [Works Progress Administration], and also working at the little saw mill below where we lived. We lived in Grandma Susan Savage's house on top of the hill [on] Fond du Lac Reserve, which is now called Houle's Hill. Dad had land below as part of his allotment. He wanted to build a home below the hill. At that time, there were logs coming down the St. Louis River. He had an old horse and got enough logs to build a home - 3 bedrooms, kitchen, dining room and front room. Also, he got lumber from the saw mill. Dad was always half farmer. We always had a big garden which was in what is now a sand pit. This was quite a distance from the house. This garden was very big. My mother did lots of canning. We also had a root cellar. It is still useable to this day. This is where we kept the winter meat and vegetables.

"We had no electricity or running water. We had a spring not far from the house where we got our water. In those days we walked everywhere. The four kids went to Sacred Heart School [now the Queen of Peace School in Cloquet] - there were no buses for us. So we walked the railroad tracks, about three miles. We went to Holy Family Church sometimes on Res. Road, other times the short cut up to Tony Defoe's.

"I remember Dad always going to Indian Meetings at Riley Thompson's. They were the R.B.C. of their times. Josephine Thompson was secretary. They were real active in trying to do good for the people of Fond du Lac Reservation.

"Dad read a lot and was quite active in many things. He had a gift for history. I remember him telling my kids of things that he experienced. They would listen with big eyes to the stories he told.

"In 1943, he sold our home to Mr. LaDuke and moved out to the Old Jarri farm. There was nine of us, seven girls and two boys. In 1957, Mom and Dad and the young girls moved back to a small house on the old Jesse place, where Dad added rooms. This was the first time in their life they had electricity and running water. After Mom died in 1966, Dad moved into the Fond du Lac HUD Housing, the FDL compound. He lived a long life, he was 95 when he passed away. During his later days, he did work with Barbara Sommer and Betty Dahl from U.M.D. [University of Minnesota - Duluth] on historical things and places."

From A Historic Resources Inventory of the Fond du Lac Reservation by Barbara Sommer, M.A. Degree Paper, University of Minnesota, 1981.

The following tape was made with Dave Savage on the Fond du Lac Indian Reservation and at his daughter's home in Superior, Wisconsin on November 14, 16 and 20, 1978. The interviewer is Barbara Sommer.

Dave Savage was showing me the old location of the old Indian village on the Fond du Lac Reservation. The village is located on a road that ran from the Mission Church down to Cloquet following the St. Louis River. Access to the road is gained through Willy Sam Thompson's land, called the Sam Thompson Road. There is very little left of the village now. There is a cut through the trees that one can follow with a four wheel drive truck. Some additional cuts through the trees where other streets led in that are barely visible at this time; some foundations, bare spots where houses once stood and Dave was able to pick out some garden spots. Dave gave me the names of all the people who had lived in the village prior to 1910, when it was disbanded by Agent G.W. Cross, Indian Agent. At that time, the decision was made that the Indians should all go out and live on their allotments. Cross was the agent who removed the Indians from this village and forced them out onto their allotments, according to Dave.

Dave described the village by saying that originally the homes were all just shacks and then the Indians went in and were able to get lumber from the mills and build nice lumber houses. Most of the village was on land allotted to some of his relatives; people by the name of Margaret Posey, Susan Posey (who was his mother), and Joe Posey, who was his mother's brother. We started by looking at some of the homes that are across Reservation Road from the Holy Family Mission. At the time of the village, Reservation Road was not cut and was not in existence. Standing at the mission, with one's back to the mission and looking out across the field, the homes from left to right were those of John Winters and Frank Winters (brothers), Sam Wood, Lou LaPrairie, Old Man Blair (otherwise known as George Blair), Frank and Flora Whitebird, John Martin, Tom Floodwood, and, across from the mission home right next to the cemetery, was the home of Joe Petite.

On the main road of the old village, the road through which you had to access through Willy Sam Thompson's land, the homes were owned by Old Lady Christ (otherwise known as John Christ), Mrs. Emma Reed, Frank Defoe, a woman named Black Woman, otherwise Macademaquoque, Caroline Couture, and Antoine Couture, who was a blueberry buyer. The jail was next to his house, then Mrs. Joe Whitebird, Mrs. Redwing, Frank LeDuc who was chief of police, then Simon Defoe, who ran the store, Frank LaMuiex (Lemieux), John Bassett, Ben Bassett, Frank Martin, Louis Smith, and then on a branch of the road that turned off to the right, Old Man Rabideau. On a trail off the main village further down again, George Sheehy, George Winkleman, Nancy Houle, and Lizzie Laundry. Back along the main road lived Susan Posey and Dave Savage bought this house from Old Man Cadotte. Then Joe Houle and George Houle and Frank Godfrey. Then near the top of the hill were Joe Nagaunub and another Joe Houle and Tom Jackson.

Dave mentioned later about the Indian Village, St. Louis River described earlier that most houses were on the right hand side of the road as you went in. There was only one house on the left hand side that belonged to a man by the name of Tom Jackson. Finally, Dave Savage mentioned that he had drawn a map of this Indian village and identified each home on the map.

Elizabeth (Betty) Gurno

In 1977, the Duluth (Minnesota) Public Schools, Indian Education Program, published a number of interviews of Indian people done by writer David Martinson . A series of children's stories and a book, <u>A Long Time Ago Is Just Like Today</u>, resulted from his work. The book of interviews contained several of Fond du lac band members, including Betty Gurno and James Martin, whose interviews are included in this book. Permission to reprint the articles was received from the Duluth Indian Education Program.

History *(Betty Gurno)*

My great grandparents came from the Apostle Islands to Park Point. There was no Fond du Lac or Duluth. I read a little story of how Park Point was formed. The story was that a young Chippewa warrior was being chased by the Sioux from the Wisconsin to the Minnesota side of Park Point. He could go no further. Either he was going to be killed by the Sioux or drowned in the lake. The water was very cold, but he decided to go into the lake. The Great Spirit saw him, and rather than let him die when the Sioux tried to follow, he erased the sand.

That's kind of far fetched, but the Sioux were here. This is Sioux territory - all of it. As we were being pushed out of Wisconsin, Michigan and part of Canada by the white settlers, we naturally had to push somebody else. The Indians in those days were not minglers. They'd much rather be by themselves because they understood one another. They didn't know the white men and his ways.

So we pushed the Sioux out. That's the reason for the battles we had at Moose Lake, Moose Horn Lake and Hanging Horn Lake. People still find arrows there. Big Sandy – that too was strictly Sioux territory. As we moved we fought and pushed them out.

We did leave them two places. One is at Morton, Minnesota, which is near Redwood Falls, and the other is Prairie Island which is right across from Hastings. That's theirs. That's still Sioux territory. All the rest is Chippewa.

I can remember my grandmother talking about some battles. I knew that they weren't just neighborly scraps. That was something big that you talked about.

The Cloquet Fire *(Betty Gurno)*

1918? It was horrid. Fire and me just don't see eye to eye. I respect fire, but that too is from that 1918 holocaust. It hit here about 5:00. Noon hour, my grandfather came and said to get ready. It was supposed to have been 12:00 then, but you'd have sworn it was midnight. The smoke was so thick because, of course, Brookston was already on fire. It was really terrible.

We were sitting with a blanket over us, my mother, my little brother and sister and me. My three older brothers were standing in the water dunking blankets. Burning trees were blowing down from the top of the hill, and they'd land close by.

Then one of the men would douse it with water and throw it away from us. HOT - I can remember when I opened my mouth, it was so hot that my teeth hurt! But as kids go and how nosey they are, I lifted the blankets. We were sitting between the railroad track and the river. I remember seeing the railroad tracks coming up. It looked like the rails had turned into snakes!

I remember lumber flying through the air. Those boards were strips of fire. It was a lumber yard that was on fire. And that wind! Fire was flying all over. Trees were blowing off the hill.

I remember seeing our Priest, Father Simon. He was a big man. Of course, I was tiny so maybe he wasn't as big as I remember. He had a red kerchief on his head because he didn't have any hair. He had little knots tied in the corners so it would stay down. It hadn't blown off, and his head was blistered from the intense heat. He was dressed in a cloak, and he had the Blessed Sacrament with him. He said, "Try to reassure the people that they will not perish as long as they say their prayers." He started the rosary, and that's when I peeked out. I thought, "How in the world can he say this when all this fire is flying around?"

I wasn't in the water. I was on the bank between the railroad and the river. All the younger men from the reservation were running with buckets. You could hear the people screaming. They were saying in Chippewa, "Help us."

The next morning, we knew no Indians were lost. They didn't panic, and they knew enough to seek the water. One Indian woman did die as a result of the fire, but I think she was frightened to death. She was epileptic. Now they know that it was, but in those days they didn't know what she had. She had a convulsion and she didn't come out of it.

My uncle and all his family first crawled down this big well. They had an open well with ladders down it. They had cleaned it out before the winter set in, so there wasn't too much water in there. They had the kids standing on the ladder rungs. They put on the big metal cover, and the mother held the cover down. She had reversed it so the wooden handle was on the inside so she could hang on to it. When she looked out, she saw that their house was gone. Then she said, "Run to the field. We'll bury our faces in the sand. Dig a hole. It won't be so bad."

Before the fire got bad, they knew enough to turn all the cattle loose. The cattle had gone to this open field, and that's where they were standing. They didn't lose any cattle. The chickens were all over. Now that's animal sense. There was no way that they would burn, standing on sand.

Humans didn't have enough sense. They ran where they would surely die – like going down in that well.

No, no Indian people got killed. Four hundred white people died right in this area. Right here. Hinckley was even worse off. Part of Garfield School [west end Cloquet] is still standing and my Aunt's house right downtown [Cloquet], but every other house burnt.

There was a house at the end of the road. The old lady who lived there, being a Catholic, lit a candle and took a statue of St. Anthony and then told that statue to protect her home. She ran off, but when she came back, that candle was still burning the next morning. The fire burnt right up to a certain area, and that was it. They all said that was a miracle because nothing else burnt.

Right on the top of this hill where our church [Holy Family Church on the Fond du Lac Reservation] now stands, was a cemetery, and there was a church there, too. One man and a couple of his brothers were throwing water on folks, and they could hear all these people hollering on top of the hill in Indian, "Come and get us, come and help us, we're burning."

So they all hollered back in Indian, "Come this way, down here by the river. Come this way! They ran up as far as they dared go, but they couldn't get too far. Then they heard someone hollering, "Help." They said that by this time they were at the tip of the hill, so they went up to see who it was. Oh my goodness, they couldn't imagine who was burning because everybody that lived up there was accounted for at the foot of the hill. No one was left up there! They figured out after awhile that it was the dead ones in the cemetery. They all hollered together so their voices even carried over that 90 miles an hour wind! It had to be the dead that called.

October 12, 1918 - My husband was nine years old when that happened. He couldn't remember anything. Maybe it was so bad that he wanted to wipe it out. It was awful. I wouldn't want my kids to go through that. Scary.

But God works in funny ways. He spared my great grandmother's house, and she had all the rice and apples and two barrels of flour.

Survivors of the 1918 fire. CCHS Photo

The Great Epidemic *(Betty Gurno)*

My grandmother talked about the big smallpox epidemic. Quite a few in their family had died from it. One day in the fall, they could hear howling out in the woods. I don't understand what that howling was, but they said they could hear this howling. Grandpa went out, and there was a man and a boy standing at the edge of a big field. They didn't speak the same language we spoke, but my grandfather was very good at doing sign language. The man told him that all but two of the tribe were dead. They were the only two left.

Grandpa told the man and boy to gather up all the wood they could, put it in a pile and start a fire. Then he told them to take off all their clothes and shave all their hair. He said, "I don't want any hair on you at all. Scrape your face, and do it to the little boy too. Cut your toenails and fingernails till they bleed, and then stand by the fire until you are burning on all sides. When you have done that, come over here."

Grandfather must have put out some baskets of water and some strong sand – at least I think it was sand. Then he said, "Now rub yourselves."

Later, Grandpa gave them each something to drink. He said, "Don't eat anything else, just drink this. Then go over there and do your business." Grandpa went back over to where their things were.

They were not Chippewas; I think they were Sioux. They stayed with us for two years. Then they set out to try and find their own people.

I often wonder who they were. They were the only two survivors. Whatever tribe they were, she never said for sure that they were Sioux. She just said, "Different Indians."

January Nights *(Betty Gurno)*

What do I remember about January nights? Story time. Stories don't stay with me though.

When I was a little girl, I don't remember ever going to bed. I'd always fall asleep. Probably my uncle carried me to bed – or my grandfather.

We'd sit on the floor by the fire. We had a pot belly stove, I remember that. We'd tell different things that happened. That's where I first learned about spoons and forks and clocks being invented.

They didn't know how to use the clock; I remember grandma saying she didn't know how to use that clock. She always relied on the sun. That told her truthfully what the time was – better even than the clock. She had never seen one before so she didn't know how to wind it. It was all new to her.

I remember her telling about the brand new knife that she got. It was more or less a hunting knife that grandfather had bought for her to cut up meat. The first thing she did was take off the tip of her finger with it, and she didn't want to use that knife anymore. I remember asking, "Well, what did you use?" She answered, "The one that grandfather gave me many years ago."

I think that was a bone knife, not a steel knife. What else did they have? She didn't tell me it was bone. I just assumed that if she had never seen a steel knife, she wouldn't know how much sharper steel is than bone, and she could easily cut off the tip of her finger. It must have been sharper than the one she had used, so the first one she had from grandfather must have been bone.

Then later we were talking about the fork. She said she pricked herself so many times in the mouth with the fork because she didn't know how to hold it.

Food Preservation *(Betty Gurno)*

By the time wild rice season started, you had all the potatoes dug. They were put out in the field to dry, and they were covered up with sand. Your cabbages, rutabagas and carrots were put in boxes and containers, and you put sand on top of them. They were buried in the sand. Then they were put into a root cellar because most of us like my grandfather never had a basement. They had root cellars and when it was cold enough, they even put milk in there. There was no refrigeration so if you couldn't dry the meat, you didn't take it. Same with fish. Even today we only fish what we can eat. We take no more because there will be some tomorrow. That's the way my folks did it. I don't know if that's the way people do it now.

Natural Medicine *(Betty Gurno)*

All spring we'd pick weeds. I call them weeds, but they were herbs. When I was little, I would go herb picking with my grandmother. For example, there is a certain tree that had to be chopped. She used it for just any kind of medicine. She would have maybe two or three kinds of medicine for diarrhea because all medicines do not work alike on each person. She had to try maybe three different kinds of medicine for the diarrhea. The little kids years ago were the ones that got it. They would get it bad.

We started picking herbs in March. We picked *wigob* in March and April. Now that's a fiber. It comes from basswood at just about the same time as the maple syrup comes. We'd go around then and pick this *wigob*. You can pick that till June because sap doesn't come in until then. Maple sap comes in first, then birch, and then the other trees follow.

I've got a sack of *wisugibug*. It's good for lung congestion or for a stuffy head and the chills. There's no dizziness attached to it because it's just a good tea. But you have to drink it real hot before it will do anything. Like if you're coming down with a cold and chills, boil some water. Then I steep some of those leaves, strain it, then reheat it and drink it as hot as I can. I add a little sugar to mine. Gives it a little bit more flavor. I drink that right down and into bed I go. And I don't get up – just stay put with a lot of covers on. When I finally get warm, I break my cold. So I pick that in the fall of the year. I go right down here at the corner. It's called swamp tea if you want to break it up into English.

There's a lot more than swamp tea, too. If you are out for medicinal purposes, you go into the woods and kind of smell around. You can smell wild onions, rosemary and sweet grass. Sweet grass is not a grass, it's leaves. That makes real good tea.

You can go out to Ditchbank, out along the edge of Deadfish Lake during ricing time, and pick some *wike*. That's for the throat. When Indians sing and do drumming, they usually chew this. It's also called bitterroot because it is bitter. You can take very little and you don't have laryngitis. You aren't susceptible to sore throats if you know enough to chew that root. I don't like it, but, if I think it's going to do me some good, I'll take it. If I have to do any singing, like years ago I sang in a church and during Lent we sang from

Wednesday on, I'd always chew a little *wike*. Everything was sung; you didn't say it, you sang it. But come Easter Sunday, my throat would be so sore from singing so much! We sang practically all day Saturday. That's the Catholic Church again. They don't do that anymore. Now they have rock and roll in church. They do.

There isn't a month that goes by except possibly January – no, not even January – when there's not something you can cut from something.

Treebark *(Betty Gurno)*

When you look for birchbark, you look for the bark that doesn't have many bumps. When you find what you like, you decide how big a piece you need, depending on what you're going to make. You take your knife and you just mark it. Then you slit that tree. It's kind of in layers. You slip your finger in the slit you've cut, and then you run your hand under it. It's wet and gummy. As you run your hand under the piece that you cut around, it will peel off and the whole thing will pop out.

Then you flatten it out so it will be in workable condition. You'll have to set weights on it to make it flat because it has a tendency to roll up. When you flatten it, lay it opposite of the way it was on the tree - sticky part up. When you want to work on it, then you wet it.

People made canoes. If you wanted any kind of boat to travel in or to go ricing, you had to make a boat. How were you going to get it? They were made here. Oh, a lot of people made them. Just about everybody, I guess. Of course, boards came into view when I was a kid. My husband made a boat, but I think it was made of plain wood. There is a birchbark canoe at St. Scholastica [the College of St. Scholastica in Duluth, Minnesota] that was made in Grand Portage.

There is a canoe in the church near Sawyer, but that one is made of some kind of basswood, and I think it's sewn with balsam stripping. I don't mean the bark of the balsam tree, but I mean the root. During a certain time of the year, you can chop pieces of root right from the tree. For the heck of it, pick up the root and take it and try it. Try a short one first. See what it does? You'd swear that somebody had sat there and twisted those fibers, so you would be ready to sew with nature's thread.

You stripped the tree as wide and as thick as you wanted, depending again on what you were going to use it for. If you're going to use it for baskets, then you didn't need as thick a fiber. But for canoe work or for the baskets that you're going to use for boiling sap, then there had to be a thicker material. Then you had to use balsam pitch.

Late in the summer, grandpa went through the woods until he saw a good size balsam. He blazed it. Do you know what blazing is? It means to mark it. He'd slash that tree, and out of it would come the sap or goop and form a hard bubble. Then in the fall, we would have to take bags and gunnysacks, and go with grandpa. He'd take a knife – there was no trick to it – and he'd just hit it once and it would pop right off. It looked like resin. It wasn't too heavy because I can remember carrying a bag full, and I was pretty small.

Grandpa had to have just so many for his winter's work. He'd take deer tallow and melt this pitch down. It didn't give off a pitchy smell or taste. He heated it when he needed it to sew up seams. It was leakproof.

I remember when grandfather's packsack was like the ones kids wear now to carry their books to school, only bigger. Everything went on their shoulders in those days. I suppose something must have rubbed a hole in it. He didn't know how to patch it. Where was he going to get another piece of burlap or gunnysack material? Sewing machines were not into view yet, or at least we couldn't afford one. So he took that pitch, and he took a leaf and put it over the hole in the packsack. I don't know what kind of leaf he used, but I do remember looking at him - wondering what in the world he was doing. He put a rock down, then he put the burlap packsack on top of the rock, and finally, he put this leaf on. Then he used a little paddle to put the resin on. He just patched that leaf into that burlap! Then he just let it hang there and dry. That's all there was to it. That was his patching.

I can remember him patching his overalls like that too. He'd put on some kind of a leaf, and he'd just patch it over. Probably wasn't the very best looking thing. It probably looked dirty, but it was leakproof! In those days, you wore pants till they practically stood up by themselves. Grandpa used to say, "My pants is just ripe." That meant that he had them broken in to where they were comfortable to wear. He didn't care about the dirt – that was all right – those were his "ripe pants." He would go out in the woods, and they were leakproof and waterproof. He'd come back home, and he'd take off his pants and hang them up. When he'd go back out into the woods, he'd put the same thing on again - his "ripe pants."

I still don't know what he meant by his "ripe pants." They had expressions like that. Today I don't know what they meant. I should have asked then, "What did you mean when you said this or that?"

Respect *(Betty Gurno)*

Everyone I talk to has mentioned the respect for the elders in the tribe.

Yes, that was Number One. That was implanted in you when you were born. The elders of your community and your reservation were to be respected to the highest degree. For instance, if a member of your family (a boy being girls did not go hunting) went hunting for the first time and would get a deer, he'd take the blood of the deer, splash it on his face, and then proceed to cut up the carcass. He'd save the skin and go to the oldest elder of the clan or reservation. He'd give him or her a good size portion of the first piece of meat. Then he'd go around to the other ones, sharing everything. He was not allowed, according to the tradition, to eat any of it, but he carried the mark of the blood. So the following season if he killed any game, he could keep it all. He didn't have to share, but he usually shared. That was then a teaching.

Feathers *(Betty Gurno)*

The very fact that you are born is all you are entitled to as a gift from your mother and father. You are also entitled to one feather. You are born with it. That is your heritage. This is what I learned from my great-grandmother.

A woman in her lifetime can only earn two feathers. A third one is very rarely given. The only girl I know who got the third one was the little girl, Sacajewea, who led that Louis and Clark expedition. The Shoshone tribe supposedly gave her a third feather. Now she could wear three if she wanted to, but I don't think she wore any.

A boy can wear as many feathers as he has earned, but not one more than that.

He makes his own cap. It is made out of squirrel. He first kills the squirrel, then eats the meat, and, finally, dries the hide. He shapes it to fit his head. He puts the number of feathers that he has earned on it in any shape or form that suits him. Over a period of years, if he earns more and his cap becomes too full, he can go out and repeat the process of killing the squirrel and eating the meat.

You do this by yourself. You fix the fur part up to suit you and put the feathers on the way you want.

Months *(Betty Gurno)*

Because we start fresh we call the beginning of the year the Great Spirit Month, *kitchi- manito-gisiss.* Manito refers to whichever spirit you have reverence or respect for – God, Lord, Jesus Christ. That's what it is, the Great Spirit Month.

In January, kitchi-manito-gisiss, Indian people made things with what they'd gathered last fall. Right after ricing, the men went to the woods to look for green birch trees. Of course, at that time of the year there was hardly any brush, no leaves, so they could spot a birch tree in the woods a lot easier. Then they would cut it. Now in January they had all this to work on. The men worked on birchbark and whittled spigots for maple sugaring. Days were precious because you had to do all your work in the daytime, not evenings. All we had were kerosene lamps, and they didn't give enough light to do anything with. It was just more or less not to fall over each other in the dark.

Men trapped and snared rabbits for food. My uncles were never home during kitchi-manito-gisiss. They were out getting camp ready for trapping. They would get maybe 40 or 50 rabbits and then they would come home.

I don't know where Strout is, but they went up on a train they called the "short line." Those are terms that I heard, I don't know – I think it was a train. They'd say, "I'll be back on such and such a day. Look for me."

"All right, this is the day Uncle John and Uncle Joe are coming home. We should go meet them." So we'd go down to the bottom of the hill and wait for them Just before sundown on the day that they said, we would go.

Sometimes they'd bring venison. See venison was illegal to take, but if they'd dried some earlier, they could bring that home. It was a matter of survival, I guess.

So that's what they did in January. I'm just going according to what my grandmother did. Everybody else, I don't know what everybody else did. Everybody lives different. They still don't live alike.

* * *

February is *namebini-gisiss.* Namebini means "sucker." A sucker is a fish so Namebini- gisiss means such fish month. It tells you what the fish do at that time. About that time of the year, they look for holes in the ice for air. Usually it's the suckers who find the holes first, then the bullheads come up

224

there, then the perch and even northerns. But those don't need as much air as the sucker. They're the first to smell thin ice and they'll break through.

I can hear fish; I can hear them under the ice. They make a noise like a chicken but not quite as loud. To me it sounds like they're clicking their teeth. Now, do they have teeth? They must click their little teeth or, maybe, their fins go together. But you can hear that. I know that sounds kind of far-fetched.

In February people kept on doing a lot that they did in January. There was no letup. They just kept right on. It reminds me of trying to beat the clock – seeing that they didn't have a clock system.

You had to go according to the moons. We only had so many days, then already we had to start thinking about going out to the sugarbush. "Have we got everything ready? When are you going to leave?"

And there had to be one big storm.

* * *

It would be March then. March is *onabani-gisiss*. It means the "crust on the snow." The winds have changed considerably. Because the sun is a little higher and gives more heat, the winds blow warmer and make the snow glassy. It gets shiny, icy crust. That's the "hard crust" month.

Then you can still hunt rabbits. You're not allowed to take them too close to them having their young. You have partridge this time of the year, too. They're not wormy this time of the year. It's a good time to eat.

* * *

Now, here we are in April. April is *sisibakwat-gisiss* or maple sugar harvesting month, and that is just what you do the whole month. Grandpa used to go up the second to the last week in March. Of course, that was preparing time when he pitched tent and collected the wood he would burn. The wood wasn't to keep warm but to keep that syrup boiling. He'd do that for two weeks. Of course, we always went out and checked on him and took him some food he could heat up if he wanted it.

We'd move out the first week in April. There was no chasing back and forth. We would stay right there.

Did you notice the little pussy willows? You know that they get sort of yellow and bushy? Well, that tells that the sap is done. It also meant that May is starting.

* * *

May is flower budding month. It is call *wabigoni-gisiss* or flower month. Everything is in bloom like May flowers, cowslips, and cherry and apple blossoms. Then at the end of May strawberry blossoms start, and, of course, that means June will follow.

* * *

June is strawberry month or *odeimin-gisiss* because that's the month you pick strawberries. Our canning season starts then, and you have to pick birchbark during June too.

* * *

Now July. It's just what it says, firecracker moon. It's *papashkige-gisiss* or firecracker moon. And the only reason why that is, is because of the Fourth of July. I don't know what they called it before because I was born too late. There was a celebration – usually pow-wows. They still have that. I don't know, maybe they didn't know the meaning of what they were celebrating – the Fourth of July.

* * *

August was *manomini-gisiss*. It was time to rice according to the moon, according to the tide. When the tide would come in, they'd get up, get out on the bay and get out on those little holes where at that time the rice was. First, we used to rice at Lake Minnewowa. Then Minnewowa became very poor for ricing so my folks went down to Fond du Lac. I was big then; I was 14. By that time we had a little Model A and we'd drive down. We stayed with my great aunt, *Ma-ma-nse*. *Ma-ma-nse* means little mother once removed. We stayed with her until we moved out onto the little islands. The men made the rice in and out of those little bays down there by Lake Superior. Fond du Lac.

* * *

Then we're up to September moon. Here it is *wake-baga-gisisss* or "leaves turning color" moon. It's freezy, frosty. It is also the time to take your game. We didn't use bows and arrows. I suppose in years gone by they did, but not when I was a kid. Guns were already in when I was a kid.

My folks were funny; they only took what they could eat. There was no refrigeration, and if you couldn't dry the meat, you didn't take it. Forget it, you only took what you could eat.

226

* * *

The word for October is exactly what it does - *binakwigisiss*. The leaves turn color in September. They're frozen and on the dry side. They'll fall. I say binakwan means a comb. So binakwi-gisiss means the moon when the leaves are combed out of the trees. By this time everyone is waiting for the snowfall. You've had your garden and your hunting season. You've already gathered your deer, and you've dressed it.

* * *

November is *gashkadini-gisiss* or freezing moon. Now, when you're going out in the wintertime and you're going on snowshoes, do you know how the snow crunches when it's real cold? That's what we are talking about. The word for November has nothing to do with November as we know it. It's just that's what happens during that moon – the crunching noise you make walking in the snow.

* * *

And December is Little Spirit moon or *manitogissons*. Remember January wis kitchi- manito-gisiss or Big Spirit moon? Now this is a little bitty one. It's the last of the moons, and now you have completed one year. One cycle.

I often wonder if the Chippewa people started a year in January. I don't know. I suppose once you were old enough so you understood, it just seemed that way forever. It's just a thing that followed. You became aware of the time of the year and just kept on from there.

Days of the Week *(Betty Gurno)*

Now me being of Catholic origin, I say mariegijigad or Mary's day for the Mother Mary for Saturday. That is the way I was brought up. Other places say kisibigaigijigad or scrub day. Now that is what is used on most reservations. That's what you do on that day – "scrub the floor."

* * *

Church day is anamiegijigad, prayer day.

* * *

Monday is *gi-ishkwa-anamiegijikak.* That's what it is to me on my reservation. That's Monday – past tense. It's part prayer day which automatically would make it Monday. But other reservations, they said *nitam-anokigi-jigad* or the first working day.

* * *

Tuesday is *nijogijigad* or the second day.

* * *

Wednesday is *abitosse* and it means half way. Wednesday is half way. Abita is half and abitosse is the day.

* * *

Thursday is the fourth day which would be *njoijigad.*

* * *

Friday – now here we go again – this is the Catholic origin. I would say tchibaiatigijad or cross. You know, it is holy cross day.

* * *

Then they say *mariegijigad.* They're back to Saturday again, and the week begins on Saturday.

228

Good Luck *(Betty Gurno)*

Some people don't see good luck signs, but I do because of my earlier training. If we went out to the sugarbush, out ricing, or out to the blueberry camp and we saw an owl sitting in a tree, our grandmother wouldn't let us go near it. "Stay away from that. He's the watch dog. No harm will come to us because he'll let out the first noise."

And squirrels – they never would let us get squirrels. If danger is coming, or anything is there that doesn't belong there, squirrels will chatter and scold and make all sorts of noises. As long as you stand perfectly still, they will take you for granted. Then they'll shut up – like when you are on a deer stand. But until you stand perfectly still, those little squirrels will chatter and chatter. Of course, they're warning the deer that there is something out of place.

Now a bluejay will talk to you too and make all kinds of noises. If you stand completely still, then you're supposed to be there. They too will shut up. But let a deer come, and they will let you know that there's a deer near.

I saw a deer when I was with my daughter, and I told her to raise her gun. She couldn't see anything. "Look at that, there he is. Can't you see him?" I said. It took her a good ten minutes to spot that deer in there! She shot that thing and it raised him up. That deer stood up and made a noise, whirled right around, just stood up and took off. We drew blood, but we didn't kill him. We trailed him, then it started raining. I said, "Forget it."

The next day Clyde [Atwood] went out. He said, "You couldn't have hit it too bad. I couldn't pick up his trail."

Maple sugar camp at Big Lake, 1951

Maple sugar camp at Big Lake, 1951

Maple sugar time, Ditchbank Road, Big Lake: Front, John Berthiums and Chief Beargrease. Background, Elaine (Beargrease) Isaacson.

[The following article appeared in the book, I Wish I Could Give My Son a Wild Raccoon, edited by Eliot Wigginton, published by Anchor Books/Doubleday in 1976. Permission to reprint the interview of Betty Gurno was granted by Anchor/Doubleday.]

Red is the East for the Sun

– Thomas D. Peacock and James L. White

Elizabeth Houle Gurno, a Chippewa Indian, was born in 1913 on the Fond du Lac Reservation, near Duluth, Minnesota, and was raised by her grandparents. One of her most vivid memories of those days is that of a forest fire:

I was only four or five years old but I remember it. My grandfather was a timber cruiser, and he was out in Brookston. He rode a horse out in the woods, and he knew that fire was out of control. And he raced to my mother's house and said, "Go to the river!" So my mother, my grandmother, and my great-grandmother all took blankets and some food and left everything else just as it was. Went to the river hollering as we went to the other homes on the way to get down to the river. The young boys then cleared all the underbrush and turned up the dirt so that when we sat down, we were sitting in dirt. And my brothers stood waist deep in water and dunked blankets and traded and we had blankets on top of us. They'd dry out as fast as they'd put them on. And they'd throw pails of water at us and wet the ground all around as far as they could.

I remember seeing Father Simon – he was a priest back then – he had water blisters on his head, and he had the chalice to put the blessed sacrament in, and he had Coke and he blessed us with that and he said, "You won't die. Don't be afraid." But every kid is nosey. I lifted the blankets up and looked, and I could see the railroad track from the heat just buckling, going like sort of a snake. And lumber and trees flying over us. And then there was a water tank, but below that water tank there were two barrels sitting there. And these men rolled this heavy barrel full of oil away. It was so hot that a man burned his hands, so it was near ready to explode. The water tank had a metal roof that just caved in. That's how hot it was. And the priest was blistered! He had great huge water blisters. He was very sick, and he had two black eyes. I thought, if this is the end of the world that I've heard about, then this is it. But the next morning we were all there.

Thousands of non-Indians burned to death, but not one Indian. They had the common sense that God gave them to go to the river like an animal. All the animals were there. There were bears swimming out there. I can remember seeing the bears. That was terrible. I hope I never have to live through anything like that again.

And the cemetery – there was a cemetery right by the church. And the same man that rolled that barrel down the hill heard somebody hollering for help. He made three separate trips with wet blankets. He went up hollering in English and in Indian, "Come this way! Come this way!" And he'd get to the church and it was all quiet. He said there was no church. He came down and told us the church was burnt. And when it was getting on towards morning, we heard this terrible screaming. Many voices. Not just one. Many. He went back up again. Went up three times and kept hollering in English and Indian, "Come this way! The river is this way!" And it would be quiet. I don't know what ever happened. My grandmother always said that the dead were hollering. They were burning too. There wasn't anything left.

Mrs. Gurno was educated in elementary grades in Catholic schools, and went to high school in Flandreau Indian School in South Dakota, where she took training as a practical nurse. She married in 1935 and raised three children and now has eleven grandchildren and one great-grandchild. Mrs. Gurno goes to school "piecemeal" at the University of Minnesota, Duluth, and Bemidji State, where she became a certified Ojibwa (Chippewa) language teacher. She teaches in the high school at Cloquet and she teaches language also at the University of Minnesota-Duluth. She works as a coordinator at the Cloquet high school and coordinates Indian culture programs for both Indian and non Indian students. She likes to paint and do arts and crafts such as beading, birch bark work, and some quilting.

My mother died when my sister was a year old, so I was raised by Mr. and Mrs. La Prairie, two old, old people. And I have to give credit to them. They raised four of us as Indians – Indian beliefs, rights, and traditions. So I have kept it up these many years, and I in turn have taught my children Indian things, like what living with other people means to you. Respect them, but first of all respect yourself. Their property is just as important to them as your property is to you. If you want viciousness to reign the most, then that's the way to act and it will be returned exactly. Be kind. There's a saying that an Indian will give you the shirt off his back, and that is true. If you are in need of something, they give it to you – anything. That's a sign of love – not by words, but by actions.

We had fun when I was young. Grandpa made toys for us. We didn't have many toys. There was no such thing as a dime store – no such thing as money. But he made us a ball out of deer hide. This ball was covered with deer hide and laced with deer hide like the balls you see now – more like a softball. But in it, at the dead center, was a rock as round as he could find, and he padded it all around with swamp moss, and it was packed hard. It didn't take one day, it took days to make it. And he made several at one time. And then he'd sew it with scraps that Grandma didn't have use for – real buckskin.

And he'd carve out a bat for us out of cedar. They were nothing to what kids have now, but they didn't cost a penny.

We played an awful lot of ball because my father was a ball player, and I had a couple of uncles that were very active. Dad played with the White Sox of 1910, and he always said, "I wish you had been born a boy, but I'm glad you're you." So I played baseball with half the reservation boys.

And he made barrel hoop type things that we would roll from a certain goal to another goal. I don't think you see that much any more.

And we created. We made paper dolls like they do now, but we used our heads to do that. We made dolls out of buckskin. I had about eight little buckskin dolls about six or seven inches tall. They each had an Indian name. They went to bed the same time I did. My two older sisters had dolls the same way. We only had one brother that lived with us. He was very sickly, so Grandpa catered to him. Made him a wagon out of what he found in the woods. Made the wheels and all. There wasn't one nail in these wagons that he made. He made him several. And we'd pull him in these wagons. That's how big they were.

There were a lot of kids there on the reservation. We spent our winters sliding down this big huge hill, which has since been cut down.

Of course we had to work. Grandpa had a small farm. We had cows and chickens. There was a lot of things to do. Raised potatoes and rutabagas and carrots. I worked hard as a child. Picked berries in the summertime and canned the old fashioned way. Dried meat, dried fruit and vegetables. But along with it, at the end of the day, we knew that we would be rewarded with sugar cakes. That was always our reward. Or Grandpa might be lucky enough to have some things to barter, and he would bring back fresh fruit. That was a treat. He didn't have to go very far for it, but nevertheless, that was a treat.

And then we used to eat rabbits and porcupines. A porcupine can't hear. He runs with his nose to the ground for he only senses through vibrations. You can run down a porcupine and club him. And you can make a deadfall and kill a rabbit. And, of course, we'd eat venison. We'd eat every bit of it. Indians did not take animals and just take parts and throw the rest away. They never killed an animal unless they could use all of it. They ate the meat and used the hide for clothes and tents, and then used the bones for jewelry or for sewing needles. There was something that could be made even out of antlers. If they were cut a certain way, you could make a yoke and carry two buckets of water on the prongs. The weight was on your shoulders, and all you had to do was hang onto the pails.

The Indians survived with their hunting and their garden produce. And years ago there was plenty of wild rice. There was one lake we'd stay at while we were gathering. Camp there. And that's the only place we went to make rice. We had more than enough to bring home – say, ten big sacks of rice. But then they changed it. Now you can't take rice off that lake because the non-Indians that came said they were putting that aside for the ducks so the ducks would have some rice to eat. My dad said, "Since when did you ever see a duck sit on a rice stalk and eat rice, because he's not built that way. He scoops up from the water because he's built that way. The Almighty made him with a bill to scoop – not to perch on a rice stalk!"

Wild rice has always been our mainstay of life. If you have rice, you are not hungry. Indians believed that at one time or another, we came from the water. Therefore, anything in the water is edible. You can eat it if you know how to cook it.

And then we made maple sugar. They make maple sugar this year – the junior high and the senior high school. Some of the kids had never heard of it, so we proposed a project. And that's what we were teaching the kids. They thought that you went to the tree and just wiggled this little spigot and maple syrup would come out. It takes forty-three gallons of sap to make one gallon of syrup. You have to know how to do it. I think they learned a lot.

Indians took things from Mother Earth. She gave us maple syrup. But with the left hand, we thanked her. I still do this in my family. We had quite a ceremony about that when I was growing up. Same with rice. Even if you don't ask everybody on the reservation to come in and join you, you ask a few people to come in and you give thanks. And with this wild rice, you save up enough maple syrup and sugar to mix with it. Just the two things mixed together. You eat that. That's a thanksgiving for what Mother Nature has given to you. And you don't waste it. You take it and be thankful that you got it. And then you have a dance. I can remember going by horse and buggy up to a ceremony. That year the garden produce was terrific. It was beautiful. And they danced till morning and ate in between times. I remember that. It was a give-away dance. That's a certain kind of dance they do. And they give away garden produce in baskets to the ones that they invited in to dance with.

There are many things in Indian life that nowadays you'd say don't make sense. We are associated with drums and feathers and that sort of thing. But all that makes sense to the Indians. A drum to the Indian has a place. I'd never deliberately walk up and give one a kick. It has a place. It's a symbol. That's *me*. Even though I'm a Catholic now, that's still part of me, of my heritage. My grandfather had a drum in the house. He never touched it. It had a place of respect. He'd always refer to it: "That is you and me." Nothing individual. It was all of us.

There's several types of drums. The *mide'* drum, only the *midewiwin* men can touch the drum, and a woman, no matter who she is or how high in life she is, could not touch that drum. It's just never heard of.

Then there are water drums. Now water drums, you don't find them here because we are never in want of water. We have plenty of water. You go down south and you'll find your water drums because there they pray, they dance for water. Water is a necessity of life. Therefore, what water they do have, they fill half of their drum with water and that gives a different pitch. But we have our share of water up here.

And we have feathers. We are mostly associated with lots of feathers. But a feather in our culture has to be earned. We are born with one feather. That is a gift from our parents. Now my father told me that he was given a feather at his birth, and a blanket. And that blanket did not come from J. C. Penny. It was homemade out of rabbit hide. And his mother took nine months to make it. She finished her last stitch the day the baby was born. That was her gift to the baby.

Then, as the years go by, for a female, she put away her dolls at about twelve or thirteen or fourteen years old and said, "I'm through with dolls; I am entering womanhood," she then would be given another feather. Then she could wear both of them. When she married, she took one and fastened it over her right shoulder. Then, in the course of her lifetime, maybe she became a widow. She'd take this feather and put it on her left shoulder when she went out in public. It saved a lot of asking: "Are you a widow?" "Are you married?" But at the same time, she only mourned her husband one year. After that, she put the feather back up. Even though she had maybe nine kids, she still had the right to wear her two feathers up.

But a man is different. A man has to earn each feather. Now, he alone did not decide that he was entitled to a feather. He had to prove himself. Now he could be many things and earn feathers many ways, just like Boy Scouts. He could be a runner, a hunter, a scout, or send messages by blanket, or a provider of wood, which was essential to eating and warmth; or he could be a tent builder or bow and arrow maker. He earned credit like that, but he didn't decide that he was entitled to a feather. The elders of the tribe sat in council: "Did he earn this feather? How?" And then he had to show how he earned it. Well, then they'd give him the feather.

By the time he'd reach, say, forty—possibly younger—he could go out and kill a squirrel, cure the hide himself, eat the meat, and take the squirrel hide and make a bonnet type of hat and put the feathers on himself. He had to do his own. No one else could do it for him. I couldn't make you one, for example. He made his own and put all his own feathers on it.

And now these feathers weren't just crow feathers or robin. They were eagle. Years ago, eagles were plentiful, but as the non-Indians moved in with all their concrete, the eagles went other places. I remember my father telling that they'd go on eagle hunts up in the hills. This was when he was a little boy. And they'd sort of make a bet amongst themselves that they would gather the most feathers. Now you don't kill an eagle. You gather the feathers that he sheds. They call it molting. Once a year they molt and all the feathers fall to the ground for you to pick up. And they went up in the hills in what is now Duluth – all around in there. Michigan Street and Superior Street was nothing but a cedar swamp.

And then we decorated things with porcupine quills. Those quills are very dangerous, but then they were used to decorate anything made out of birch bark. The ends have to be bent. They can go through human flesh. Very dangerous. They were dyed with chokecherries and raspberries for red, or pitch from the base of a balsam tree or a beech tree. That was boiled and it would be black. Whatever you had to dye, you'd stick it in that boiling water and then take it out and lay it to dry. The quills themselves are sort of a beige color. And they used them for decorating headbands and wristbands. And especially on birch bark baskets because they made a prettier design and were easier to work with. My grandmother had an art with birch bark that she chewed a design into the thin bark that my uncle would then in turn sew it onto another basket. There are a few in a Chicago museum that she had done. She would fold the birch bark a certain way and chew on it, then unfold it and look at it, and if it didn't suit her right, she'd fold it up another way and chew on it. Just as quick. And she'd come out with the most beautiful designs: flowers, leaves. She did beautiful work.

And she worked in the true Indian spirit. An Indian always has several things in mind when he does things: first, that he's busy with his hands doing something and not wasting his or anybody else's time. Then, that he's making something useful and something beautiful to look at – not just an eyesore. And then that he's making something that will tell a story. It had to have meaning. For him to sit down and spend hours, there had to be a reason for it. In the end, it would tell something – like my headband. I have fixed roses on it. Took me a while to make it. It's pretty. It's going to be useful. But I can't wear it yet. I was born in 1913, and each rose represents ten years of my life, so when I am sixty, I will wear it. Until then, I can't.

The sacred colors are white, red, black, yellow, and blue. White is for the north, for the white snow. That, in turn, gives you strength. Red is the east for the sun. Yellow is for the south – for the heat that ripens our staff of life, the corn. And black is for the west. If a storm is coming, look to the west and there will be black clouds. The storm originates in the west. And blue represents man. So in doing any type of work, we try to include one or all of the colors depending on what we're making.

I think it's nice that the kids are trying to recover some of that now. I'm glad for them. But their mothers and fathers often don't know enough. That's where the hitch is. The mothers and fathers are going to have to be educated first. You don't read those things in books. You see, years back, it was a downright sin to be known as an Indian. It was something to be ashamed of. I couldn't go along with that because my grandmother spoke nothing but Chippewa. I lived in an Indian home. That's the way I breathed. The others picked up English. Then they in turn didn't want their children to speak Chippewa because the government agent told us that was wrong: "You don't look like a white man but you got to live like one. You have to live like a white man now."

But I'm Indian. I believe Indian ways. They know I'm Indian and that's it. I cannot erase me. I'm here to stay.

But I think it's wonderful that the kids feel more firmly about Indian ways now. Life will be a little more meaningful for them. And I always stress respect, because that was taught to me from the year one. Respect your elders. They have lived longer than you have; therefore, they are wiser.

I think the kids are trying real hard, but they cannot learn overnight what for years has been driven out of them. I never was ashamed to be an Indian. I'm still Indian. Be the best darn Indian you can be. That's the way I look at it. In my eyes, that's right. And the kids are the same way. Some of these kids have beautiful thoughts.

[The following interview with John and Mary LaFave was published in a 1976 book, I Wish I Could Give My Son a Wild Raccoon, edited by Elliot Wigginton. Permission to reprint the interview was received from the publisher, Anchor/Doubleday.]

It makes shivers go up your back
– Thomas D. Peacock and James L. White

Mary LaFave was born on February 2, 1909. Her mother was a Chippewa Indian and her father was a white man who had been adopted by the tribe. She attended a public school until the sixth grade, and then went to a boarding school in Hayward, Wisconsin, for two years. She and her husband, John, now live in Cloquet, Minnesota.

MARY LAFAVE: My mother was a full-blooded Indian. Her maiden name was Liza Keene. She was Catholic. But both of her parents were pagan. All of her people on that side were pagan. There was a family of ten, and she was the only one that wasn't.

We went over and saw my mother's father and mother in 1918. My grandfather died in 1918. He had cancer of the back. A bear had caught him when he was young and scratched his back. He developed cancer there and that's what he died from. This happened when he was young but as he got older it got bigger and bigger, I suppose. They only spoke Chippewa, and that's all I learned until I went to school and was taught English. I went to the public school till I was in sixth grade.

We didn't know what discrimination was at one time, but when we went to school at public school, we knew. I know they used to call us squaws and big Indian, and, boy, we'd get mad. After a while the white kids wouldn't even bother. After the sixth grade, I went to Hayward. It was a boarding school. They furnished us food, and we stayed there nine months. Then we had permission to go back to the reservation till the end of vacation. Then in the fall they'd come after us.

We weren't allowed to speak Chippewa, but us girls used to speak Chippewa when we were alone. Anytime the employees heard us speak Chippewa, they'd punish us. Oh, they'd give us demerits. Then we couldn't go to town on Saturday. If we had more than five demerits we had to stay and work them off on Saturday afternoon. We had the military style there. We used to have to march to the dining hall and march back, all in formation; and we'd have to drill about fifteen minutes before we ate.

I remember when I was an officer there and we had to take these kids in and sign them in and take their names. And then we had to see that they were cleaned up and had their haircuts. Nobody was allowed to have long hair. The girls, too, their hair was cut short 'cause it was easy to keep clean.

For subjects we had English and geography. We never did have Indian history. Oh, we had some, but it was always bad about Indians, you know. Never anything good. That they were hostile and all that. And they had a farm on the Indian school, and they'd keep some of the children in the summer, to keep the farm and can.

Anyway, that was my schooling and how I learned to speak English.

Now my mother became Catholic when she married my dad. I have two other sisters. I was born February 2, 1909. And when I was a kid my dad used to tell us all about the Indian religion. He was no Indian himself, but he was raised by the Indians. He had full knowledge of the Indian way of life, and he could talk it, but still, he wasn't an Indian; he was a white man. He was adopted by the Indians and the one he claimed to be his mother had light hair and was light complected, and during the war with the Sioux, he said they were riding down the river and when they'd see him with his mother, they didn't bother them because they were so light. He had red hair. And the Sioux didn't bother them.

My dad used to work for the town. He drove a school wagon – a covered wagon.

I didn't think it was too bad back then because my father was a farmer and he had a good house. He kept things there, a lot of food. Oh, there was potatoes and cabbage and carrots and things like that you know, so we weren't too bad off. We never knew a day's poverty when we were kids.

And Indian children respected their elders. They never made fun of anyone. They were real good children at that time – well, they're still good children, but I mean they respected their elders in every way. We were told to respect our elders and not make fun of other people.

I remember a lot of happiness and a lot of rituals. In one, we went into

241

a wigwam. There was nothing going on in there, but boy you should see the pretty things they had up. Nice blankets and nice beadwork they had up in there around the inside of the wigwam. I don't know if they done this for people to see, but I sure thought it was pretty. They had beaded belts and everything up there. They had deerskins that were tanned. They had some kind of baskets where they used to keep their tobacco. There was great big beadwork that they put over their shoulders.

Another time I went to a wake and we stayed a couple nights there. They'd have great big water drums.

JOHN LAFAVE: They are hollow and they got water in there and they pound on them all night long and they tell Indian stories. They go around in a big circle. One tells a story, then another one, then another one.

MARY: We stayed there two nights and then they had the funeral. They have big feasts every night and they put a mat on the floor, and they eat on the floor. They have rice, and maybe deer meat and dumplings, Indian hominy.

JOHN: They never carry a body out through a door, always through a window and feet first. And when someone is buried you take all the clothes make a bundle and put it into the casket.

MARY: And they have a little pot for tea and a pot for something else. And that head beater tells the body which way to go, not to look back, and whenever you get to this river to go across it. It was really something to hear, how they chant these songs. It makes shivers go up your back and your hair stands on end. It's beautiful all right.

JOHN: At the grave, every fall they'd put something near it, like sugar. In the spring of the year they'd put sugar and, in the fall of the year they'd put wild rice and raisins and sometimes they'd put tobacco. A big bunch of boys would go and pick up the tobacco. The chief told me, "If you want that rice and things, go get it. That's what it's there for, to eat."

MARY: I remember a lot about those days.

My aunt used to go out to the sugarbush, used to make sugar. They had to go about four miles to get to the sugarbush. That's what they called it. And I know several times us girls went out there to help her to carry sap to those great big kettles they had. And they stirred these kettles to make their syrup.

They'd have to boil it a length of time before it can be syrup. They had to have so many gallons of that sap before it could make a gallon of syrup. It's a tedious job, but good if you have a lot of help. They'd go to every tree and empty it into the buckets and then they'd bring it over to the big kettles. Make a lot of friends that way.

You know, a lot of Indians, even though they're Catholic, still cling to their old ways. I think it's good. I think that in this day and age these Indians should know the good ways of living they had. Of course, the Indians always had good ways of living. They lived out in the open, never hardly stayed in the house. I don't know why some of the white people say the Indians are dirty. I don't think they were dirty. They had water! And I'm sure that if the Indians nowadays went back to some of their old ways, I think it would be better in some ways.

JOHN: If they don't follow it now, it'll die out anyway. Later on it will die off. Some has already.

Maple Sugaring

– James Martin

(From <u>A Long Time Ago Is Just Like Today</u>, published by Duluth Indian Education Committee in 1976)

I started sugaring when I was just knee-high to a grasshopper with my parents. That was in Sawyer. We used to live out by Deadfish Lake. There were a lot of maple trees about three miles south of Deadfish Lake, and my parents used to do a lot of tapping there. They didn't have a drill like people have now; they used axes for notches. They notched the tree, stuck a piece of oval-shaped iron underneath, and pound it in. That's how they made spouts. They were pretty good, but they lost a lot of sap. Sometimes that flat spout wasn't in far enough and they'd lose a lot of sap because it would leak out on either side of it. You start tapping trees when the trunk of the tree was bare – you know, when all the snow around it is melted. Even when you had snow 2 1/2, 3 feet deep. You wait till the trunk of the tree is bare. Then you tap it.

White people say that the sap will flow any time after an extended freeze. Then when it warms up to about 40 degrees again, it will flow. So that could even be in November and December.

Sometimes people say you should tap when the pussy willows come out but that's probably a little too late. Even when the buds start forming here now, we see that our trees stop flowing in the mornings. Then in about an hour and a half they start again, but after flowing for awhile, they stop again just that quick. Yes, I think when the pussy willows come out it's a little too late to tap any trees.

We used cast iron kettles when I was a boy. That one, way on the other side belongs to my wife. Her dad used to own it. Her dad died when he was 98 years old. Before him, his dad owned it; that was the grandfather. His grandfather owned it before his dad. Third generation. It has been passed on that long. I don't know how old that thing is. I don't know where those cast iron kettles come from. But they got them anyway. At Sawyer, we had six – my mother had four and her brother had two.

They used to get salt pork in barrels a long time ago. The Indian people were rationed out some salt pork through the government, and they used to ask for these barrels. We had eight barrels when my parents were maple sugaring and eight barrels we'd fill up right away. In the mornings the kettles would be all ready to start boiling by the time we'd get out there. They'd be all filled up. All we'd do was start the fire. As the kettles boil down, we'd empty maybe two or three barrels. My brothers, my dad, and my uncle were all out there gathering sap. They just kept on filling up the barrels as we emptied them. It's a long process and takes a lot of work. Sometimes you have a short season – I mean only ten or twelve days.

I cannot remember anyone using birchbark containers to boil sap. My wife has seen that done. I talked to a lady who saw it done in Sawyer. She's making some containers right now, and they're going to be trying it out next week. They've got the birch all ready, and she says she thinks she remembers how to fold it and seal it. You don't have to put any pitch on it. I guess because it will seal if you fold it the right way. She told me that birch would never burn as long as you had liquid inside of it. That's what my wife said too. She has told me quite a bit about it, but she doesn't know how to seal it. She has seen them do it, but she wouldn't know how to seal them herself. It has to be whole – a big tree.

They used spruce roots for handles. Some way they cured it so it had a bend on the handle. They hooked that birchbark to a low fire and the thing would start to boil without catching fire. The outside, the white part would catch, but the minute the fire contacts the liquid, it stops burning. They claim it was a slow process, but they made their sugar that way.

They used to have a feast after the first batch of sap was boiled down. Everybody is forbidden to even take a sip out of the can or whatever container you had. You were forbidden to even taste it.

So they waited until the first batch. When that was done, they made sugar. After that, they'd gather, and they'd pass out tobacco to different people. The spokesman told everyone what the tobacco was for. He said it was to give thanks to our Creator because He provided this from the trees so our Indian people could live on it and eat syrup or whatever they made from it. The people gave thanks to the Creator for that purpose. That's just what we did here. Then we had a feast. Everybody that was invited brought different stuff. When you did that, the following years, you'd get good results. The Creator answered our asking.

245

People gave thanks by putting food and tobacco out. We got tobacco before the white man entered this continent. We don't know where from – maybe from some leaves. We generally put out tobacco to give thanks to the Creator and that the Creator had provided this for us. We have done that ever since I can remember.

We make candy out of the syrup. We made some from the first batch. When the sap turns white, that's when it started to boil. We used to boil it down into maple syrup, sugar, whatever, and at that time, that's when we give our thanks. We put our tobacco out again. We give thanks to everything we use to process this syrup – even our kettles, pails, and containers. There's a lot of things we give thanks for. Even the snakes next to the sugar camp because there are a lot of snakes. We ask the Creator to remove these little creatures to other places. Our prayers were answered, and we didn't see any snakes around our camp anymore.

We give thanks that the Almighty has provided all that for us to use. I'm very much thankful. In my mind when I put that tobacco in the fire, I thought about the Creator. I might as well give Him the best of what I know about.

Interview with Cecelia Robinson (c. 1976)

– Carol Jaakola

Cecelia Robinson, a full-blood Chippewa Indian, was born March 11, 1895. I interviewed her one day after her 83rd birthday. She was born at a maple-sugar-making camp in a birch bark wigwam in an area called the "Ditchbanks" near Sawyer, Minnesota. This area is included in the Fond du Lac Reservation.

She lived most of her young life in a log cabin on Deadfish Lake also near Sawyer, with her grandfather, Wa-ba-no, and grandmother. When she spoke of her Grandfather, she said she had to add "bun" to the end of his name (Wa-ba-no-bun) since he was dead. She did not mention her grandmother's name or her parents names.

Cecelia was 17 years old when she married, first by Indian custom, then later "the Catholic way" with a state license. She bore seven children in her life time. Only a son and a daughter are now living. The daughter lives in Louisiana and the son lives in Deer River, Minnesota. Two children died as babies; one only 12 days old, from pneumonia, and another at 2 1/2, due to high fever from the measles. One son was killed in war and one son died last year, shortly after Cecelia had a stroke. She attributed his slowness of getting well to her grief.

She has more than 100 grandchildren, and has found it impossible to count her great and great-great grandchildren because of their many number and because she has little contact with many of them. We talked about how wonderful it would be for her to have a family reunion.

Cecelia lived in a very small tarpaper covered home, built by her husband in 1926, until about two or three years ago, when Community Action Program (CAP) workers completed a new home for her only a few steps from her old one. She wasn't very happy about moving into this new home, but finally seems to have become accustomed to it. She gets around well enough, appears quite healthy, except for a sore between her toes (which the doctor has suggested she go barefoot to heal) and does her own cooking. Someone comes to clean house for her twice a week. She says that is plenty.

Shortly before I got there, a neighbor, Herman Wise, had just brought her three waboose (rabbits). She said he was very good to her and watched out for her. She planned on making soup with some of the rabbit and would probably roast some. Seeing the frozen rabbits in a dish pan, feet up, reminded me of times of when I would try "snaring" rabbits when I was young. I never did have any luck that I can remember.

I was really amazed at how Cecelia told me she had given birth to all of her children. In the customary Indian way, poles were set up, one on each side of her, with one across that she would hold on to. There would be a hole dug underneath her with straw laid in it with clean cloths over it. She would then kneel over the hole and hang onto the pole while giving birth, with her mother at the back of her and the midwife at the front of her. She recalled, with a twinge of bashfulness, how she thought her first baby was going to pass through her navel to be born and how her mother had said later, "Oh, my daughter, I should have told you!"

Cecelia made wild rice up until three years ago, when a drunken partner tipped their canoe over and she fell head first into Perch Lake – one of the main wild rice lakes on the Fond du Lac Reservation.

Cecelia said, "It was a good thing I didn't drown, I fell in head first but I knew what to do," and described something like treading water. She said a man on shore was "just white" and Frank Whitebird, who was a committeeman for wild rice season, "he was scared."

She was quite proud to have in her possession a very old ice box, which is brown with age, and a picture of the Dionne quintuplets hanging on her living room wall which she considers antiques. She also has a picture of herself at about 20 years old in full Indian costume, with an eagle feather headdress made in 1913 by her brother.

Cecelia mentioned being on movie film in full dress at Sawyer one time, and has also danced in a program at a local television studio in Duluth. She belongs to the Chippewa religious group in the area and they have many ceremonies throughout the year. She says the religious ceremonies are held during the day and a big pan of many good foods is set out to eat three times a day. A pow-wow is held in the evening for all who wish to attend. A ceremony and a pow-wow will be held in April for one of the elders of the community, Mike Shabiash.

Cecelia sometimes gathered maple syrup sap all alone when she was young, while men gathered her wood. This season she is going to aid her nephew, Ralph Fairbanks, the Chippewa language instructor at both UMD and St. Scholastica, in making maple syrup. Some of her helpful tips in the boiling of sap include how to prevent it from boiling over with a balsam branch or strips of pork on the end of a stick, and also not to use poplar wood, as it makes too much ash.

Many people are interested in her storehouse of knowledge, many seek advice from her, ask of the old ways, how to pronounce Ojibwe words and like myself, a few document her historical life as one of our original Americans, the Anishinabe. She says there are no swear words in the Chippewa language. Animosh (dog) is about as bad as you can call someone. Coffee (mak e de mash kiki waaboo) is called "black medicine water" and is not very good for you. Also, a teaspoon of maple syrup can help one to fall asleep.

Cecelia says the Indians like the old customs and they are going back to the "old ways." The young people want to wear Indian things. She was pleased because an Indian boy who had visited her the day before wore a bandanna around his head, "Indian style." She likes to live according to the season. Maple sugar making in the spring, planting and harvesting in the summer, wild rice gathering in the fall and fishing through the ice in the winter. She recalled one time long ago when she was fishing through the ice and was pulling them out one after another, while others around her were getting nothing. She revealed to me she had been using rabbit bait and the others had been using pork. This was all very amusing to her. She probably never once thought of how important her role was in the acquiring of food.

Writers note: My apologies if I have in any way misinterpreted my interview with Cecelia. It was one of the greatest experiences of my life and [I] would like to visit her many more times. Many gaps in the story are not filled as it is very difficult in one interview.

Rupert Smith
–Elizabeth (Smith) Albert

My Dad, also known as Sonny, Butch, Smitty and Rupert Michael Smith, was born November 19, 1922, on the Red Cliff Reservation in Bayfield, Wisconsin to Jay Smith and Lizzie Bear.

He lived between Fond du Lac and Red Cliff, spending a lot of time with his grandparents, Michael (Moniang) Bear and Charlotte (Otchipwe) Bear. The Otchipwe name is now spelled Ojibwe or Ojibway. Moniang interpretation is " from Canada."

**Rupert Michael Smith
(Sonny, Butch, Smitty)**

I will refer to my dad as "Sonny" throughout this story because that's what his family and most of his friends called him. As a child, Sonny was the marble champ of the school and the reservation. He was a handsome child and well liked. His cousins were his best friends growing up and most of them remained his friends throughout his lifetime.

Sonny was sent to a Catholic Mission boarding school in Odanah, Wisconsin, when he was seven years old. His cousins were sent to Ashland. I doubt very much if his family had a car at that time, because he told me that he didn't see his family for a year. He said he was sent there because they told Grandma that the food was better and he would be better taken care of. He said they still ate oatmeal and corn soup and it sure wasn't as good as Grandma's. I am sure that the institutional care was not the same as a parent's love either. He got sick and was sent home, and he would never talk about what happened at that school.

In many pictures of him as a child, he is dressed in suits, black pants, and often is wearing a cap. There was an organization in Bayfield that sent clothes to the reservation for special occasions (must have been a Catholic organization). For his first communion picture, all of the children (Native American) are dressed in suits and white dresses.

He was well known for his charm and charisma, and he loved to dance

250

and loved music. He was very handsome (to me he was handsome his whole life; even at 74 he still flirted), he was a heart throb. Marge (Newago) Pascale told me that she had an awful crush on him as a teenager, but when she would see him coming down the road, she would jump in the ditch and hide because she was so shy.

Growing up, he was a hard worker. He cut grass every Saturday (an area the size of a field) in exchange for a movie ticket. One summer he painted three Catholic churches; Red Cliff, Bayfield and the Town of Russell. He continued to work hard, he always had a second job or went to night school. Even after he retired, he continued to work his second job. Many of you remember him calling bingo at the Fond du Lac Ojibway School, the gym, and at Black Bear Casino for 14 years.

Sonny graduated eighth grade from Red Cliff Missionary School, a school where I became the Tribal Head Start Director, 60 years later. He gave me his veteran's eagle feather to hang in the school for spiritual harmony and balance. This feather was presented to him at the Fond du Lac Veteran's Pow wow and he was very proud of it. Many of his friends came to the Dedication Ceremony, but he was unable to attend.

He went to Cloquet High School until 10th grade, then to Flandreau Indian Vocational School in Flandreau, South Dakota, where he graduated. He drove heavy equipment, making logging roads and whatever else was asked of him during the summers for the Civilian Conservation Corps.

Sonny played the trumpet. Some of you may remember him playing at night on the reservation when he was a teenager. He would sit out on a rock in the field and play. The next day, people would comment and ask if you heard him playing, and smile. He played the trumpet throughout his life, played in a band and he played taps at most of the veteran's funerals for the VFW-American Legion Honor Guard. When he couldn't reach the high notes anymore, they began to use tapes. He was a member of the American Legion Drum and Bugle Corps and was in many parades throughout the area.

Sonny joined the Army (1943-1946) and was in Company D, 544th Engineer Boat and Shore Regiment. He served in the Philippines, New Guinea, Northern Solomons, and Luzon during World War II. He was decorated with the Philippine Liberation Ribbon, a Bronze Star, a Bronze Arrowhead, Good

Conduct Medal and the Asiatic-Pacific Theater Service Ribbon.

He was a member of the Cloquet VFW 3979, past commander, All-State Quarter Master National aide-de-camp and District 8 Adjutant. He was an active member of the American Legion Post 262, Moose Lodge 1274, Disabled Veterans and Cooties.

He had a Cootie's Cap with hundreds of bugs on it. A person can't buy  his own; they have to be gifts from someone else. He was really proud of that cap, but someone stole it when he was at a convention in California. He got another hat and began to fill that one up too.

Sonny was very dedicated to the veterans. He drove the VFW van to St. Cloud and Minneapolis for years, bringing veterans to their medical appointments. He helped with the special events the VFW sponsored and was presented an award for Minnesota Volunteer of the Year for his continuous effort and community involvement. He was proud to have served his country and to be a veteran; he loved parades and marching bands.

When I was a small child, I remember a black trunk that was kept in the sun porch. It was filled with pictures, newspaper clippings, medals, and all the memorabilia that Dad had saved. The pictures were of beautiful Asian women. Dad said they were his "old girlfriends." A few months before he died, we were reminiscing and I asked him about that trunk and those old pictures. His wife Bertha said, "Oh he still has all of those pictures." I exclaimed, "Dad, really?" He looked at us and smiled, and he said, "Proof!"

Sonny also told a story of going to visit Simon Whitebird when he was overseas. Simon was in the hospital with malaria and he traveled to visit him. He said Simon was really surprised to see him. They both made it back from the war, but many of their friends didn't. Ironically, Simon died only a few months after Sonny died.

When Sonny was discharged from the Army, he married Mary Lou Leimer and they had five children. They were married for ten years. He went to night school and worked days at the Wood Conversion, later named Conwed, and known today as U.S.G. He worked there until he retired (38 years).

Sonny married Bertha Chiemileski (May 7, 1960) and moved back to Fond du Lac. They had two children. They purchased the "nurse's home" next to the Fond du Lac Indian Hospital. At that time the hospital was vacant and later demolished, but the house had been used by nurses that worked at the hospital. Sonny's mother, Lizzy, had worked at the hospital as a cook for many years. I was born in that hospital and was named after her. My grandmother was a hard worker. She had 10 children. Edward, the third child, died in infancy. My grandfather worked at the Wood Conversion, and retired from there. They had a garden and raised chickens, ducks and pigs. Often on Sunday, Grandpa would kill a chicken and we would have it for dinner. It was fun to pull on the tendons of the chicken feet and watch them turn into claws!

We attended the Holy Family Church and I remember sitting in the choir loft on many Sundays. Dave Savage rang the church bells. There is no other singing like the Indian women singing Catholic songs with an Indian accent; it was almost like wailing. Josephine Thompson, Mary Savage, Stella Morrissette, Betty Gurno and others sang, while Grandma played the organ and sang. My uncle, Roger Smith, had a habit of pulling chairs out from under people before they sat down, so there was always laughter in the choir loft and lots of noise.

Janie Savage always teased me because my mother made us wear these brimmed hats to church around Easter, so of course my two sisters and I really stood out! Often I would forget to bring a scarf, but Grandma always had an extra veil in her pocket. Summers we went to Catechism in an old building near the church. Nuns would come, and we made our first confessions, communions, and confirmations. It was also a great time to have fun with relatives and friends. Spitballs and bobby-pin snapping! I spent a lot of summers at Grandma and Grandpa's, but lived in town. The Holy Family Church was a big part of my grandma's life; she cleaned for the priests, cooked for them, and they boarded horses in my grandparent's front yard (field). She even had 8″x 10″ pictures of the priests hanging in the living room – Father Clements and Father Jude. I don't remember anything Indian on the walls, but there were crucifixes in every room except the kitchen. She also had beautiful peonies and other flowers in her yard, and big trees; a special huge weeping willow.

The St. Louis River was behind her house and we went to the "rock" and fished, went in the woods and peeled poplar trees, and picked hazel nuts and put them in a sock and hit them against a big rock to get the pickers off of them. It was great staying at Grandma's house.

One of the Ojibwe traditions that I really miss is the New Year's Day tradition of going from house to house to make amends, start the new year out with friends and family, to socialize and renew friendships. My grandma always baked lemon meringue pies, tarts, homemade bread, and she had little cups of candy for the kids. Everyone knew who would be home with the coffee and tea on and who would be going house to house. There were a few that would give you kisses – remember Alice Plug [Alice Payquette]? I recollect jumping under the covers with a cousin of mine to hide, but she found us anyway!

Sonny loved to fish and deer hunt; as he got older, his sons, brothers and nephews would put him in a stand and drive the deer to him. They also brought him venison when he wasn't able to hunt anymore. I asked him what it was like during the depression. He said that Grandpa stood in line for rations and he remembered that even rabbits were scarce at that time. He also told me that they lived in almost every house on the reservation. People would move away for awhile and they would move into their house. When the people came back, they would find another house that was vacant or the family was moving out.

He and Bertha riced together for over 30 years. They finished it and were known for their excellent rice. They took pride in their garden and had a beautiful yard. They canned, pickled and froze the things they grew. They loved to sit on the front porch and listen to the birds and sounds of nature and to visit with family and friends. He loved storytelling and had a wonderful sense of humor. He always had a joke to share.

I never heard my dad say a bad thing about anyone. He was a very proud man and he had every right to be. He worked hard, enjoyed his grand-children and was a good husband. He was loved by his family and his friends. We really miss him and we know that he is with the Creator and probably telling Him stories!

Rupert Smith

(Re-printed from Nah-Gah-Chi-Wa-Nong Di-Bah-Ji-Mo-Win-Nan)

A Profile of Fred Pellerin
FDL Veteran of D-Day Invasion, Battle of the Bulge, will be on hand for Veteran's Pow-Wow
– by Frank Thompson, with Michael LeGarde

Like communities around the United States, the Fond du Lac Reservation will honor its World War II veterans this summer at a Pow-wow planned for July 30 and 31 on the grounds adjacent to the Fond du Lac gymnasium. Those being honored in person will be all surviving Fond du Lac members who saw service in the U.S. armed forces during World War II. Those members who gave their lives in that war or who have subsequently passed away will also be honored through remembrance and memorial.

One of those former servicemen who'll be on hand for the July Pow-wow will be Fred Pellerin. The highly decorated former combat soldier spent three years in the army in Europe after being drafted at age 19. Fighting as a non-commissioned officer with a respected Airborne Division, Pellerin, now 71, was awarded the coveted Bronze Star with three battle stars and a Purple Heart.

Action, the former graduate of the Flandreau Indian School says he saw plenty, from his participation in the D-Day Invasion, 50 years ago this month, to his front line position during the historic Battle of the Bulge, the desperation move of Hitler's army in the closing months of the war. Pellerin was part of the airborne parachute drop behind the Normandy lines in the French countryside on D-Day, June 6, 1944.

He was later wounded when he took part in the drop of the 101st Airborne's famed "Screaming Eagles" attempt to rescue the American troops in Bastogne when they were surrounded by advancing German troops. That was the Third Reich's surprising, but hopeless, effort of Christmas 1944 to drive a wedge in the Allied lines that came to be known in history as the Battle of the Bulge.

The wounded Pellerin was shipped to England to recover and he was there when the war in Europe was declared over by President Harry S. Truman in May 1945. He ended his service days in Washington D.C. before being mustered out and back to civilian life.

257

With his combat jumps behind him and five campaign ribbons to his credit, Pellerin returned to build a new life in post-war America. However, he didn't turn his back on those wartime experiences that had done so much to shape his life as a young man. He became a life member of the Disabled Veterans of America and a life member of the American Legion.

While Fred Pellerin has never regretted his being in the U.S. Army during those war years, he does recall that it wasn't his first choice. At the time, Pellerin had filled out the papers necessary for enlisting in the U.S. Navy, but was too slow in getting the naval papers signed. Before he knew it, he had been drafted into the army.

(Re-printed from Nah-Gah-Chi-Wa-Nong Di-Bah-Ji-Mo-Win-Nan, 1994)
WWII Veteran, Rob Northrup:
"My biggest fear was being strafed by enemy aircraft..."

In Anishinabeg society, as well as other tribal societies, the warrior has always been held in high esteem. They were the ones who risked their lives so that others may live. In more recent history, the warriors have fought on the side of the United States.

One warrior, Robert "Rob" Northrup, served in the 835th Combat Engineering Unit during World War II. Having just turned 75, Northrup looks back some to years ago when he was in another place, in another time, apart from the world he knew back home.

"I have been through many different experiences," said Northrup who now resides at the Fond du Lac Elder's Complex. "I was in a convoy that went by the great pyramids in Egypt and I had wanted to take some pictures and send them home, but they (security forces) wouldn't allow that."

Having seen the pyramids, he still wonders how an ancient civilization could accomplish such a feat without modern construction equipment. The wonderment is natural since his military unit was in charge of building bridges, command posts and other needed structures once the infantry secured captured territory.

In addition to meeting construction needs, Northrup's unit also had the task of making sure the area was clear of land mines, booby traps, and ammunition that retreating forces had left behind. The work was dangerous and time consuming. And if land mines weren't troublesome enough, there was also the threat of being shot by attacking aircraft.

"A buddy and myself were cleaning up, digging out land mines, that type of thing. It took us three hours to go two blocks, so you really had to concentrate on what you were doing. My buddy tripped a wire and was killed instantly." Northrup sadly explained. "My biggest fear, however, was being strafed by enemy aircraft because a lot of the work was done out in the open, making you an open target. I lost several friends to both land mines and enemy aircraft."

Northrup stated that he was lucky to survive the war, as were most of his brothers (now deceased) who also served in the armed forces. Four of five

259

Northrup brothers saw action in the European Theater of Operations. Of those, it was Stanley who was the one to suffer a minor, nonlethal, wound.

For the 32 months that he served overseas, Northrup received three commendations – Battle Stars – for his participation in armed confrontations with the opposition in battle zones. He took part in the Anzio Beach landing, one of the biggest offensives at the beginning of WWII. He also served in the North African campaign, where the engineering unit had to be ever watchful for the "Desert Fox," German Field Marshall Erwin Rommel, notorious for his direction of tank warfare units in the African theater.

With the defeat of the Nazis, and with the surrender of the Japanese, Northrup's next service station was Italy, and it was there that he ran into someone he knew from home – Adam Barney.

"I ran into Adam Barney right after the end of the war," Northrup fondly remembered. "He was the only guy I knew and saw that was from back home while I was overseas. I was really surprised and glad to see him. Needless to say, after his platoon was dismissed, we went and celebrated the end of the war and also the chance meeting of two friends."

Northrup, originally from Sawyer, is one of 25 surviving veterans from Fond du Lac who served overseas during WWII. This July he will be among those who will be honored for their wartime service at the First Annual Fond du Lac WWII Veteran's Pow-wow.

(Re-printed from Nah-Gah-Chi-Wa-Nong Di-Bah-Ji-Mo-Win-Nan, 1994)

"Gooder Man"

If you heard someone talking about the "Gooder Man," who is the first person who comes to mind?

Your only answer would have to be Simon Whitebird, an elder of the Fond du Lac Reservation, who will be one of the 25 World War II veterans to be honored at the WWII Veteran's Pow-wow at the end of July. Simon, 85, currently resides at the Elder's Complex on the Reservation.

A man known for his quick and very funny sense of humor, there is another side of the Elder that many don't realize: he is a decorated WWII veteran.

Simon "Gooderman" Whitebird

Whitebird went through boot camp at Fort Leonard, Missouri in the 6th Division, 63rd Infantry. After marching 750 miles through North Carolina, Georgia, and South Carolina, he was told to go home because he was "too old and couldn't keep up with the younger guys." He was 32 years old at the time.

So, home to the Fond du Lac Reservation he went. It was here, while having a beer, talking with friends, that he heard of the news of Pearl Harbor. It was soon after that he received his orders to report back to his old outfit, the one from which he was dismissed for being too old. On his return to his outfit, he found his old bunk ready and made and awaiting his return.

It was at Camp Mc Coy, Wisconsin, where his division received further training, and once that was over, more training at Palm Springs, California, where they received instruction in desert fighting techniques. Whitebird and his fellow corpsmen were originally to be shipped to Africa, but by the time they finished with the required training, the war in Africa was brought under control. The Division was then shipped to Hawaii on the U.S.S. Henry Berg, a converted cargo ship that managed a speed of 15 knots. The reason they went to Hawaii was for more training, this time for jungle training.

From Hawaii, the division's campaign began in New Guinea and the Philippines, where the fighting was intense. While some of his buddies got some R & R, Whitebird was point man on patrol. It was in the island jungles that Whitebird caught a case of malaria that put him in the hospital for a short while. The hospital was an open-air stadium, and while he was recuperating, he had a visit from Rupert Smith, who is also from Fond du Lac.

Once he was given a clean bill of health, Whitebird was soon returned to his outfit and resumed fighting, which by this time was fierce and constantly moving. It was a defining moment for Whitebird as he suffered being shot in the leg, but his outfit was on the advance so he never bothered to see how badly wounded he was. A shot in the leg, malaria, a case of elephantiasis, eating "C" rations for the duration, and, to top it off, "jungle rot," would take their toll on most people, but Whitebird kept going.

Some of his most vivid memories are Japanese aircraft strafing his outfit. He describes how they would go into their dives and then spray the ground with bullets. He also described a few instances when American fighters were able to down enemy aircraft as he watched them crash into the sea.

Whitebird may have been a long way from home, but he ran into others from the Cloquet area (besides the already mentioned Rupert Smith). He met up with two members of the Ecklund family and a member of the Joseph family who were all assigned to the artillery, and he also saw an old friend from Grand Portage, Lex Porter. He may have been overseas, but he met enough people to shrink the distance between the continents.

He laughs while he describes that all they had to wear while overseas were the fatigues that they were shipped out in. It wasn't until two years after he was discharged that he received a military dress uniform.

As a result of his battle experience (s), Whitebird received several commendations. He is especially proud of his Combat Infantry Badge, the two Battle Stars that are attached to his Asiatic Pacific Campaign Ribbon and another Battle Star for another campaign. He also received the Bronze Star and a Good Conduct Medal, but it wasn't until ten years after his discharge that he was awarded those.

He also mentioned something about a "Ruptured Duck."

The Gooder Man, Simon Whitebird, honored Elder of Fond du Lac, had only this to say, summing up his experiences, "Holy miracula!"

Les Northrup
– Brenda Pollak

Today is Thursday. March 5, 1992, and I (Brenda Pollack) am talking with Les Northrup on the Relocation Program.

"My name is Leslie Gerald Northrup, Sr., born June 26, 1937 in the Fond du Lac Indian Public Health Service Hospital. I lived on the Reservation from 1937-41, and then moved to town (Cloquet) during the war. In 1946-49 moved back to the Reservation. In 1949, I moved to Duluth and went back and forth to Cloquet schools. Completed the ninth grade in Duluth, at which time I quit school in 1953 and did odd jobs, bowling alley, golf course, delivered telegrams, any job I could do. In 1955, I got a job in construction at Silver Bay, Minnesota, putting in the taconite plant. I worked there for two years, until the job was finished and I got laid off. After that, I went to work for Western Electric in Duluth, Minnesota doing electrical wiring, soldering, solder inspecting, reading blue prints and adjusting relays for telephones. This gave me good experience in electrical assembly work. I worked there from 1957-58 until I was laid off, went back to Cloquet and lived at the nurses' cottage, next to the Indian Public Health Services Hospital on the Fond du Lac Reservation."

Reservation, the summer of 1958

"At this time, my brother Darwin Bishop, found out about the relocation program and went out to Oakland, California. In about August, he called and told me there was so much work out there that you can quit one job today and go on another one tomorrow. So he said to come out on relocation. I could go to Oakland, San Francisco or San Jose. I decided to go to San Jose, which is 45 miles south of Oakland and about the same distance from San Francisco. At that time, my wife and two daughters went to Sacramento, California to be with their grandmother (my wife's mother). I was going to night school and had taken the test to get my high school diploma. I had also taken all the manual dexterity and another test for aptitude in math, writing and science. The employment service did the testing, and passing qualified me to go on relocation, I guess. So about January 1959, my wife and two children came back to Cloquet."

When checking into relocation in Cloquet, Les talked to Pete DeFoe, Sr., who gave him the number for Rex Mayotte, the relocation officer in Cass

Lake, Minnesota. He came down and filled out the applications at Les' home with him. Les went off to San Jose. With help from a social worker, his wife and children got a big apartment for $125 a month, which he noted was quite a bit of money in 1959. He later moved to a less expensive ($65 a month) apartment. He was working full time.

The Bureau of Indian Affairs (BIA) gave him one month rent and two weeks worth of groceries. He doesn't recall getting any clothing or safety clothes, etc. The BIA had counselors available to help you find jobs, take the bus, etc., but he didn't use them; he did things on his own. Les worked at the Container Corporation of America in Santa Clara for about a month, and then took a job with Hiller Aircraft.

In the meantime, he had contacted his parents and all his relatives back in Cloquet and told them about all the opportunities for work in California and encouraged them to come. He met someone from the apartments who worked for the Palo Alto Volkswagen Garage and told him what a good mechanic his father was. The fellow said he would hire him if he came out. Another friend knew the personnel director from Locke and said they'd hire his mother. His sister, Clara Northrup, (who married Vern Skoglund), had typing skills, had graduated from high school and UMD, and had an Elementary Education degree. She worked for the State Employment Service for four or five years. She died from cancer in 1971.

His parents were living in Duluth at the time Les approached them about relocating, and they were both unemployed (not too many people were employed at the time).

His dad, mother, and Uncle Mike came out on relocation and he had jobs waiting for all of them. They all got money to travel because they came out on the relocation program.

He indicated that he was aware of some other Indians who weren't able to make it on their own for various reasons, such as inability to read, and they were sent back home.

He went to the Oakland Indian Center and saw Indians: Sioux, Arizona Indians, Navaho, some from the western states and a lot of Alaskan Indians. There were other Indian centers in San Francisco and he thinks also in San Jose. They held cultural events: pow-wows and meetings and politicing. In San

Francisco he was asked to apply for one of the directorships. He was aware they were going through political hassles and he refused, saying he had to work and go to school, and would rather do that.

In 1960 he moved back to Duluth with his two daughters, Mary and Charlotte and moved from there to Cleveland, Ohio in 1961. He was on unemployment while in Duluth. He worked in Cleveland almost a year. It was very different from life in California: it was a very rough area, mostly blacks and whites. By this time his brother Darwin was living up around San Jose. He suggested Les come back out there and he would have a job waiting for him.

In Cleveland, he obtained employment on his own. He had gone there with Elwin Benton and Les' two daughters, because his cousins, Charlie (Chuck) Diver, Don Diver, and "Little" Dick Diver were there. He bought a 1949 Ford for $35, took out the back seat to make room for a mattress and clothes, and drove to Cleveland. He got a job right away and Elwin was babysitting for him until he got a job. Gene Thompson lived there also, and Les chummed around with him.

Later, young Billy Diver and Dick Diver came and they used to go to the bars together. It was rough. People carried guns and Les used to get into a lot of fights. He decided he better get out of Cleveland before he got killed or put in jail or hurt somebody. He came back to Cloquet with his two daughters.

His brother Darwin called from California and had another job for him at an aircraft place about 15-20 miles from his old job. He moved in with his brother and later moved into a bungalow for about six months and later bought a house in Sunnyville, California where his brother lived from 1962-65.

When the aircraft plant closed down Les decided to go back to school. He went to the BIA Office and told them he was laid off and would like to go to school. He was tested again and the man who tested him had lots of confidence in Les. He said that Les knew a lot and had at least a ninth grade education, and high school equivalency.

Relocation was a big deal. It gave Les a lot of opportunities and got him started. This is a program that he would like to see come back and be utilized by Indian people. He realizes a lot of people don't like it because it takes Indians off the reservations and puts them in strange cities. But he feels that if a person doesn't have the ability to function off the reservation or away from home, and can't hack being on his own, then he shouldn't go.

B.P.: "Do you think it's changed now, with more Indian people going on to further their education, and those who go to live off the reservations becoming more successful because of the opportunities that exist today that didn't back prior to relocation?"

L.N.: Back in 1963 or '64 up until 1975, his sister Clara was one of only two Indians in the state of Minnesota to graduate from a college (UMD). In his immediate family she was the first to graduate, then Les, and two of his daughters.

Education is advantageous to Indian people. When you go to another state they recognize you as having work ethics, higher education, more motivation and being hardier people. He, as an Indian, was classified like that. A lot of other Indians he met weren't as assertive, aggressive and extroverted as he was. He was always proud to be an Indian and never denied being an Indian. He even fought the agencies and the Police Department in Duluth on treatment of Indians (brutality, housing, and general treatment).

B.P.: "Were you lonesome when you moved out to California?"

L.N.: "Well, not totally lonesome, because my brother Darwin lived out there and I went to see him every weekend." This was prior to his parents coming out. His family came out and they all were lined up with jobs, (father, mother, sister and Uncle Mike).

After working, for several weeks, Les suggested that his family go to the BIA because they would be given a month's rent and food for two weeks, and clothes. They went to the San Jose office, but the man at the Bureau was angry because he said they were to have been there two or three weeks ago. He told them that they were supposed to come for orientation to teach them how to use the phone and these sort of things. Les's dad got angry at him and stated they knew how to use the phone, take a bus, and drive, and that they were working and had only come to get their subsistence. The man from the Bureau was amazed that they were all working and had done this on their own. Les's father was very offended because the man was treating them like kids. They did receive their subsistence. Bureau of Indian Affairs procedure was for people on relocation to report to them and they would send a message back to the reservation saying that you had arrived. Prior to leaving the reservation, word was sent to the city you were relocating to that they knew you were coming and they would be waiting for you to arrive. They had been expecting his family and were upset initially.

Les stayed out there until the end of the 1960's. He moved back to the Cloquet area for a while, later returning to California for additional training. But in the end, he came back and stayed.

The decision to move back home came about on a Sunday afternoon when they were sitting around having a few beers and someone just brought up the idea of going home, and that's all it took. He doesn't recall who said it, and they gave their two week notices at work. By this time his uncle Billy Diver had come out also, so coming back there was a caravan of about four cars.

His second time on relocation to California was for training. He had no problems when he moved back out there in 1967. Soon after his training he moved back to the Cloquet area, where he worked for the forestry service, then the Reservation.

Les feels relocation gave him a good idea of what was going on in other parts of the country and a greater insight of the importance of education, along with all the work experience he gained. He feels he could find a job any place, from assembly work to teaching. Moreover, he felt the experience he gained from working different jobs gave him the freedom to move back and forth. It really opened the doors. In 1973-75 he went to school full time. In 1978 he graduated from college with a degree in teaching history. He didn't want to be poor like he was growing up as a kid. He didn't want his kids to have to live like that. Everyone in his family was ambitious, no one was lazy.

The Christmas of 1927

(As told to Bonnie Wallace by her mother, Delia Moreland, and aunt Pat Novacinski.)

Our stockings were always filled by Santa, but in those days we were given oranges, apples, nuts, ribbon candy and other hard candies. Oranges were a very special treat.

Ma (Liz DuFault) would put about 15 candles on the tree and would call everyone into the big room to see the candles lit. It was a sight. The whole tree would just light up. It was beautiful, but Ma only kept them lit for a short time. I would say, "Oh, ma that is so pretty, is Santa going to come?" Ma and Pa (Pete DuFault) would assure us "that you've all been pretty good." When ma would blow out the candles it would be smoky and blue in the room. No presents were ever put under the tree before Christmas morning and when our parents said "go to bed," we went to bed. When Pa talked that was the law.

There were two bedrooms upstairs and one downstairs in our house in Sawyer. Prayers were said every night. Ma would sit in a chair and we would all kneel down by her. We'd all say goodnight, don't let the bedbugs bite. As poor as we were though, our stockings were always filled.

Pat said: "One year Delia was the only one to hang her stocking and all she got was a big switch. She cried and cried to Pa. 'Why? Why didn't I get oranges, apples, nuts and candy?' Pa laughed and held her, 'Oh my girl, it isn't Christmas, it's the 4th of July.' I think Delia was just too young to realize the difference in holidays. In the end, it was me who put the old willow stick in her stocking."

Delia laughed: "Yeah, I felt mad, sad and glad, all at the same time!"

Growing up in Sawyer, "Kidsplay"

(As told to Bonnie Wallace by her mother, Delia Moreland, and aunt, Pat Novacinski.)

Ma and Pa had the post office and grocery store in Sawyer and it was connected right to our house. Ma was actually a federal employee. When she and Pa would leave in the morning, she would hide all the scissors, matches or anything that us kids might get into. One morning after we had finished eating our pancakes and Ma and Pa left to work in the post office and store, our brother Bob and sister Esther sat Pat, who was just the baby, in the middle of the kitchen table and began pouring cups of syrup over her little head. They were having all kinds of fun, including Pat, even though they made a big mess. Boy, when Pa and Ma came home and saw that they were really mad. It took a long time to clean up not only Pat, but also the kitchen, as there was syrup everywhere.

One other time they did the same thing to Pat, only with flour. God, poor Pat was just coughing and gasping for breath, all the while Bob and Esther thought it was great fun.

Jennie Ding Dong Bell

– Told by Delia and Pat

When Delia was born in the old house in Sawyer, Grandma Scott helped deliver her. Old Lady Isaacson said when Delia was born she let everyone know by crying so loud you could hear it for miles around. Anyway, Pa said to the three kids, Pat, Bob and Esther, "Come upstairs to see and meet your new baby sister." She was so tiny. Pa asked the three kids, "What would you like to name her?"

Well, Ma and Pa used to have this old cow named Jennie with a bell tied around her neck. The poor old cow got hit by a train and died and Pat (age four at the time) seemed to take it the hardest. She insisted Ma and Pa name the new baby, Jennie Ding Dong Bell. To this day (summer 1997), Delia still shares this story with her kids and they tease her to no end calling her Jennie Ding Dong Bell. What if Ma and Pa really would have named her that?

As told to Bonnie Wallace
— by her mother, Delia Moreland, Summer 1997.

Ma used to always tell us kids to not drink her vinegar but, boy, as soon as her back was turned we'd make our own pop. We'd mix vinegar, water and sugar...then add baking soda and it would fizz, just like soda pop. Boy, was that a treat.

Delia's Mirage

I was about 8 years old when I saw the whole town of Sawyer in the sky. I remember it being a very bright, cold winter day, not a cloud in the sky. Pa was outside cutting wood and most of the kids were outside playing and that's where I wanted to be. But Ma had different plans for me. She was making me a dress and I had to stay in.

I was waiting for Ma to call me to try it on when I looked outside the window, and there was the whole town of Sawyer in the sky. Ma called for me to come try on the dress, but I was frozen to that spot. Believe me, I could see the post office, store, the old school, kids playing, even Pa cutting wood.

Ma kept calling for me and I finally said to her, "Ma come quick, I can see the whole town of Sawyer in the sky." She didn't come right away, and by the time she did get to the window the whole thing was gone.

It was like Ma didn't believe me and neither did anyone else. But I know what I saw, and I stuck to my story, even to this day. Well, many years later when I was going to Carlton School, Harry Newby was our science teacher and we were talking about mirages. When he explained what they were, I told him my story. It finally felt like someone believed me and there was an explanation after all.

Delia Moreland's parents

Ma was 20 years younger than Pa, and it was an arranged marriage. They were married when she was 16 and Pa died when he was 74, so they were married for 38 years. Ma was a widow at age 54, and years later she did remarry.

During her marriage to Pa, he was always encouraging and supportive of her going off on all these trips alone. Sometimes she would hitchhike to places far away, and us kids were always worried. We wondered why Pa would just let her go like that. He told us, "Let your mom go. She never had any fun because we married when she was so young. I've had all my fun, so it's your

272

mom's turn. Don't be mad at her."

When I think about that today, Pa was really ahead of his time. He might have been considered a "feminist" by today's standards. He was really supportive of women and treated all women with great respect. He was always polite.

Delia's story about her "bouquet"

In our day there wasn't much talk about a woman's time of the month. Ma never really talked to us about it either, and when it arrived she would just tell us, "You finally got your bouquet of flowers." She said, "If your brother's clothes are on the floor, don't step over them, go around them. Stay away from boys." She kept us pretty isolated.

She told me how Grandma Lyons made a wigwam way out on their property every berry picking season, she would put her daughter(s) in there and feed them only soup for about a week. All we were told is that Indians believed you had to isolate the girl, especially if it was her first "bouquet."

Leo Rabideaux

– Michael Rabideaux

In the oral tradition of the American Indian, storytelling continues to preserve and transmit our culture and values. This in itself is astonishing when considering all the influences placed upon generations of American Indians. Elders have stories to share that do reveal tribal and family history, and their personal contributions to the larger society. It is through these stories/collected memories that we too develop a greater appreciation and respect.

Leo Francis Rabideaux was born in 1927 at the Fond du Lac Indian Hospital located on the Fond du Lac Reservation. He was the youngest of three children, having a brother Clifton and a sister Genevieve. Leo was raised primarily by his grandfather John Whitebird, (FDL enrollee) and grandmother Michelle Petite, (Bad River enrollee) because his mother Stella Rabideaux worked full-time as a nurse for Dr. Monserud at the Fond du Lac Hospital. Leo's father, Alec Rabideaux, had died when Leo was four or five years of age. Grandfather and Grandmother had five children including Stella (Leo's mother), Jenny, Frank, Leo and Felix. Stella and Leo are the only remaining children living. Stella was remarried to Ed Morrissette and had two more children Ed and Robert. At that time Leo moved back to live with his parents.

Leo attended school in Cloquet, and recalls vividly how he was sent home the first day of school because he could not speak or understand English. His grandfather and grandmother spoke no English and spoke only Ojibwe. The task of teaching English to Leo became the responsibility of his Uncle Leo and his wife Mary, who were living with the grandparents as well. It took two years for Leo to learn English. As a result, he soon forgot most of his first language, Ojibwe.

Many Fond du Lac Indians attended school in Cloquet at either Leach or Jefferson Schools. A county nurse made sure that kids went to school by visiting homes on the Reservation and asking parents/grandparents why their kids weren't in school. Sometimes kids didn't have clothing, so in some cases the nurse would provide clothing. But many of the Fond du Lac families did make their own clothing from World War I Army fatigues. It was during this time that most of the Reservation kids looked like "Army guys."

Leo remembers his experience as positive during his school days in

Cloquet. One time he was sent to Jefferson, and because he didn't want to attend school there, he walked back to Leach. The school allowed him to make this decision (grade 5). Most of this had to do with the fact that he was a police-boy. In fact, he was a police boy captain who supervised other young police boys. Police boys wore badges, and worked as crossing guards among other duties. Each year, the police boys would be taken to Jay Cooke State Park for a picnic to reward them for their service. At one such gathering, Leo won the annual peanut pick-up contest. It's an event where a hole is made in the bottom of a large burlap peanut bag, and then the bag is dragged across the ground. Kids scramble in the wake to gather as many peanuts as possible.

As a little guy, ("little guy" is a term used often by Leo; in fact, his nickname is Bitty, meaning "little guy"), Leo remembers well the sugar bush, ricing, hunting and fishing, working in the gardens, and gathering berries. He remembers fondly working with his grandfather and grandmother for weeks in the ricing and sugar bush camps.

He remembers well the first trip he made to East Lake to help his grandparents harvest rice.

Toward evening when everyone was quitting for the day, he noticed campfires beginning to burn across the lake. The flames from the fires sparkled against the water and soon he heard the drums begin to echo. It seemed the drums were talking to one another and then the campfires began to go out, being replaced by one large fire that flared-up and the drums were suddenly beating at one fire. His grandmother walked with him to the fire, and he fell asleep to the beating drums. Throughout the night he remembers hearing owls hooting in the distance; his grandmother would smile, telling him that they were watching him to make sure he fell asleep.

Leo also remembers how his grandparents gathered maple sugar sap near the ditchbanks. At one sugar bush camp, he remembers walking to the creek to get a pail of water for his grandmother. Much to his surprise, a large moose was standing in the creekbed. He was so excited that he raced back to the camp and attempted to tell his Uncle Leo what he had seen, but he was so excited he could barely speak. Uncle Leo went back to the creek and soon Leo heard a couple of shots. The moose was big, so Uncle Leo had to get help to get it out of the creek. Everyone who helped get the moose out enjoyed a feast for many days.

Grandfather and Grandmother were very self-sufficient. They didn't need many goods from the store, other than flour, baking soda, salt, sugar, and tobacco. The land provided what they needed. They worked a garden that produced potatoes, cabbage, onions and greens. Grandfather often hunted the woods for game, including rabbit, partridge, and deer. Leo, too, learned how to hunt from his grandfather. When Grandfather needed something from the store he would walk with a backpack to the Co-op store located in Cloquet. Considering the grandparents lived near the old village, it was quite a walk.

During his teenage years on the Reservation, Leo worked for two years on the St. Louis River as a motorboat operator. His job was to run up the river from Cloquet and meet the men who were raising deadhead logs from the bottom of the river. The logs, which had been in the river for about two or three years, were then towed down to Cloquet to a planing camp. For Leo, it was exciting work because the level of the river would sometimes rise quickly, making navigation extremely difficult in the swirling currents. Many of the loggers did not want the motorboat job because they felt it was too dangerous.

In 1944, when he was 17 years old, Leo left school, enlisted in the Navy, and held rank in the Landing Ship Tanks Division. He was stationed in the Pacific, and served on the USS George Clymer. After serving two years in the armed service, he was honorably discharged. He returned to Cloquet High School and graduated in 1947. While in high school, he played in the High School Band and the City Marching Band.

After high school Leo attended the university located in Duluth, Minnesota, and when his GI bill ran out he attended the Electronic Radio and Technical Institute in Minneapolis. After one year he was offered a job as a telegrapher for the Omaha Railroad in 1948. At that time he married and moved to Spooner, Wisconsin.

Leo relocated to Whitefish, Montana, to work with the Great Northern Railroad. From 1949 through 1951 he moved twice more due to railroad mergers, relocating to Garret, Indiana, and San Antonio, Texas. Not only were the railroads merging, but they were also undergoing a change in technology – teletypes and computers were replacing telegraphers.

An automobile injury hospitalized Leo for about two years in 1959 and

1960. After he got out of the hospital he returned to the Reservation. He began working on the Great Lakes as a WheelMaster who navigated a ship. From 1963 to 1968 he worked on the merchant marine ships that carried ammunition from North Carolina to the armed services stationed in Vietnam. Finally, in 1968, he returned to San Antonio, Texas, and worked as a railyard tower operator until 1974 when he retired from the railroad.

Leo has since moved back to the Fond du Lac Reservation and lives at the Elders Complex located in the Cloquet District. The five children he had with his wife Barbara (deceased) live in New York, Australia, and in the Wrenshall, Minnesota area. He is the grandfather of seven children.

[From Helen Carlson, Linda LeGarde Grover and Daniel W. Anderson, with the assistance of Bonnie Cusick, <u>A Childhood in Minnesota, Exploring the Lives of Ojibwe and Immigrant Families, 1880s - 1920s</u>. A. M. Chisholm Museum, Duluth Minnesota 1994. A description of several Fond du Lac families' lives.]

Where Did Families Live?

Clem Beargrease: "We had birch bark houses, wigwams. You used cedar branches and bent them like this. You put birch bark over this, and it didn't leak a bit. We had a hole in the middle for a fire. It could be forty degrees below zero outside but it was nice and warm inside. We heated rocks in the fire and took them to sleep with us. It kept everyone warm. Everybody lived in the village together."

Joseph Naganub, Jr.: In Fond du Lac village, "There were 37 comfortable frame dwelling houses in said village and upon this land, several of them costing as much as five hundred dollars. I have lived in a comfortable house thereon all of my life as did my father and father's family; that my house as it now stands was built in 1888 of pine lumber from the mills in Cloquet and at a cost of some $400.00; that the house is one-and-one-half-stories high, 16 by 21 feet, divided into two rooms below and one above; that the house is comfortably furnished and represents my earnings for life, and the same could not be moved without large expense. There are many other houses in the Indian village better than mine and better furnished, some of them with carpets upon the floor, an organ and a sewing machine. It would be a great hardship and great expense and loss as well to remove the buildings constituting this village. Many of the villagers, in addition to comfortable houses, have enclosures of cultivated ground running from one-half to two acres of land, with outbuildings, wells, cellars, shade trees, etc. fenced in with good fences, and from which a large amount of their support is derived. All the Indians in said village, at least 150 in number, have made their homes there, built houses and improved their homes with the full belief that the tract of land on which the village is built had been used and would be secured to them free from all molestation, and that they would never be disturbed in their settlements."

Source: Words of Joseph Naganab, Jr., Fond du Lac, from a 1897 court case related to allotment issues (NAC).

Top: John Godfrey, John Bassett
Bottom: Louie Godfrey

**Mr. and Mrs.
Frank Houle**

MHS Photo

1910 – Men drinking.

1948 – 30th Anniversary (married 7-2-48), Ben Loons, Julia (Northrup) Loons. Donated by his daughter Joyce (nee Loons) Troset, and granddaughter Mary Northrup.

Left to Right: Ben Loons, John ?, John LaPrairie and Frank Houle

**Left to Right: Liza Danielson, Dorothy Marie Danielson
and Gideon Danielson**

Dead Fish Lake

Eliza

LEFT: Mary Beargrease Connors, born in the Cloquet area in 1875. Left is Elizabeth Danielson, born October 1888 in field just west of Holy Family Church. Mary, her mother, was on the way to pick cranberries and delivered Elizabeth on a blanket on the ground, wrapped her up, took her down the hill to Squaw Creek to wash her off. Washed her off and continued on her way to the cranberry bog.

Ben and Adeline Bassett's 50th Anniversary: Front row; Adeline, Mildred, Adeline (Mother), Marcelline, and Beatrice: Back row; Robert, Everett, Arnold, Ben (Father), Wilfred, and Burton.

Vets Pow wow - 1994: (Left to Right), Harvey Danielson, Everett Bsssett, Truman (Joe) Bassett and Bobby Bassett.

1994 – Everett and Bobby Bassett.

Mr. and Mrs. Dave Savage and children Mary, Agnes and Truman,Kate Savage Lyzeme Jr., Blaze.

Boys in front of Holy Family Church: front row Dan Savage, Glen Thompson, ?, Chuck Smith and Frank Thompson; back row; ?, Harvey Danielson, ?, Truman Savage, ?.

Connors Road 1938 (Danielson Road)

Sawyer Church – the oldest Catholic church in the area.

Chief Nagahnub's tombstone in the Sawyer Cemetery.

Holy Family Church congregation, early 1950's.

Chippewa Indians beating wild rice to break the husk.
Note the birch bark baskets.

1944 – Leo Rabideaux, US Navy
LST 797 (Landing Ship Tank)

Leo Whitebird, Indian Guide at the dock
of a lodge in Walker, Minnesota.

Chapter Seven:
Calling Each Other Names

Almost everyone has a rez name. Mine (Tom Peacock) is 'Auk'. Since I went off to school and became over-educated, some people now call me 'Doc Auk'. I think the name Auk originated from one of those characters in an early television horror show. Auk was a regular on "Shock Theater." My brothers thought I looked like that early version of Igor. Hence, I have been called Auk ever since.

But there are other names as well. Many of us also have Ojibwe names. Here is a story of one naming.

When it was time for my children to receive their Indian names my wife and I asked their Uncle Freddie Tonce, who was from Inger. And we offered him tobacco and asked him if he would give names to them and he said he would.

"I'll come down in a few weeks and we can do it then," he said.

Now in the language of elders a few weeks can mean anywhere from a week to a month, or more, and it is part of our learning these things to know that. Never once have I heard one of the traditional elders say, "I'll be there next Sunday at 2:00 in the afternoon."

We saw him again when he was in Cass Lake and he said he would be over to see us in a week. My wife prepared a feast of meat, wild rice and fry bread and we got a pouch of tobacco. And he came over that day and gave the children their names. I remember him sitting there in the living room and asking the children to come over to him and he took them separately by both hands and talked to them in Ojibwe and in English. He talked about his dreams and gave them their names. We set out a separate plate of food with some tobacco, which later was brought out into the woods.

Later I said of my boy's name, "What does it mean?" and he said, "You are walking in the woods and out of the corner of your eye you see a wolf. And you look over toward where it should be and it is not there."

Good thing that name is in Ojibwe.

A long time ago Ojibwe children were given names by a namesake, or way'ay', because it was believed that if they died without a name they would not be able to make the journey west into the land where our ancestors have gone. Moreover, the Creator (Gitchi Manito) could not answer the prayers of those who didn't have their name because he would not know who was speaking to him.

Usually the person selected as namesake was an old person, and always an old person who had not been ill during his or her life. This was because it was believed the child would then be healthy. Children who were sickly were sometimes given two or more names from different namesakes for this same reason. Namesakes could be either men or women and there did not seem to be a limit on the number of children that they would name; however, the namesake always gave a different name because each name was dreamed. There was always a feast held when a child was named in which venison and wild rice were prepared by the parents. Guests were often invited to the naming ceremony.

– T. Peacock, Editor

Part One:
Names of Fond du Lac People (1800's)
– (unknown source)

Names	Translation	Name in English	No. In Family
Margaret Shingop (Chief)		The Balsam tree	2
Mekwamiwigiji	The Icy Sky		1
Charlotte Mekwamiwigijig	The Icy Sky		3
Bawitigokwe	Maid of the Falls		2
Marie Belair	Mary Belair		1
Chiwiso			2
Misami			1
Makade mikokwe	Maid of the Black Beaver		4
Louise Menabojo	Louise Menabojo		2
Ogimabinens	The King Bird		2
Manidons	The Young Spirit		4
Madjiiasinokwe	The Maid Who Sails Away		2
Giwegijig	The Home Sky		2
John B. Bibonish	Who Winters Through	John B. Bibonish	6
Louise Bibonish	Who Winters Through	Louise Bibonish	2
Frank Bibonish	Who Winters Through	Frank Bibonish	1
Charlotte Bibonish	Who Winters Through		
Charlotte Lyons			8
Minweweshkang			2
Frank St. John		Frank St. John	6
Gebiose	He Who Walks Through to the End		2
Ozawakondib	The Yellow Headed		1
Anastasie			2
Edward Mangons	Ed Young Loon		3
Songakamig	The Hardened Ground		5
John B. Songakamig	The Hardened Ground		1
Cecil Durfee		Cecil Durfee	5
Frank Houle		Frank Houle	6
Biwabikobinens	The Iron Bird		
Joseph Lagarde			3
Joseph Charette (2)			
Joseph Charette			3
Anamuhsung (Chief)	The Receding Light		4

293

Mijakigijig	The Dipping Sky		2
Madjigwanibi	The Moving Feather		2
Wimigwans	The Small Feather		3
Akiwen	The Old Man		4
Sagigwanebi			2
Debasiwide	He Who Bears Downwards		3
Wewijigwanebi	He Who Sits Proudly Feathered		3
Gedagigwanebi	He Who Sits Spotted Feathered		5
Dedabashitang			5
Biowewegijig	The Approaching Voice of the Sky		1
Beshabikokwe	Maid of the Striped Rock		4
Wabishkibinens	The White Bird		4
Bijiw	The Lynx		4
			(White Man)
Wisag	Bitter		1
Thomas			2
Mijakikamigokwe	Maid of the Dip to the Earth		7
Minjwakwe			1
Sagimakwe			3
Shabwewegijigokwe	Maid Whose Voice Pierce the Sky		1
William Coffey		William Coffey	1
James A. Coffey		James A. Coffey	1
Ayishkinjig	Fac-simile of the Eye		2
Makons	The Young Bear		6
Gitchi Gwewizens	The Big Boy		1
			(White Man)
Wabishkash	He Who Sails in White		1
Medwekamigishkang	Whose Tread Upon the Ground Maketh Sound		1
Ogijins	The Lively Acting		4
			(White Man)
Wabishkishkinjig	The White Eye		4
Banodj			1
Louis Couture		Louis Couture	4
			(White Man)
Netawashikwe	Maid Who is an Adept to Sail		4
Frank Roussain		Frank Roussain	4
Joseph Obigwad (Chief)		Joseph Obigwad	2
Bemigijig	The Passing Sky		2

Shewebinens		2
Minjinawe	The Messenger	2
Makade Gegik	The Black Hawk	1
Mokaamokwe	Maid of the Rising Sun	2
Anamah Sung	The Receding Light	3
Ogima		3
Nijoiash	He Who Sails Doubly	2
Eshkweosekwe	Maid Who Walks in the Rear	2
Charlotte Minjinawe	Charlotte Messenger	3
Wabishkabikwe	Maid Who Sits in White	1
Gwekabikwe	Maid Who Sits Around	4
Songakamig	The Hardened Ground	
Joseph Petit		3
		(White Man)
Anodagan	The Servant	
Michel Petit		3
Frank Dufault		4
Bitawadanikwe		1
Josette Dufault		2
		(White Man)
Joseph Charette		2
Sophie Petit		1
Mannadis		1
Sowe Bibonish	Sowe He Who Winters Through	1
Chaigijig	The Fair Sky	1
Wabisnkigwanebikwe	Maid of the White Feather	3
Onijish	The Good Looking	2
Nijogijig	The Two Skies	1
Wabaneiasang	Illuminate the One Side	1
Odishkweiashikwe	Maid Sailing in the Rear	
Ojawashkokekek (Chief)	The Green Hawk	4
Wabano		2
Adisokan	The Fictitious Story	4
Memiskwange	The Red Winged	3
Akawegijigokwe	Maid of the Retained Sky	1
Sagwandagaikwe	Maid of the Thick Woods	1
Gidaiganikwe	Maid of the Gun Worm	2
Chiganikwe	Maid Who is Foremost	3
Ozawigijigokwe	Maid of the Yellow Sky	2

Nijobikwe	Maid Who Sits Double	1
	(White Man)	
Elizabeth Badger		1
Louise Badger		1
John Michel		2
Lucy Dingley		1
Chido		1
Medweiadjiwang	The Roaring Rapids	1
Ikwensish	The Little Woman	4
	(White Man)	
John Ozagi (Chief)		3
Margaret Ozagi		1
Frank Lemieux		3
Joseph Lemieux		2
Joseph Lavierge		4
Margaret Lemieux		4
Peter Lemieux		3
Catherine Ozagi		3
Charles Allard		2
Leon Allard		2
Antoine Gakabishi		1
Joseph Gakabashi		1
Midnjimans		1
Omakakins	The Toad	2
Wigon		3
Akwagonkwe		1
Naganab (Chief)	He Who Sits Foremost	2
Paul Naganab	" " " "	2
Louise Naganab	" " " "	3
Antoine Naganab	" " " "	5
Naganabins	" " " " (Young)	
Sophie Belanger		2
Louis Belanger		1
Sowians		1
Menwabikwe	Maid Who Is Well Seated	1
Josette Landri		6

296

Part Two:
FDL Nicknames

– Bonnie Wallace, Carol Jaakola and Rick Smith

One of the wonderful things about reservation life is that almost everyone has a nickname. Here is a sampling of nicknames of present and past reservation residents, including a few non-Fond du Lac enrollees. The list doesn't include every resident's nickname; however, it gives enough of them to give readers a flavor for the variety of names we think up to call each other. **We left a lot of space on the side so you can add other nicknames.**

Beanie (Geraldine Savage Diver)

Bone (Alan Abramowski)

Junior (Carl Abramowski Jr.)

Bokok (Ida Anamahsung)

QuakeQuake (Mary Anamahsung)

Bunker (Robert Barney Jr.)

Rabbit (Bob Bassett)

Bado (Clayton Bassett)

Bergie (Mary Bassett)

Spitty (Scot Bassett)

Snake (Terry Bassett)

Jiggs (Wilfred Bassett)

Mead (Bassett)

Scoop (Oliver Bassett)

Pee Wee (Marie Benton)

Bubbie Berglund (Kathryn Peil)

Sis (Kathryn Sheehy Berglund)

Punkin (Daryold Blacketter)

Bope (James Blacketter Sr.)

Diz (Sylvia Blacketter)

Sun (Delmar Campbell)

Gran Hex (Pat Campbell)

Weazer (Billy Carpenter)

Stick (Lawrence Coffey)

Chief (Cleo Coffey)

Java (Leo Coffey)

Weasel (James Couture)

Dapper Dan (Darrell Danielson)

Peggy (Delma Danielson)

Anna Banana (Anna DeFoe)

Umitz (Garrett DeFoe)

Zero or Dutch (Leroy DeFoe)

Halfpint (Harvey DeFoe)

Bage (Roberta Defoe)

Weeshgob (Joe DeFoe)

Homzee (Anna L. Diver)

Gog (Agnes Diver)

Jib (John Diver)

Cook Em Upper (Art Diver)

Bum (Beverly Diver)

Billy Boy (William Diver)

Duckie (Doug Diver)

Weedy (Eleanor Diver)

Ching (Eleanor Diver)

Bit (Liz Mullen Diver)

Tiny (Eugene Diver)

Sketties (Fabian Diver)

Sandy (George Diver)

Junior (Harold Diver)

Bullhead (John Diver Sr. & Jr.)

Beaver (Norman Diver)

Maang (Raymond Diver)

Moo Moo (Willy Diver)

Miseeayne (Ed DuFault)

Ginty (Karen Petite DuFault)

Porky (Vincent DuFault)

Ba-Sah (Vince DuFault)

Ainty (Raymond DuFault)

Tipper (Duane Dupuis)

Sam (James Dupius)

Corky (Wayne Dupuis Sr.)

Bimbo (Wayne Dupuis Jr.)

Poogidi (Gordon Dupuis)

Toddy (Florence Eno)

Bimbo (Blake Evans)

Son Son (Tom Foldesi, Jr.)

Homzee (Anna Lorraine Diver/Freidman)

Punkin (Norma Graves)

Sunny (Jacob Greensky Jr.)

Jug (Sharon Greensky)

Geepush (Mike Greensky)

Sweetie (Ardith Greensky)

Aubie (Leonard Gurno)

Dubbie (David Gurno)

Tykie (Nadine Gurno King)

Speed (Norman Houle)

Mudd (Phillip Houle)

Dodee (Carol Jaakola)

Pinky (Ed Jaakola)

Bunny (Julia Jaakola)

Diamond Dick (Ed LaFave)

Jenny Lahook (LaFave)

Midnight (Lloyd LaFave)

Smotty (Robert LaFave)

Chick (George LaPrairie Sr.)

Bird Dog (George LaPrairie, Jr.)

Jay-ogg (Bruce LaPrairie)

Skinno (Louie LaPrairie)

Bonzo (Michael J. LaPrairie)

Skunk (Joe Laundry)

Butler (Louie Laundry)

Buckles (Lemieux)

The Colonel (Charlie Loons)

Bayem (Jim Loons Jr.)

Bug (John Loons)

Zeke (Richard Loons)

Muck (Bill Lyons)

Jii ogg (James Martin)

Beesko (Frank Martin)

Birdie (Alberta Martin)

Hanny (Francis Martineau)

Turk (Gene Martineau)

Chetty (Kathy Martineau)

Nukka (Juanita Martineau)

Butch (Vincent Martineau)

Susan Mudd (Susan Mudwayash)

Deelo (Delores Misquadace)

Chig (Edward Misquadace)

Shanood (Charlotte Northrup)

Tahdah (Charlotte Diver Northrup)

Teetums (Darwin Bishop Northrup)

Bope (Jim Northrup, Sr.)

Puskie (Sylvester Northrup)

Tootsie (Les Northrup)

Sunny (Les Northrup, Jr.)

Hayman (Ernest Northrup)

Moosh skin (Mary Northrup)

Gabbi (Viola Northrup Foldesi)

Bun (Gordon Ojibway)

Cobby or Bopo (Jerrad Ojibway)

Brow or Jerry Eyebrow (Jerry Ojibway)

Muggins (Margaret Ojibway)

Bucky (Carl Olson, Jr.)

Alice Plug (Alice Paquette)

Putt Putt (Harvey Paquette)

Mum (Barb Peacock)

Bitsy (Elizabeth Peacock)

Dozer (Emeron Peacock)

Sonny (Robert Peacock)

Friday (Robert Peacock Sr.)

Buckskin (John Peacock)

Peanuts (Michael Peacock)

Auk (Tom Peacock)

Jimbo (Jim Peil Jr.)

Skip (Ed Pelerin)

Scoop (Michael Petite)

Red (Fred Petite)

Poker (Albert Porter)

Hambone (Moses Posey)

Chuck (Charles Rabideaux)

Kiffie or Crow (Clifton Rabideaux)

Dummy (Clifton Rabideaux, Sr.)

Rafferty (Don Rabideaux)

The King (Leo Rabideaux)

Rocky (Earl Rennquist Jr.)

Mooner (Darrell Reynolds)

Peach (Ernest Reynolds)

Man Head (Gene Reynolds)

Popeye (Simon Tony Roy)

Stinky (Dennis St. John)

Janquish (Frankie St. John)

Skip (Ray Sandman)

Sunshine (Isabelle Savage)

Monk (Jerry Savage)

Sloopy (Simon Savage)

Smokey (Lyzme Savage, Sr.)

Moe (Muriel Savage)

Toddy (Henry Sheehy)

Dooksie (Clara Northrup Skoglund)

Chunkie (Ann Smith Sheehy)

Coon (LaVerne Shotley)

Muck (Gene Shotley)

Billy or Singing (Raymond Smith)

Deer Leg (Kelly Smith)

Buddha (Roger Smith Jr.)

Chick (Ronald Smith)

Chuck (Clarence Smith)

Rub or Poochie (Rollin Smith)

Rick (Rupert Smith)

Smitty or Sonny (Rupert Smith)

Dip Smith (Terry Smith)

Rat (Tommy Stevenette)

Chuck (Charley Thompson)

Bit (Henry Thompson Sr.)

Junior (Henry Thompson Jr.)

Chico (Clifford Thompson)

Juggie or Jughead (Riley Thompson)

Dottie (Doris Tibbetts)

Lee Dog (Lee Tibbetts)

Tootie (Renard Trotterchaude)

Big Boy (Hubert Urrutia)

Bugsy (Clinton Waite)

Bibsy (Robert Wallace)

Corny (Jack Wallace)

Goggin (Roy Welsand)

Boozer (Darrell Welsand)

The Gooder Man (Simon Whitebird)

Rocky (Roger Wilkinson)

Abe (Herman Wise)

Sunny or Rubberlegs (Johnny Woods)

Slim (Elizabeth Woods)

Roundman (Billy Wuollett)

Beebo (Vivian Wuollet)

Duck (Donald Wuollett)

Wiggy (Vern Zacher)

Epilogue: A Forever Story

– T. Peacock

When I was nine years old I went on my first camping trip up the St. Louis River in the company of my cousin Bird Dog (George LaPrairie, Jr.), and our mutual friend, Dutch (Leroy DeFoe). I was the youngest of the three: Bird Dog was the oldest at 11, and Dutch was about 10 years old.

In those days we didn't have sleeping bags and it was our practice to use patch quilts and army blankets in an attempt to keep warm. They never accomplished their intended duty because I never remember being warm. Camp food always included a generous supply of government commodities (spam, powdered eggs, powdered milk, oat meal, lard, and something we called "Gravy Train," which was a beef gravy concoction) and tea.

On this first camping trip we made camp on the river at a place known as the Pipeline, located just down the hill from the Reservation church. Things went well for part of the evening. We gathered a large amount of dry firewood, put out numerous set lines for catfish and made a big pot of tea with river water. There is no way I can describe the taste of tea made with river water. To paraphrase an old Grape Nuts cereal ad, the river water gave it "that nutty taste."

After dark we sat around the fire and told stories, or more correctly Bird Dog told stories, because he was a wonderful storyteller. We talked about summer catechism (a uniquely Catholic experience), other camping trips Bird Dog and Dutch had gone on, and practical jokes Bird Dog had played on a large variety of friends and relatives. At one point, nature called Dutch away from the fire and he was gone just long enough for Bird Dog to arrange a clever plan.

"Let's pretend we peed in the tea and then offer some to Dutch."

So the plan was agreed upon and when Dutch returned to the campfire area, Bird Dog offered him some tea from a recycled peanut butter jar. Dutch gladly accepted. Bird Dog even put sugar in it for him.

"This is good tea."

"It should be. We peed in it while you were gone."

At this point, Dutch became very upset and continued to be so until Bird Dog assured him the tea was only made with river water. Only river water.

If we had known then the river water was contaminated with mercury and other harmful chemicals from acid rain, run-off and ground water contamination...we probably would have drank it anyway.

From that point on the evening, everything settled into a comfortable routine, or so it seemed. Bird Dog prepared a curious mix of powdered scrambled eggs (hydrated with river water) with Spam and another batch of tea. Around midnight the catfish started to bite and we were kept busy checking our set lines. Life was good.

At one point in the evening, a bear decided to wander down from the hills and proceeded to make all kinds of noise out near the railroad tracks, several hundred feet from us.

"There's a bear out there. What are we going to do?" wondered Bird Dog.

Intense group fear set in and a hastily implemented plan was put into effect. First, we would build up the fire. Bears didn't like fire and that might keep it from wandering into camp and eating us. Second, we would pray. And pray we did, kneeling around the fire saying our "Hail Mary's" over and over and over again. The plan worked and as proof I offer this story.

Years later I walk the hills and woods and pastures that overlook the river that flows through Nagachiwanang and I think of those bears and tea days. I think of Bird Dog, who would, as a young man complete his circle on this earth as the result of a car accident, after serving two tours of service to his Nation in Vietnam. He survived one war only to lose his life in another.

Now as a grandfather, I still go up the river. I don't set catfish lines anymore, but fish for walleye instead. And I don't camp along the river bank anymore. Instead, I drive up along the railroad tracks on an ATV and return home in the evening to the comfort of my bed.

I have traveled there lately with my youngest son. We stop often, and I tell him how places got their names. I tell them the locations of the natural springs that flow out of the hills. We've walked up the hill to the old Fond du Lac Village site, and I have told him the story of that place. I tell him where the graves are on the sides of the hills so he knows why certain places feel the way they do. It seems such a long time ago when other people showed me the same places and told me the same stories.

My hope, of course, is that he will have in him the same love and sense of responsibility I have for this place, as it was for my parents, grandparents and great grandparents. This, you see, is truly a forever story.

– T. Peacock, Editor